THE

EUROPEAN

UNION

THE

EUROPEAN

UNION

Readings on the Theory and Practice of European Integration

edited by
Brent F. Nelsen
Alexander C-G. Stubb

LYNNE
RIENNER
PUBLISHERS

BOULDER
LONDON

Published in the United States of America in 1994 by
Lynne Rienner Publishers, Inc.
1800 30th Street, Boulder, Colorado 80301

Library of Congress Cataloging-in-Publication Data
The European Union : readings on the theory and practice of European
    integration / edited by Brent F. Nelsen and Alexander C-G. Stubb.
    p. cm.
    Includes index.
    ISBN 1-55587-505-X (alk. paper)
    ISBN 1-55587-506-8 (pb) (alk. paper)
    1. European federation.   2. European Economic Community.
3. Europe—Economic integration.   I. Nelsen, Brent F.   II. Stubb,
Alexander C-G.
JN15.E88   1994
341.24'2—dc20   94-19158
                                                              CIP

Printed and bound in the United States of America

       The paper used in this publication meets the requirements
  ∞   of the American National Standard for Permanence of
       Paper for Printed Library Materials Z39.48-1984.

Published and distributed in Europe exclusively and outside
the Americas, Japan, and Australasia nonexclusively by
MACMILLAN PRESS LTD
Houndmills, Basingstoke, Hampshire RG21 2XS and London
Companies and representatives throughout the world

ISBN 0-333-64675-4

A catalogue record for this book is available from the
British Library

5 4 3

Contents

Preface

Necessity is the mother of invention, and, perhaps, college textbooks. Or so it was with this book.

It all started in the fall of 1992 when the professor among us (we will call him Nelsen) began planning for a new course he was scheduled to teach in the spring entitled "The European Community." Nelsen was under the crazy impression that students would understand the European Community (now the European Union) better if readings taken from key Community documents, the writings of its founders and political leaders, and important academic works were used to supplement the standard textbooks on the EC. When it became apparent that no such reader was on the market, he determined to put together his own packet of readings for the course. With the help of his star student and research assistant (we will call him Stubb, pronounced *Styb*), Nelsen waded through the vast amount of material available in the English language and compiled a course packet that was as expensive (royalties and all) as it was large and unwieldy. It became clear at some point during this process that the price for making important materials available to the class was too high for the instructor and the students (or should we say their parents?). Thus, amidst the piles of books and photocopied articles, a textbook was conceived.

The twenty Furman University students (including Stubb) who paid an exorbitant price to be guinea pigs in that first EC class deserve the highest praise. Their close, critical reading of the supplementary material and their practical input helped us determine which readings worked and which did not. After the students had their say, we took valuable advice from a number of scholars in the field, including Desmond Dinan, Cleveland Fraser, James Guth, Christine Ingebritsen, Pauli Järvenpää, Janne Haaland Matlary, Martin Sæter, and two anonymous reviewers. Although we followed many of their suggestions, we, of course, take full responsibility for the final product.

Many other people contributed significantly to this project. Margaret Crisp and her legion of student helpers, including Maureen Atta,

Lori Hall, Kerry Harike, Sandra Padgett, and Tonya Smith, provided essential secretarial services. Sharon Dilworth and Carolyn Sims also did much typing. Bozhidar Dimitrov helped us get the scanner working, and Lilli Ann Dill and Steve Richardson helped us with countless library searches. Lynne Rienner, from the moment she laid eyes on the project, offered superb advice without ever demanding control. She proved to us the value of a good publisher.

The Duke Endowment and the Knight Foundation, via Furman University's Research and Professional Growth Committee and the Furman Advantage Program, provided generous financial support for this project. Emotional support and personal sacrifices were freely offered by many family members and friends who will remain un-named—but not unthanked.

Finally, each of us, in different ways, owes a debt of gratitude to our friends and colleagues—faculty, students, and staff—in the Department of Political Science at Furman University. To them we dedicate this book.

—B.F.N.
—A.C-G.S.

Introduction

This book is primarily designed to supplement standard textbooks on the history, theory, and practice of European integration. Its purpose is threefold. First, in Part 1, it invites students (and their instructors) to join the primary shapers of the European Union in a nearly five-decades-long conversation about Europe. In their own voices, Winston Churchill, Robert Schuman, Jean Monnet, Charles de Gaulle, Margaret Thatcher, Jacques Delors, and the authors of the preambles to the important Community treaties explain why Europe must unite and what a united Europe must look like. Their visions of a united Europe differ, in some cases because the authors differ in their fundamental views on human nature, national sovereignty, the role of government, and international relations, in other cases because time has changed the context in which Europe must exist. We enter this conversation to understand better the historical development of the European Union and the ideas that still inform its shapers.

The second purpose of this book (principally Parts 2, 3, and 4) is to encourage students to think about why and how nations come together by tracing the evolution of integration theory in the postwar period. The social scientific impulse to explain human behavior, and encourage it in certain directions, motivated theorists in the 1950s and 1960s both to explain why Europe was uniting and to describe how it should be done. When theoretical explanations and prescriptions seemed to falter in the 1970s, social scientists turned their attention to the more mundane decisionmaking processes that characterized the European Community during its "stagnant" years. When the Community took off again in the mid-1980s, these studies informed a new wave of theorizing that has yielded less elegant and less comprehensive, but more realistic, explanations of integration.

The third purpose of this book, also met primarily in Parts 3 and 4, is to add depth to the existing knowledge students may have of particular actors, institutions, or issues—for example, the European mass public, national elites, European interest groups, the 1992 project, monetary union, and the Maastricht treaty. The intent here is not to present research on every aspect of the European Union, but to provide articles that offer both empirical information of practical value and interesting theoretical conclusions.

Readers will find this book more useful if they keep in mind two important points concerning its construction. First, a short introduction precedes each chapter that (1) places the selection in context and (2) summarizes the argument. The prologues are designed to amplify the dialogue among the authors of the texts. They should not substitute for a broader discussion of the historical or theoretical contexts, nor should they replace a close reading of each piece. Second, the editors have abridged each selection. Centered bullets (· · ·) mark significant abridgments; minor abridgments go unmarked; brackets [ ] mark editors' additions; and all notes are omitted. The editors have taken great care to preserve the core—and much more—of each author's argument, but readers should consider the original sources before making definitive (i.e., published) statements about the selections reprinted here.

PART 1

Visions of a United Europe

1 The Tragedy of Europe

Winston S. Churchill

Winston Churchill (1874–1965), the great wartime prime minister of Britain, found himself leader of the Conservative opposition in Parliament after Labour's victory in the 1945 General Election. Despite his removal from office, Churchill remained a key architect of the postwar world by identifying the dangers facing the West and articulating a clear strategy for defending Western interests and values.

Churchill's speech at Zurich University on 19 September 1946 profoundly influenced the shape of postwar Europe. He began this speech with the refrain common to all the postwar integrationists: Europe must unite before war destroys the continent, its glorious civilization, and perhaps much of the rest of the world. He called specifically for a "United States of Europe" led by Europe's former antagonists, France and Germany, but he did not outline a detailed program for achieving unity. Rather, he argued simply and powerfully for Europe to adopt an ideal to style its future. Interestingly, Churchill seemed to exclude Britain from his grand European project, thus reflecting an ambiguity toward Europe that remains strong in Britain today.

Churchill's stature forced European leaders to take his Zurich call seriously. His efforts eventually led to the Hague Congress of May 1948 and the creation of the Council of Europe in 1949, both milestones in European integration.

I wish to speak to you today about the tragedy of Europe. This noble continent, comprising on the whole the fairest and the most

Reprinted with permission from *Winston S. Churchill: His Complete Speeches, 1897–1963*, Vol. VII, 1943–1949, ed. Robert Rhodes James (Chelsea House Publishers, 1974). Copyright 1974 by Chelsea House Publishers.

cultivated regions of the earth, enjoying a temperate and equable climate, is the home of all the great parent races of the western world. It is the fountain of Christian faith and Christian ethics. It is the origin of most of the culture, arts, philosophy, and science both of ancient and modern times. If Europe were once united in the sharing of its common inheritance, there would be no limit to the happiness, to the prosperity and glory which its three or four hundred million people would enjoy. Yet it is from Europe that have sprung that series of frightful nationalistic quarrels, originated by the Teutonic nations, which we have seen even in this twentieth century and in our lifetime, wreck the peace and mar the prospects of all mankind.

And what is the plight to which Europe has been reduced? Some of the smaller states have indeed made a good recovery, but over wide areas a vast quivering mass of tormented, hungry, care-worn and bewildered human beings gape at the ruins of their cities and homes, and scan the dark horizons for the approach of some new peril, tyranny or terror. Among the victors there is a babel of jarring voices; among the vanquished a sullen silence of despair. That is all that Europeans, grouped in so many ancient states and nations, that is all that the Germanic Powers have got by tearing each other to pieces and spreading havoc far and wide. Indeed, but for the fact that the great Republic across the Atlantic Ocean has at length realized that the ruin or enslavement of Europe would involve their own fate as well, and has stretched out hands of succor and guidance, the Dark Ages would have returned in all their cruelty and squalor. They may still return.

Yet all the while there is a remedy which, if it were generally and spontaneously adopted, would as if by a miracle transform the whole scene, and would in a few years make all Europe, or the greater part of it, as free and as happy as Switzerland is today. What is this sovereign remedy? It is to recreate the European Family or as much of it as we can, and provide it with a structure under which it can dwell in peace, in safety and in freedom. We must build a kind of United States of Europe. In this way only will hundreds of millions of toilers be able to regain the simple joys and hopes which make life worth living. The process is simple. All that is needed is the resolve of hundreds of millions of men and women to do right instead of wrong and gain as their reward blessing instead of cursing.

Much work has been done upon this task by the exertions of the Pan-European Union which owes so much to Count Coudenhove-Kalergi and which commanded the services of the famous French patriot and statesman, Aristide Briand. There is also that immense body of doctrine and procedure, which was brought into being amid high hopes after the first world war, as the League of Nations. The League of

Nations did not fail because of its principles or conceptions. It failed because these principles were deserted by those states who had brought it into being. It failed because the governments of those days feared to face the facts, and act while time remained. This disaster must not be repeated. There is therefore much knowledge and material with which to build; and also bitter dear-bought experience.

I was very glad to read in the newspapers two days ago that my friend President Truman had expressed his interest and sympathy with this great design. There is no reason why a regional organization of Europe should in any way conflict with the world organization of the United Nations. On the contrary, I believe that the larger synthesis will only survive if it is founded upon coherent natural groupings. There is already a natural grouping in the Western Hemisphere. We British have our own Commonwealth of Nations. These do not weaken, on the contrary they strengthen, the world organization. They are in fact its main support. And why should there not be a European group which could give a sense of enlarged patriotism and common citizenship to the distracted peoples of this turbulent and mighty continent and why should it not take its rightful place with other great groupings in shaping the destinies of men? In order that this should be accomplished there must be an act of faith in which millions of families speaking many languages must consciously take part.

We all know that the two world wars through which we have passed arose out of the vain passion of a newly-united Germany to play the dominating part in the world. In this last struggle crimes and massacres have been committed for which there is no parallel since the invasions of the Mongols in the fourteenth century and no equal at any time in human history. The guilty must be punished. Germany must be deprived of the power to rearm and make another aggressive war. But when all this has been done, as it will be done, as it is being done, there must be an end to retribution. There must be what Mr. Gladstone many years ago called "a blessed act of oblivion." We must all turn our backs upon the horrors of the past. We must look to the future. We cannot afford to drag forward across the years that are to come the hatreds and revenges which have sprung from the injuries of the past. If Europe is to be saved from infinite misery, and indeed from final doom, there must be an act of faith in the European family and an act of oblivion against all the crimes and follies of the past.

Can the free peoples of Europe rise to the height of these resolves of the soul and instincts of the spirit of man? If they can, the wrongs and injuries which have been inflicted will have been washed away on all sides by the miseries which have been endured. Is there any need for further floods of agony? Is it the only lesson of history that mankind is unteachable? Let there be justice, mercy and freedom. The peoples have to will it, and all will achieve their hearts' desire.

I am now going to say something that will astonish you. The first step in the recreation of the European family must be a partnership between France and Germany. In this way only can France recover the moral leadership of Europe. There can be no revival of Europe without a spiritually great France and a spiritually great Germany. The structure of the United States of Europe, if well and truly built, will be such as to make the material strength of a single state less important. Small nations will count as much as large ones and gain their honor by their contribution to the common cause. The ancient states and principalities of Germany, freely joined together for mutual convenience in a federal system, might each take their individual place among the United States of Europe. I shall not try to make a detailed program for hundreds of millions of people who want to be happy and free, prosperous and safe, who wish to enjoy the four freedoms of which the great President Roosevelt spoke, and live in accordance with the principles embodied in the Atlantic Charter. If this is their wish, they have only to say so, and means can certainly be found, and machinery erected, to carry that wish into full fruition.

But I must give you a warning. Time may be short. At present there is a breathing space. The cannon have ceased firing. The fighting has stopped; but the dangers have not stopped. If we are to form the United States of Europe or whatever name or form it may take, we must begin now.

In these present days we dwell strangely and precariously under the shield and protection of the atomic bomb. The atomic bomb is still only in the hands of a state and nation which we know will never use it except in the cause of right and freedom. But it may well be that in a few years this awful agency of destruction will be widespread and the catastrophe following from its use by several warring nations will not only bring to an end all that we call civilization, but may possibly disintegrate the globe itself.

I must now sum up the propositions which are before you. Our constant aim must be to build and fortify the strength of [the United Nations]. Under and within that world concept we must recreate the European family in a regional structure called, it may be, the United States of Europe. The first step is to form a Council of Europe. If at first all the states of Europe are not willing or able to join the union, we must nevertheless proceed to assemble and combine those who will and those who can. The salvation of the common people of every race and of every land from war or servitude must be established on solid foundations and must be guarded by the readiness of all men and women to die rather than submit to tyranny. In all this urgent work, France and Germany must take the lead together. Great Britain, the British Commonwealth of Nations, mighty America, and I trust Soviet Russia—for then indeed all would be well—must be the friends and sponsors of the new Europe and must champion its right to live and shine.

2 The Schuman Declaration

ROBERT SCHUMAN

Efforts in the 1940s to realize Churchill's vision of a united Europe led to increased economic and political cooperation but did not yield anything like a United States of Europe. European leaders needed a new strategy to achieve such a goal. On 9 May 1950, Robert Schuman (1886–1963), France's foreign minister, outlined a plan to unite under a single authority the coal and steel industries of Europe's bitterest enemies, France and Germany. The purpose of the plan, which was developed by Jean Monnet, was to begin building a peaceful, united Europe one step at a time. European governments would start with two industries essential to the making of war, coal and steel, then add other economic and political sectors until all major decisions were taken at a European level. This would create, in Schuman's words, a "de facto solidarity" that would ultimately make war between France and Germany "materially impossible." The practical approach of Schuman and Monnet won favor on the European continent; France, Germany, Italy, and the Benelux countries eventually responded by creating the European Coal and Steel Community in 1952.

World peace cannot be safeguarded without the making of creative efforts proportionate to the dangers which threaten it.

The contribution which an organized and living Europe can bring to civilization is indispensable to the maintenance of peaceful relations. In taking upon herself for more than 20 years the role of champion of a united Europe, France has always had as her essential aim the service of peace. A united Europe was not achieved and we had war.

Reprinted with permission from *Europe—A Fresh Start: The Schuman Declaration, 1950-90* (Office for Official Publications of the European Communities, 1990). Copyright 1990 by the European Communities.

Europe will not be made all at once, or according to a single plan. It will be built through concrete achievements which first create a *de facto* solidarity. The coming together of the nations of Europe requires the elimination of the age-old opposition of France and Germany. Any action taken must in the first place concern these two countries.

With this aim in view, the French government proposes that action be taken immediately on one limited but decisive point. It proposes that Franco-German production of coal and steel as a whole be placed under a common High Authority, within the framework of an organization open to the participation of the other countries of Europe.

The pooling of coal and steel production should immediately provide for the setting up of common foundations for economic development as a first step in the federation of Europe, and will change the destinies of those regions which have long been devoted to the manufacture of munitions of war, of which they have been the most constant victims.

The solidarity in production thus established will make it plain that any war between France and Germany becomes not merely unthinkable, but materially impossible. The setting up of this powerful productive unit, open to all countries willing to take part and bound ultimately to provide all the member countries with the basic elements of industrial production on the same terms, will lay a true foundation for their economic unification.

This production will be offered to the world as a whole without distinction or exception, with the aim of contributing to raising living standards and to promoting peaceful achievements.

In this way, there will be realized simply and speedily that fusion of interests which is indispensable to the establishment of a common economic system; it may be the leaven from which may grow a wider and deeper community between countries long opposed to one another by sanguinary divisions.

By pooling basic production and by instituting a new High Authority, whose decisions will bind France, Germany and other member countries, this proposal will lead to the realization of the first concrete foundation of a European federation indispensable to the preservation of peace.

. . .

3 Preambles to the Treaties of Rome

On 25 March 1957, the six member countries of the European Coal and Steel Community (ECSC) signed treaties establishing the European Economic Community (EEC) and the European Atomic Energy Community (EURATOM). The three treaties together are commonly referred to as the Treaty of Rome.

The preambles to each of the treaties reflect the founders' vision for building, through economic integration, "an ever closer union among the peoples of Europe." The deep desire for peace on the continent runs through each of the preambles and links them to the visions articulated by Churchill, Schuman, Monnet, and many others. But the documents also represent a subtle shift in emphasis away from peace to economic prosperity as the driving motive for unity. We can detect the shift in the Schuman Declaration and its parallel, the preamble to the ECSC treaty, but it becomes more evident in the preamble to the EEC treaty, where "economic and social progress" seems to take precedence over preserving and strengthening "peace and liberty." European leaders, though mindful of the dangers of violent conflict in Western Europe, were becoming more concerned with the material improvement of life on a peaceful continent.

• EUROPEAN COAL AND STEEL COMMUNITY

. . .

CONSIDERING that world peace can be safeguarded only by creative efforts commensurate with the dangers that threaten it,

Reprinted with permission from *Treaties Establishing the European Communities (ECSC, EEC, EAEC), Single European Act, Other Basic Instruments*, abridged edition (Office for Official Publications of the European Communities, 1987). Copyright 1987 by the European Communities.

CONVINCED that the contribution which an organized and vital Europe can make to civilization is indispensable to the maintenance of peaceful relations,

RECOGNIZING that Europe can be built only through practical achievements which will first of all create real solidarity, and through the establishment of common bases for economic development,

ANXIOUS to help, by expanding their basic production, to raise the standard of living and further the works of peace,

RESOLVED to substitute for age-old rivalries the merging of their essential interests; to create, by establishing an economic community, the basis for a broader and deeper community among peoples long divided by bloody conflicts; and to lay the foundations for institutions which will give direction to a destiny henceforward shared,

HAVE DECIDED to create a European Coal and Steel Community.

. . .

• EUROPEAN ECONOMIC COMMUNITY

. . .

DETERMINED to lay the foundations of an ever closer union among the peoples of Europe,

RESOLVED to ensure the economic and social progress of their countries by common action to eliminate the barriers which divide Europe,

AFFIRMING as the essential objective of their efforts the constant improvement of the living and working conditions of their peoples,

RECOGNIZING that the removal of existing obstacles calls for concerted action in order to guarantee steady expansion, balanced trade and fair competition,

ANXIOUS to strengthen the unity of their economies and to ensure their harmonious development by reducing the differences existing between the various regions and the backwardness of the less favored regions,

DESIRING to contribute, by means of a common commercial policy, to the progressive abolition of restrictions on international trade,

INTENDING to confirm the solidarity which binds Europe and the overseas countries and desiring to ensure the development of their prosperity, in accordance with the principles of the Charter of the United Nations,

RESOLVED by thus pooling their resources to preserve and

strengthen peace and liberty, and calling upon the other peoples of Europe who share their ideal to join in their efforts,

HAVE DECIDED to create a European Economic Community.

.   .   .

- **EUROPEAN ATOMIC ENERGY COMMUNITY**

.   .   .

RECOGNIZING that nuclear energy represents an essential resource for the development and invigoration of industry and will permit the advancement of the cause of peace,

CONVINCED that only a joint effort undertaken without delay can offer the prospect of achievements commensurate with the creative capacities or their countries,

RESOLVED to create the conditions necessary for the development of a powerful nuclear industry which will provide extensive energy resources, lead to the modernization of technical processes and contribute, through its many other applications, to the prosperity of their peoples,

ANXIOUS to create the conditions of safety necessary to eliminate hazards to the life and health of the public,

DESIRING to associate other countries with their work and to cooperate with international organizations concerned with the peaceful development of atomic energy,

HAVE DECIDED to create a European Atomic Energy Community (EURATOM).

.   .   .

4 A Ferment of Change

JEAN MONNET

*Jean Monnet (1888–1979) was the "father of Europe." No single indi-
vidual influenced the shape of the European Union more than this
French civil servant and diplomat. Monnet convinced Robert Schuman
to propose the European Coal and Steel Community and became the first
president of its High Authority; he also convinced Johan Willem Beyen
and Paul-Henri Spaak to propose EURATOM and the EEC, and then established the influential Action Committee for a United States of Europe to
pressure governments to accept the proposals. Monnet worked hard,
and eventually successfully, to enlarge the Community by adding
Britain, Ireland, and Denmark. And finally, shortly before his death, he
persuaded EC governments to turn their regular summits into the European Council.[1] So great was this man's influence that The Economist
suggested naming the future common European currency the "monnet."*

*Monnet drew on the functionalism of David Mitrany (see Chapter
11) for his vision of Europe. He argued that problems of insecurity and
human need in the world, and in Europe in particular, required radical
changes in the way people thought about solving these problems.
Nations, he believed, should adopt common rules governing their
behavior and create common institutions to apply these rules. Such a
strategy, even if applied on a small scale, would create a "silent
revolution in men's minds" that would change the way people thought
and acted. For Monnet, the European Communities of the early 1960s
demonstrated that small collective steps set off "a chain reaction, a
ferment where one change induces another." This ferment, he asserted,
would not lead to another nineteenth-century-style great power—
although a united Europe would be able to shoulder an equal burden of
leadership with the United States—nor would it be confined to Europe.*

Reprinted with permission from *Journal of Common Market Studies*, 1(1)(1962):
203-211. Copyright 1962 by Blackwell Publishers.

Integration was a process that may have started in Europe but would soon have to include the West at first, and then the rest of the world, if humanity was to "escape destruction."

This century has probably changed the manner of life more for everyone of us than all the thousands of years of man's progress put together. In the past, men were largely at the mercy of nature. Today in our industrial countries of the Western world and elsewhere, we are acquiring an unprecedented mastery over nature. Natural resources are no longer a limitation now that we control more and more forms of energy and can use raw materials in more and more ways. We are entering the age of abundance where work, as we know it, will only be one of many human activities. For the first time we in the West are witnessing the emergence of a truly mass society marked by mass consumption, mass education and even mass culture.

We are moving, in the West, from a society where privilege was part of nature to one where the enjoyment of human rights and human dignity are common to all. Unfortunately, two-thirds of mankind have not shared in this process.

And now, on the very eve of creating unprecedented conditions of abundance, we are suddenly faced with the consequences of our extraordinary mastery over the physical forces of nature. Modern medicine is steadily increasing our prospects of life, so that the population of the world is increasing fantastically fast. This revolution is creating new explosive pressures of all kinds in the world. At the same time, science is repeatedly creating new powers of destruction. This faces us with the greatest threat humanity has ever had to deal with. The issue today is no longer peace or war, but the triumph or destruction of civilized life.

We cannot assume that we shall avoid such destruction. We have only to look back on the last fifty years to see how constant the risk of upheaval has become. No region of the world has escaped violence. One-third of mankind has become Communist, another third has obtained independence from colonialism, and even among the remaining third nearly all countries have undergone revolutions or wars. True, atomic bombs have made nuclear war so catastrophic that I am convinced no country wishes to resort to it. But I am equally convinced that we are at the mercy of an error of judgment or a technical breakdown, the source of which no man may ever know.

We are then in a world of rapid change, in which men and nations must learn to control themselves in their relations with others. This, to my mind, can only be done through institutions: and it is this need for common institutions that we have learnt in Europe since the war.

We are used to thinking that major changes in the traditional relations between countries only take place violently, through conquest or revolution. We are so accustomed to this that we find it hard to appreciate those that are taking place peacefully in Europe even though they have begun to affect the world. We can see the communist revolution, because it has been violent and because we have been living with it for nearly fifty years. We can see the revolution in the ex-colonial areas because power is plainly changing hands. But we tend to miss the magnitude of the change in Europe because it is taking place by the constitutional and democratic methods which govern our countries.

Yet we have only to look at the difference between 1945 and today to see what an immense transformation has been taking place under our very eyes, here in what used to be called the old world. After the war, the nations of continental Europe were divided and crippled, their national resources were depleted and, in most of them, the peoples had little faith in the future. During the last fifteen years, these countries have lost their empires. It might have been expected they would be further depressed by what many considered the loss of past greatness and prestige.

And yet, after all these upheavals, the countries of continental Europe, which have fought each other so often in the past and which, even in peacetime, organized their economies as potential instruments of war, are now uniting in a Common Market which is laying the foundations for political union. Britain is negotiating to enter this European Community and by this very fact changing the tradition of centuries. And now the President of the United States is already asking Congress for powers to negotiate with the enlarged European Common Market.

To understand this extraordinary change in all its basic simplicity, we must go back to 1950, only five years after the war. For five years, the whole French nation had been making efforts to recreate the bases of production, but it became evident that to go beyond recovery towards steady expansion and higher standards of life for all, the resources of a single nation were not sufficient. It was necessary to transcend the national framework.

The need was political as well as economic. The Europeans had to overcome the mistrust born of centuries of feuds and wars. The governments and peoples of Europe still thought in the old terms of victors and vanquished. Yet, if a basis for peace in the world was to be established, these notions had to be eliminated. Here again, one had to go beyond the nation and the conception of national interest as an end in itself.

We thought that both these objectives could in time be reached if conditions were created enabling these countries to increase their resources by merging them in a large and dynamic common market; and if these same countries could be made to consider that their problems were no longer solely of national concern, but were mutual European responsibilities.

Obviously this could not be done all at once. It was not possible to create a large dynamic market immediately nor to produce trust between recent enemies overnight. After several unsuccessful attempts, the French Government through its Foreign Minister, M. Robert Schuman, proposed in 1950 what many people today would regard as a modest beginning but which seemed very bold at the time: and the parliaments of France, Germany, Italy and Benelux voted that, for coal and steel, their countries would form a single common market, run by common institutions administering common rules, very much as within a single nation. The European Coal and Steel Community was set up. In itself this was a technical step, but its new procedures, under common institutions, created a silent revolution in men's minds. It proved decisive in persuading businessmen, civil servants, politicians and trade unionists that such an approach could work and that the economic and political advantages of unity over division were immense. Once they were convinced, they were ready to take further steps forward.

In 1957, only three years after the failure of the European Army, the six parliaments ratified the Treaty of Rome which extended the Common Market from coal and steel to an economic union embracing all goods. Today, the Common Market, with its 170 million people that will become 225 million when Britain joins, is creating in Europe a huge continental market on the American scale.

The large market does not prejudge the future economic systems of Europe. Most of the Six have a nationalized sector as large as the British and some also have planning procedures. These are just as compatible with private enterprise on the large market as they are within a single nation. The contribution of the Common Market is to create new opportunities of expansion for all the members, which make it easier to solve any problems that arise, and to provide the rest of the world with prospects of growing trade that would not exist without it. In Europe, an open society looking to the future is replacing a defensive one regretting the past.

The profound change is being made possible essentially by the new method of common action which is the core of the European Community. To establish this new method of common action, we adapted to our situation the methods which have allowed individuals to live together in society: common rules which each member is committed to respect, and common institutions to watch over the application of these rules. Nations have applied this method within their frontiers for centuries, but they have never yet been applied between them. After a period of trial and error, this method has become a permanent dialogue between a single European body, responsible for expressing the view of the general interest of the Community, and the national governments expressing the national views. The resulting procedure for collective decisions is something quite new and, as far as I know, has no analogy in any traditional system. It is not federal because there is no central government; the nations take their decisions together in the Council of Ministers. On the other hand, the independent European body proposes policies, and the common element is further underlined by the European Parliament and the European Court of Justice.

This system leads to a completely changed approach to common action. In the past, the nations felt no irrevocable commitment. Their responsibility was strictly to themselves, not to any common interest. They had to rely on themselves alone. Relations took the form either of domination if one country was much stronger than the others, or of the trading of advantages if there was a balance of powers between them. This balance was necessarily unstable and the concessions made in an agreement one year could always be retracted the next.

But in the European Communities, common rules applied by joint institutions give each a responsibility for the effective working of the Community as a whole. This leads the nations, within the discipline of the Community, to seek a solution to the problems themselves, instead of trading temporary advantages. It is this method which explains the dramatic change in the relations of Germany with France and the other Common Market countries. Looking forward to a common future has made them agree to live down the feuds of the past. Today people have almost forgotten that the Saar was ever a problem and yet from 1919 to 1950 it was a major bone of contention between France and Germany. European unity has made it seem an anachronism. And today, at French invitation, German troops are training on French soil.

. . .

We have seen that Europe has overcome the attitude of domination which ruled state policies for so many centuries. But quite apart from what this means for us in the old continent, this is a fact of world importance. It is obvious that countries and peoples who are overcoming this state of mind between themselves will bring the same mentality to their relations with others, outside Europe. The new method of action developed in Europe replaces the efforts at domination of nation states by a constant process of collective adaptation to new conditions, a chain reaction, a ferment where one change induces another.

Look at the effect the Common Market has already had on world tariffs. When it was set up, it was widely assumed the member countries would want to protect themselves and become, as some put it, an inward-looking group. Yet everything that has happened since has shown this view to be wrong. The Six have reduced the tariffs between themselves and towards other countries faster than expected. Now President Kennedy proposes America and Europe should cut tariffs on manufactures by half, and the Common Market will certainly welcome it. This leads to a situation where tariffs throughout the major trading areas of the world will be lower than they have ever been.

These changes inside and outside Europe would not have taken place without the driving force of the Common Market. It opens new prospects for dealing with problems the solution of which was becoming increasingly urgent. I am thinking of world agriculture in a more and more industrial civilization; of links between the new and the long-established industrial regions, and in particular of the need for growing trade between Japan and the United States and Europe together.

Naturally, increasing trade will also benefit the Commonwealth. The prospect of Britain's future entry into the Common Market has already made the Continent more aware than ever before of the problems of the Commonwealth. Clearly, for countries whose major need is to obtain more capital for development, the fact that Britain is part of a rapidly developing Europe holds great promise of future progress.

Similarly, problems are arising that only Europe and the United States together have the resources to deal with. The need to develop policies of sustained growth, which in large part depend on maintaining international monetary stability, is an example. Increasing the aid of the West to the underdeveloped areas on a large scale is another. Separately, the European nations have inevitably taken divergent views of aid policies. But tomorrow, the nations of Europe by acting together can make a decisive contribution. The necessary precondition of such a partnership between America and Europe is that Europe should be united and thus be able to deploy resources on the same scale as America. This is what is in the course of happening today.

That we have begun to cooperate on these affairs at the Atlantic level is a great step forward. It is evident that we must soon go a good deal further towards an Atlantic Community. The creation of a united Europe brings this nearer by making it possible for America and Europe to act as partners on an equal footing. I am convinced that ultimately, the United States too will delegate powers of effective action to common institutions, even on political questions. Just as the United States in their own day found it necessary to unite, just as Europe is now in the process of uniting, so the West must move towards some kind of union. This is not an end in itself. It is the beginning on the road to the more orderly world we must have if we are to escape destruction.

The discussions on peace today are dominated by the question of disarmament. The world will be more and more threatened by destruction as long as bombs continue to pile up on both sides. Many therefore feel that the hopes for peace in the world depend on as early an agreement on armaments as possible, particularly an agreement on nuclear arms. Of course we must continue to negotiate on these questions. But it is too simple to hope the problems that arise out of philosophic conflicts could be settled without a change in the view which people take of the future. For what is the Soviet objective? It is to achieve a Communist world, as Mr. Kruschev has told us many times. When this becomes so obviously impossible that nobody, even within a closed society, can any longer believe it — when the partnership of America and a United Europe makes it plain to all that the West may change from within but that others cannot change it by outside pressures, then Mr. Kruschev or his successor will accept the facts, and the conditions will at last exist for turning so-called peaceful coexistence into genuine peace. Then at last real disarmament will become possible.

Personally, I do not think we shall have to wait long for this change. The history of European unification shows that when people become convinced a change is taking place that creates a new situation, they act on their revised estimate before that situation is established. After all, Britain has asked to join the Common Market before it was complete. The President of the United States is seeking powers to negotiate with the European Community on steps to an Atlantic partnership even before Britain has joined. Can we not expect a similar phenomenon in the future relations with the Soviet Union?

What conclusions can we draw from all these thoughts?

One impression predominates in my mind over all others. It is this: unity in Europe does not create a new kind of great power; it is a method for introducing change in Europe and consequently in the world. People, more often outside the European Community than within, are tempted to see the European Community as a potential nineteenth-century state with all the overtones of power this implies. But we are not in the nineteenth century, and the Europeans have built up the European Community precisely in order to find a way out of the conflicts to which the nineteenth-century power philosophy gave rise. The natural attitude of a European Community based on the exercise by nations of common responsibilities will be to make these nations also aware of their responsibilities, as a Community, to the world. In fact, we already see this sense of world responsibilities developing as unity in Europe begins to affect Britain, America and many other areas of the world. European unity is not a blueprint, it is not a theory, it is a process that has already begun, of bringing peoples and nations together to adapt themselves jointly to changing circumstances.

European unity is the most important event in the West since the war, not because it is a new great power, but because the new institutional method it introduces is permanently modifying relations between nations and men. Human nature does not change, but when nations and men accept the same rule and the same institutions to make sure that they are applied, their behavior towards each other changes. This is the process of civilization itself.

• NOTE

1. Richard Mayne, "Gray Eminence," in *Jean Monnet: The Path to European Unity*, ed. Douglas Brinkley and Clifford Hackett (New York: St. Martin's Press, 1991), 114–116.

A Concert of European States

CHARLES DE GAULLE

Charles de Gaulle (1890–1970), World War II resistance leader and first president of France's fifth republic, was first and foremost a French nationalist. His overriding objective after the humiliation of World War II was to reestablish France as a great power, free from domination by the superpowers and once again the source of Western civilization's cultural and spiritual strength. De Gaulle's vision of France profoundly shaped his vision of Europe, which differed markedly from the views held by the founders of the European Communities, most noticeably Jean Monnet.

De Gaulle believed in European unity, but he criticized the supranational vision of Europe as unrealistic and undesirable. He argued instead for a "concert of European states" in which states coordinated their policies extensively but did not give up their rights as sovereign entities to a European "superstate." De Gaulle's unwillingness to concede France's right to control its vital affairs led to the 1965 crisis in the Communities and eventually the Luxembourg compromise that, in practice, gave every member state the right to veto Community decisions. In effect, the Six were forced to accept de Gaulle's vision of an intergovernmental Europe.

War gives birth and brings death to nations. In the meantime, it never ceases to loom over their existence. For us French, the development of our national life, our political regimes and our world position from 1815 to 1870 was determined by the hostile coalition which united the nations of Europe against the Revolution, the dazzling victories and then the downfall of Napoleon, and finally the disastrous treaties which

Reprinted from "Europe," in *Memoirs of Hope: Renewal and Endeavor*, trans. Terence Kilmartin (Simon and Schuster, 1971).

sanctioned so many battles. Thereafter, during the forty-four years of the "armed truce," it was our defeat, our secret desire to avenge it, but also the fear that a united Germany might inflict another on us, that dominated our actions at home and abroad. Although the gigantic effort put forth by our people in the First World War opened the way to renewal, we closed it upon ourselves by failing to consolidate our military victory, by forgoing the reparations which would have provided us with the means of industrializing our country and thus compensating for our enormous human and material losses, and, finally, by withdrawing into a passive strategic and foreign policy which left Europe a prey to Hitler's ambitions. Now, in the aftermath of the last conflict in which she had all but perished, on what premises was France to base her progress and her actions?

The first of these premises was that, in spite of everything, she was alive, sovereign and victorious. That was undoubtedly a marvel. Who would have thought that, after suffering an unparalleled disaster, after witnessing the subjection of her rulers to the authority of the enemy, after undergoing the ravages of the two greatest battles of the war and, in the meantime, prolonged plundering by the invader, after enduring the systematic abasement inflicted on her by a regime founded on surrender and humiliation, she would ever heal the wounds inflicted on her body and her soul? Who would not have sworn that her liberation, if it was to come, would be due to foreigners alone and that they would decide what was to become of her at home and abroad? Who, in the almost total extinction of her resistance, had not condemned as absurd the hope that one day the enemy would surrender to her at the same time as to her allies? Nevertheless, in the end she had emerged from the struggle with her frontiers and her unity intact, in control of her own affairs, and in the ranks of the victors. There was nothing, therefore, to prevent her now from being what she intended to be and doing what she wished to do.

This was all the more true because, for the first time in her history, she was unhampered by any threat from her immediate neighbors. Germany, dismembered, had ceased to be a formidable and domineering power. Italy regretted having turned her ambitions against us. The alliance with England, preserved by Free France, and the process of decolonization which had removed old grievances, ensured that the wind of mistrust no longer blew across the English Channel. Bonds of affection and common interest were bringing a serene France and a pacified Spain closer together across the Pyrenees. And what enmities could possibly spring up from the friendly lands of Belgium, Luxembourg, Holland or neutral Switzerland? Thus we were relieved of the state of constant tension in which dangerous neighbors once held us and which gravely hampered our activities.

It is true that, while France had lost her special vocation of being constantly in danger, the whole world was now haunted by the permanent fear of global conflict. Two empires, the American and the Soviet, now become giants in comparison with the old powers, confronted each other with their forces, their hegemonies and their ideologies. Both were in possession of nuclear armaments which could at any moment shake the entire world, and which made each of them omnipotent protectors in their respective camps. This perilous balance was liable to tip over eventually into limitless war unless it evolved into a general *détente*. For France, reduced in wealth and power by the conflicts in which she had been engaged over the past two centuries, dangerously exposed by her geographical position at the edge of the Old World and facing the New, mortally vulnerable by reason of her size and population, peace was obviously of vital importance. And, as it happened, circumstances now ordained that she should appoint herself its champion. For she was in the singular position of having no claims on what others possessed while they had nothing to claim from her, and of harboring no grievances on her own behalf against either of the giants, for whose peoples she cherished a traditional friendship confirmed by recent events, while they felt an exceptional attachment to her. In short, if there was a voice that might be listened to and a policy that might be effective with a view to setting up a new order to replace the Cold War, that voice and that policy were pre-eminently those of France. But only on condition that they were really her own and that the hand she held out in friendship was free.

At the same time, France now enjoyed a vast fund of interest and trust among peoples whose future was in gestation but who refused to pay allegiance to either of the rival dominations. China, endowed with such reserves of manpower and resources, that limitless possibilities were open to her for the future; Japan, recreating an independent world role on the basis of economic strength; India, at grips with problems of subsistence as vast as her size, but ultimately destined to turn towards the outside world; a great number of old and new states in Africa, Asia and Latin America which accepted aid from either or both of the two camps for the immediate needs of their development, but refused to align themselves—all these now looked by choice towards France. True, until she had completed the process of decolonization, they bitterly criticized her, but the criticisms soon ceased when she had liberated her former possessions. It remained for her to exploit the potential of respect, admiration and prestige which existed in her favor over a large part of the globe provided that, as the world expected of her, she served the universal cause of human dignity and progress.

Thus the same destiny which had enabled France to survive the terrible crisis of the war, offered to her afterwards, in spite of all she had lost over the past two centuries in terms of relative power and wealth, a leading international role which suited her genius, responded to her interests and matched her means. I was naturally determined that she should play this role, the more so since I believed that the internal transformation, the political stability and the social progress without which she would unquestionably be doomed to disorder and decline demanded that she should once again feel herself invested with world responsibility. Such was my philosophy. What was my policy to be as regards the practical problems that faced our country abroad?

Apart from that of Algeria and our colonies, which was for us to settle on our own, these problems were of such scope and range that their solution would be a very lengthy undertaking, unless a new war should chance to come and cut the Gordian knots tied by the previous one. Hence a sustained and continuous policy was required to deal with them, and this was precisely what, in contrast to the unending shifts and changes of the past, our new institutions made possible.

But what exactly were these problems? First of all there was Germany, divided into three by the existence of a parliamentary republic in the West, a Communist dictatorship in the East, and a special status for Berlin, a prey to the internal strains imposed by this state of affairs and the principal pawn in the rivalry between the two camps. There was Europe, impelled by reason and sentiment towards unification after the terrible convulsions which had torn it apart but radically divided by the Iron Curtain, the Cold War and the enforced subjection of its eastern half to Soviet domination. There was the organization imposed on the Atlantic alliance, which amounted to the military and political subordination of Western Europe to the United States of America. There was the problem of aid for the development of the Third World, which was used by Washington and Moscow as a battleground for their rivalry. There were crises in the East, in Africa, in Asia and in Latin America, which the rival interventions of the two giants rendered chronic and incurable. And there were the international institutions in which the two opposing camps polarized judgments on all subjects and prohibited impartiality.

In each of these fields, I wanted France to play an active part. In this poor world which deserved to be handled gently and each of whose leaders was weighed down with grave difficulties, we had to advance step by step, acting as circumstances demanded and respecting the susceptibilities of all. I myself had struck many a blow in my time, but never at the pride of a people nor at the dignity of its leaders. Yet it was essential that what we did and said should be independent of others. From the moment of my return to power, that was our rule—such a complete change of attitude on the part of our country that the world political scene was suddenly and profoundly transformed.

It is true that the Eastern camp at first confined itself to watching to see what new attitude emerged in Paris. But our Western partners, among whom up till then official France had submissively taken its place under the hegemony known as Atlantic solidarity, could not help being put out. However, they would eventually resign themselves to the new situation. It must be said that the experience of dealing with de Gaulle which some of them had had during the war, and all of them after it, meant that they did not expect this Republic to be as easy to handle as the previous one. Still, there was a general feeling in their chancelleries, their parliaments and their newspapers that the ordeal would be a brief one, that de Gaulle would inevitably disappear after a while, and that everything would then be as it had been before. On the other hand, there was no lack of people in these countries, especially among the masses, who were not at all displeased by France's recovery and who felt a certain satisfaction, or envy perhaps, when they saw her shaking off a supremacy which weighed heavily on the whole of the Old World. Added to this were the feelings which foreign crowds were kind enough to entertain for me personally and which, each time I came in contact with them, they demonstrated with a fervor that impressed their governments. On the whole, in spite of the annoyance that was felt, the malicious remarks that were made, the unfavorable articles and aggressive caricatures that proliferated, the outside world would soon accommodate itself to a France who was once more behaving like a great power, and henceforth would follow her every action and her every word with an attention that had long been lacking.

I was to find rather less resignation in what was said and written in quarters which had hitherto been looked upon as the fountainhead of French political thought. For there it had long been more or less taken for granted that our country should take no action that was not dictated to it from outside. No doubt this attitude of mind dated from the time when the dangers which threatened France forced her continually to seek support from abroad, and when the instability of the political regime prevented the government from taking upon itself the risks of major decisions. Even before the First World War, in its alliance with Russia, the Third Republic had had to undertake to respect the Treaty of Frankfurt and let St. Petersburg lead the way rather than Paris. It is true that, during the long battle subsequently fought on our soil in alliance with the English, the Belgians and finally the Americans, the leading role and then the supreme command fell to the French, who in fact provided the principal effort. But was it not primarily the Anglo-Saxons' cry of "Halt!" that brought the sudden cessation of hostilities on 11 November 1918, at the very moment when we were about to pluck the fruits of victory? Were not the wishes and promises of the

American President the dominant factor in the Treaty of Versailles, which admittedly restored Alsace and Lorraine to us but left the enemy's unity, territory and resources intact? And afterwards, was it not to gratify the wishes of Washington and London that the government in Paris surrendered the guarantees we had secured and renounced the reparations which Germany owed us in exchange for specious schemes offered to us by America? When the Hitlerian threat appeared and the Führer ventured to move his troops into the Rhineland, and preventive or repressive action on our part would have been enough to bring about his retreat and discomfiture at a time when he was still short of armaments, did not our ministers remain passive because England failed to take the initiative? At the time of the Austrian Anschluss, then the dismemberment and annexation of Czechoslovakia by the Reich, from whence did French acquiescence stem if not from the example of the English? In the surrender of Vichy to the invader's law and in the "collaboration" designed to make our country participate in a so-called European order which in fact was purely Germanic, was there not a trace of this long inurement to satellite status? At the same time, even as I strove to preserve France's sovereign rights in relation to our allies while fighting the common enemy, whence sprang the reprobation voiced by even those closest to me, if not from the idea that we should always give way?

After so many lessons, it might have been thought that once the war was over, those who claimed to lead public opinion would be less inclined towards subordination. Far from it: for the leading school of thought in each political party, national self-effacement had become an established and flaunted doctrine. While for the Communists it was an absolute rule that Moscow is always right, all the old party formations professed the doctrine of "supranationalism," in other words France's submission to a law that was not her own. Hence the support for "Europe" seen as an edifice in which technocrats forming an "executive" and parliamentarians assuming legislative powers—the great majority of both being foreigners—would have the authority to decide the fate of the French people. Hence, too, the passion for the Atlantic organization which would put the security and therefore the policy of our country at the disposal of another. Hence, again, the eagerness to submit the acts of our government to the approval of international organizations in which, under a semblance of collective deliberation, the authority of the protector reigned supreme in every field, whether political, military, economic, technical or monetary, and in which our representatives would never dare to say "we want" but simply confine themselves to "pleading France's cause." Hence, finally, the constant fury aroused among the party-political breed by my actions in the name of an independent nation.

Nevertheless, I was to find no lack of support. Emotionally, I would have the backing of the French people, who, without being in the least inclined to arrogance, were determined to preserve their own identity, all the more so because they had nearly lost it and because others everywhere were ardently affirming theirs, whether in terms of sovereignty, language, culture, production or even sport. Whenever I expressed myself in public on these matters I felt a quiver of response. Politically, the organization which had been formed to follow me above and beyond all the old parties, and which had had a numerous and compact group elected to parliament, was to accompany me through thick and thin. Practically, I would have a stable government at my side, whose Prime Minister was convinced of France's right and duty to act on a world scale, and whose Foreign Minister displayed in his field an ability which few have equalled in the course of our arduous history.

Maurice Couve de Murville had the required gifts. Amid a welter of interlocking problems and tangled arguments he was immediately able to distinguish the essential from the accessory, so that he was clear and precise in matters which others deliberately made as obscure and ambiguous as possible. He had the experience, having dealt with many of the issues of the day and known most of the men in command in the course of a distinguished career. He had the confidence, certain as he was that the post to which I had nominated him would be his for a long time. He had the manner, being skillful at making contact by listening, observing and taking note, and then excelling, at the critical moment, in the authoritative formulation of a position from which he would never be deflected. He had the necessary faith, convinced as he was that France could survive only in the first rank of nations, that de Gaulle could put her back there, and that nothing in life was more important than working towards this goal.

This was what we were aiming for in the vast arena of Europe. I myself had always felt, and now more than ever, how much the nations which peopled it had in common. Being all of the same white race, with the same Christian origins and the same way of life, linked to one another since time immemorial by countless ties of thought, art, science, politics and trade, it was natural that they should come to form a whole, with its own character and organization in relation to the rest of the world. It was in pursuance of this destiny that the Roman emperors reigned over it, that Charlemagne, Charles V and Napoleon attempted to unite it, that Hitler sought to impose upon it his crashing domination. But it is a fact of some significance that not one of these federators succeeded in inducing the subject countries to surrender their individuality. On the contrary, arbitrary centralization always provoked an upsurge of violent nationalism by way of reaction. It was my belief that a united Europe could not today, any more than in previous times, be a fusion of its peoples, but that it could and should result from a systematic *rapprochement*. Everything prompted them towards this in an age of proliferating trade, international enterprises, science and technology which know no frontiers, rapid communications and widespread travel. My policy therefore aimed at the setting up of a concert of European states which in developing all sorts of ties between them would increase their interdependence and solidarity. From this starting point, there was every reason to believe that the process of evolution might lead to their confederation, especially if they were one day to be threatened from the same source.

In practice this led us to put the European Economic Community into effect; to encourage the Six to concert together regularly in political matters; to prevent certain others, in particular Great Britain, from dragging the West into an Atlantic system which would be totally incompatible with a European Europe, and indeed to persuade these centrifugal elements to integrate themselves with the Continent by changing their outlook, their habits and their customers; and finally to set an example of *détente* followed by understanding and cooperation with the countries of the Eastern bloc, in the belief that beyond all the prejudices and preconceptions of ideology and propaganda, it was peace and progress that answered the needs and desires of the inhabitants of both halves of an accidentally divided Europe.

At the heart of the problem and at the center of the continent lay Germany. It was her destiny to be the keystone of any European edifice, and yet her misdeeds had contributed more than anything else to tearing the Old World apart. True, now that she was sliced into three segments, with the forces of her conquerors stationed in each, she was no longer a direct threat to anyone. But how could the memory of her ambition, her audacity, her power and her tyranny be effaced from peoples' memories—an ambition which only yesterday had unleashed a military machine capable of crushing with one blow the armies of France and her allies; an audacity which, thanks to Italy's complicity, had carried her armies as far as Africa and the Nile basin; a power which, driving across Poland and Russia with Italian, Hungarian, Bulgarian and Rumanian aid, had reached the gates of Moscow and the foothills of the Caucasus; a tyranny whose reign had brought oppression, plunder and crime wherever the fortune of war took the German flag? Henceforth, every precaution must be taken to prevent Germany's evil genius from breaking loose again. But how could a real and lasting peace be built on foundations that were unacceptable to this great people? How could a genuine union of the continent be established without Germany being a part of it? How could the age-old threat of ruin and death be finally dispelled on either side of the Rhine as long as the old enmity remained?

On the all-important question of Germany's future, my mind was made up. First of all, I believed that it would be unjust and dangerous to revise the *de facto* frontiers which the war had imposed on her. This meant that the Oder-Neisse line which separates her from Poland should remain her definitive boundary, that nothing should remain of her former claims in respect of Czechoslovakia, and that a new Anschluss in whatever form must be precluded. Furthermore, the right to possess or to manufacture atomic weapons—which in any case she had declared her intention to renounce—must in no circumstances be granted to her. This being so, I considered it essential that she should form an integral part of the organized system of cooperation between states which I envisaged for the whole of our continent. In this way the security of all nations between the Atlantic and the Urals would be guaranteed, and a change brought about in circumstances, attitudes and relationships which would doubtless ultimately permit the reunion of the three segments of the German people. In the meantime, the Federal Republic would have an essential role to play within the Economic Community and, should it ever materialize, in the political concert of the Six. Finally, I intended that France should weave a network of preferential ties with Germany, which would gradually lead the two peoples towards the mutual understanding and appreciation to which their natural instinct prompts them when they are no longer using up their energies in fighting each other.

. . .

Cooperation between the two former enemies [France and Germany] was a necessary but by no means a sufficient precondition for organized European cooperation. It is true that, judging merely by the spate of speeches and articles on the subject, the unification of our Continent might well appear to be a matter as simple as it was foreordained. But when the realities of needs, interests and preconceptions came into play, things took on an altogether different aspect. While fruitless bargaining with the British showed the fledgling Community that good intentions are not enough to reconcile the irreconcilable, the Six found that even in the economic sphere alone the adjustment of their respective positions bristled with difficulties which could not be resolved solely in terms of the treaties concluded to that end. It had to be acknowledged that the so-called executives installed at the head of common institutions by virtue of the delusions of integration which had prevailed before my return, were helpless when it came to making and enforcing decisions, that only governments were in a position to do this, and then only as a result of negotiations carried out in due form between ministers or ambassadors.

In the case of the European Coal and Steel Community, for example, once it had used up the birthday presents bestowed upon it by its member states, none of them, be it said, for our benefit—French relinquishment of coke from the Ruhr, deliveries of coal and iron to Italy, financial subventions to the Benelux mines—the High Authority, although vested with very extensive theoretical powers and considerable resources, was soon overwhelmed by the problems presented by competing national requirements. Whether it was a matter of fixing the price of steel, or regulating fuel purchases from outside, or converting the collieries of the Borinage, the areopagus enthroned in Luxembourg was powerless to legislate. The result was a chronic decline in that organization, whose prime mover, Jean Monnet, had moreover resigned the presidency.

At the same time, in the case of EURATOM, there seemed an irremediable disparity between the situation of France, equipped for some fifteen years past with an active Atomic Energy Commissariat, provided with numerous installations and already engaged in precise and far-reaching programs of research and development, and that of the other countries which, having done nothing on their own account, now wanted to use the funds of the common budget to obtain what they lacked by placing orders with American suppliers.

Lastly, in the case of the Economic Community, the adoption of the agricultural regulations in conjunction with the lowering of industrial tariffs raised obstacles which the Brussels Commission was unable to overcome on its own. It must be said that in this respect the spirit and terms of the Treaty of Rome did not meet our country's requirements. The industrial provisions were as precise and explicit as those concerning agriculture were vague. This was evidently due to the fact that our negotiators in 1957, caught up in the dream of a supranational Europe and anxious at any price to settle for something approaching it, had not felt it their duty to insist that a French interest, no matter how crucial, should receive satisfaction at the outset. It would, therefore, be necessary either to obtain it *en route*, or to liquidate the Common Market. Meanwhile, determined though it was to have its way in the end, the French government was able to allow the machinery of the Treaty of Rome to be set in motion thanks to the recovery of our balance of payments and the stabilization of the franc. In December 1958 it announced that it would implement the inaugural measures which were scheduled for New Year's Day, in particular a 10 percent tariff cut and a 20 percent quota increase.

Once initiated, the implementation of the Common Market was to give rise to a vast outgrowth of not only technical but also diplomatic activity. For, irrespective of its very wide economic scope, the operation proved to be hedged about with specifically political intentions calcu-lated to prevent our country from being its own master. Hence, while the Community was taking shape, I was obliged on several occasions to intervene in order to repel the threats which overshadowed our cause.

The first arose from the original ambivalence of the institution. Was its objective—in itself momentous enough—the harmonization of the practical interests of the six states, their economic solidarity in face of the outside world and, if possible, their cooperation in foreign policy? Or did it aim to achieve the total fusion of their respective economies and policies in a single entity with its own government, parliament and laws, ruling in every respect its French, German, Italian, Dutch, Belgian and Luxembourg subjects, who would become fellow citizens of an artificial motherland, the brainchild of the technocrats? Needless to say, having no taste for make believe, I adopted the former conception. But the latter carried all the hopes and illusions of the supranational school.

For these champions of integration, the European executive was already alive and kicking: it was the Commission of the Economic Community, made up, admittedly, of representatives nominated by the six states but, thereafter, in no way dependent on them. Judging by the chorus of those who wanted Europe to be a federation, albeit without a federator, all the authority, initiative and control of the exchequer which are the prerogatives of government in the economic sphere must in future belong to this brigade of experts, not only within the Commu-nity but also—and this could be indefinitely extensible—from the point of view of relations with other countries. As for the national ministers, who could not as yet be dispensed with in their executive capacity, they had only to be summoned periodically to Brussels, where they would receive the Commission's instructions in their specialized fields. At the same time, the mythmongers wanted to exhibit the Assembly in Strasbourg, consisting of deputies and senators delegated by the legisla-tures of the member countries, as a "European parliament" which, while having no effective power, provided the Brussels "executive" with a semblance of democratic responsibility.

Walter Hallstein was the Chairman of the Commission. He was ardently wedded to the thesis of the superstate, and bent all his skillful efforts towards giving the Community the character and appearance of one. He had made Brussels, where he resided, into a sort of capital. There he sat, surrounded with all the trappings of sovereignty, directing his colleagues, allocating jobs among them, controlling several thousand officials who were appointed, promoted and remunerated at his discre-tion, receiving the credentials of foreign ambassadors, laying claim to high honors on the occasion of his official visits, concerned above all to further the amalgamation of the Six, believing that the pressure of events would bring about what he envisaged. But after meeting him more than once and observing his activities, I felt that although Walter Hallstein was in his way a sincere European, he was first and foremost a German who was ambitious for his own country. For in the Europe that he sought lay the framework in which his country could first of all regain, free of charge, the respectability and equality of rights which the frenzy and defeat of Hitler had cost it, then acquire the preponderant influence which its economic strength would no doubt earn it, and finally ensure that the cause of its frontiers and its unity was backed by a powerful coalition in accordance with the doctrine to which, as Foreign Minister of the Federal Republic, he had formerly given his name. These factors did not alter my esteem and regard for Walter Hallstein, but the goals I was pursuing on behalf of France were incompatible with such projects.

The fundamental divergence between the way the Brussels Commission conceived its role and my own government's insistence, while looking to the Commission for expert advice, that important measures should be subordinated to the decisions of the individual states, nurtured an atmosphere of latent discord. But since the Treaty specified that during the inaugural period no decision was valid unless unanimous, it was enough to enforce its application to ensure that there was no infringement of French sovereignty. So during this period the institution took wing in what was and must remain the economic sphere without being subjected to any mortal political crisis, in spite of frequent clashes. Moreover, in November 1959, at the initiative of Paris, it was decided that the six foreign ministers should meet at three-monthly intervals to examine the overall situation and its various implications and to report back to their own governments, which would have the last word if the need arose. It may be imagined that ours did not allow itself to be led.

But it was not only from the political angle that the newfledged Community had to undergo the truth test. Even in the economic sphere two formidable obstacles, secreting all kinds of contradictory interests and calculations, threatened to bar its way. These were, of course, the external tariff and agriculture, which were closely bound up with one another. True, on signing the Treaty, our partners had seemed to accept that common taxes should be imposed upon foreign goods as customs duties were reduced within the Community. But although they all recognized in principle that this procedure was essential to their solidarity, some of them were nonetheless irked by it because it deprived them of trade facilities which had hitherto been intrinsic to their existence. They therefore wanted the common external tariff to be as low as possible and in any case so elastic that their habits would not be disturbed. The same countries, for the same reasons, were in no hurry to see the Six take upon themselves the consumption and, therefore, the cost of continental farm products, nearly half of which happened to be French. For instance Germany, nearly two-thirds of whose food was imported cheaply from outside the Community in exchange for manufactured goods, would have liked to see a Common Market for industrial goods only, in which case the Federal Republic would inevitably have had an overwhelming advantage. This was unacceptable to France. We therefore had to put up a fight in Brussels.

The battle was long and hard. Our partners, who bitterly regretted our having changed Republics, had been counting on us once again to sacrifice our own cause to "European integration," as had happened successively with the Coal and Steel Community, in which all the advantages went to others at our expense; with EURATOM, for which our country put up practically the entire stake without a *quid pro quo,* and, moreover submitted her atomic assets to foreign supervision; and with the Treaty of Rome, which did not settle the agricultural question which was of paramount importance to ourselves. But now France was determined to get what she needed, and in any case her demands were consistent with the logic of the Community system. So her requirements were eventually met.

In May 1960, at our urgent insistence, the Six agreed to establish the external tariff and to adopt a timetable for the decisions to be taken on agricultural policy. In December of the same year, while urging an acceleration of the process of lowering customs barriers between them, they agreed that all imports of foodstuffs from elsewhere should be liable to an enormous financial levy at the expense of the purchasing state. And in January 1962 they adopted the decisive resolutions.

For at this date, now that the first phase of application was completed, it had to be decided whether or not, in pursuance of the terms of the Treaty, to proceed to the second phase, a kind of point of no return, involving a 50 percent reduction in customs duties. We French were determined to seize the opportunity to tear aside the veil and induce our partners to make formal commitments on what we regarded as essential. When they proved reluctant to give way, and indeed showed signs of some disquieting reservations, I judged that now or never was the moment to take the bull by the horns. Our ministers in Brussels, Couve de Murville, Baumgartner and Pisani, made it quite clear that we were prepared to withdraw from the Community if our requirements were not met. I myself wrote in similar terms to Chancellor Adenauer, whose government was our principal antagonist in this matter, and repeated it by formal telegram on the evening of the final debate. Feeling ran high in the capitals of the Six. In France, the parties and most of the newspapers, echoing foreign opinion, were disturbed and scandalized by the attitude of General de Gaulle, whose intransigence was threatening "the hopes of Europe." But France and common sense prevailed. During the night of 13–14 January 1962, after some dramatic exchanges, the Council of Ministers of the six states formally decided to admit agriculture into the Common Market, laid down there and then a broad basis for its implementation, and made the necessary arrangements to establish the agricultural regulations on the same footing and at the same time as the rest. Whereupon the implementation of the Treaty was able to enter its second phase.

But how far could it go, in view of the difficulties which the British were doing their utmost to raise, and the tendency of our five partners to submit to their influence? It was not surprising that Great Britain should be radically opposed to the whole venture, since by virtue of her geography—and therefore her policy, she has never been willing to see the Continent united or to merge with it herself. In a sense it might almost be said that therein lay the whole history of Europe for the past eight hundred years. As for the present, our neighbors across the Channel, adapted to free trade by the maritime nature of their economic life, could not sincerely agree to shut themselves up behind a continental tariff wall, still less to buy their food dear from us rather than import it cheap from everywhere else, for example the Commonwealth. But without the common tariff and agricultural preference, there could be no valid European Community. Hence at the time of the preliminary studies and discussions that led up to the Treaty of Rome, the London government, which was represented at the outset, had soon withdrawn. Then, with the intention of undermining the project of the Six, it had proposed that they should join a vast European free trade area with itself and various others. Things had reached this stage when I returned to power.

As early as 29 June 1958, Prime Minister Harold Macmillan had come to see me in Paris. In the midst of our friendly discussions which touched upon a great many topics, he suddenly declared with great feeling: "The Common Market is the Continental System all over again. Britain cannot accept it. I beg you to give it up. Otherwise, we shall be embarking on a war which will doubtless be economic at first but which runs the risk of gradually spreading into other fields." Ignoring the overstatement, I tried to pacify the English premier, at the same time asking him why the United Kingdom should object to seeing the Six establish a system of preference such as existed inside the Commonwealth. Meanwhile, his minister Reginald Maudling was actively engaged inside the so-called Organization for European Economic Cooperation, to which Britain belonged, in negotiations which were keeping the Six in suspense, and delaying the launching of the Community by proposing that the latter should be absorbed and, consequently, dissolved in a free trade area. Harold Macmillan wrote me a number of very pressing letters in an effort to obtain my compliance. But my government broke the spell, and made it clear that it would not agree to anything which did not include the common external tariff and an agricultural arrangement. London then appeared to abandon its policy of obstruction and, suddenly changing course, set up its own European Free Trade Association, with the Scandinavians, Portugal, Switzerland and Austria. At once, our Brussels partners dropped all their hesitations and set about launching the Common Market.

But the match had merely been postponed. In the middle of 1961 the British returned to the offensive. Having failed from without to prevent the birth of the Community, they now planned to paralyze it from within. Instead of calling for an end to it, they now declared that they themselves were eager to join, and proposed examining the conditions on which they might do so, "provided that their special relationships with the Commonwealth and their associates in the free trade area were taken into consideration, as well as their special interests in respect of agriculture." To submit to this would obviously have meant abandoning the Common Market as originally conceived. Our partners could not bring themselves to do so. But, on the other hand, it was beyond their power to say "No" to England. So, affecting to believe that the squaring of the circle was a practical proposition, they proceeded to discuss a series of projects and counter-projects in Brussels with the British minister Edward Heath, which threw nothing but doubt on the future of the Community. I could see the day approaching when I should either have to remove the obstruction and put an end to the tergiversation, or else extricate France from an enterprise which had gone astray almost as soon as it had begun. At all events, as could have been foreseen, it was now clear to all that in order to achieve the unification of Europe, individual states are the only valid elements, that when their national interest is at stake nothing and nobody must be allowed to force their hands, and that cooperation between them is the only road that will lead anywhere.

In this respect what is true of economics is even truer of politics. And this is no more than natural. What depths of illusion or prejudice would have to be plumbed in order to believe that European nations forged through long centuries by endless exertion and suffering, each with its own geography, history, language, traditions and institutions, could cease to be themselves and form a single entity? What a perfunctory view is reflected in the parallel often naively drawn between what Europe ought to do and what the United States have done, when the latter was created from nothing in a completely new territory by successive waves of uprooted colonists? For the Six in particular, how was it conceivable that their external aims should suddenly become identical when their origins, situations and ambitions were so very different? In the matter of decolonization, which France was about to bring to a conclusion, what part could her neighbors play? If, from time immemorial, it had been in her nature to accomplish "God's work," to disseminate freedom of thought, to be a champion of humanity, why should it *ipso facto* become the concern of her partners? Germany, balked by defeat of her hopes of supremacy, divided at present and suspected by many of seeking her revenge, was now a wounded giant. By what token should her wounds automatically be shared by others? Given the fact that Italy, having ceased to be an annex of the Germanic or the French empires, and thwarted of her Balkan ambitions, remained a peninsular power confined to the Mediterranean and naturally located within the orbit of the maritime nations, why should she throw in her lot with the Continentals? By what miracle would the Netherlands, which had always owed its livelihood to shipping and its independence to overseas resources, allow itself to be swallowed up by the land powers? How could Belgium, hard put to it to maintain the juxtaposition of Flemings and Walloons in a single entity ever since a compromise between rival powers had turned her into a State, genuinely devote herself to anything else? Lying at the center of the territorial arrangements which had succeeded the rivalries of the two great countries bordering on the Moselle, what major concern could the people of Luxembourg have other than the survival of Luxembourg?

On the other hand, while recognizing that each of these countries had its own national personality which it must preserve, there was no reason why they should not organize concerted action in every sphere, arrange for their ministers to meet regularly and their Heads of State or Government periodically, set up permanent organs to discuss politics, economics, culture and defense, have these subjects debated in the normal way by an assembly of delegates from their respective parliaments, acquire the taste and habit of examining together problems of common interest, and as far as possible adopt a united attitude towards them. Linked with what was already being practiced in the economic sphere in Brussels and Luxembourg, might not this general cooperation lead to a European policy as regards progress, security, influence, external relations, aid to the developing countries, and finally and above all as regards peace? Might not the grouping thus formed by the Six gradually attract the other states of the Continent into joining in on the same terms? And perhaps in this way, by opposing war, which is the history of men, that united Europe which is the dream of the wise might ultimately be achieved.

. . .

In the course of a press conference on 5 September [1960], after saying that "to build Europe, which means to unite Europe, is an essential aim of our policy," I declared that to this end it was necessary "to proceed, not on the basis of dreams, but in accordance with realities. Now, what are the realities of Europe? What are the pillars on which it can be built? The truth is that those pillars are the states of Europe . . . states each of which, indeed, has its own genius, history and language, its own sorrows, glories and ambitions; but states that are the only entities with the right to give orders and the power to be obeyed." Then, while recognizing "the technical value of certain more or less extranational or supranational organisms," I pointed out that they were not and could not be politically effective, as was proved by what was happening at that very moment in the European Coal and Steel Community, EURATOM and the Brussels Community. I insisted that, "although it is perfectly natural for the states of Europe to have specialist bodies available to prepare and whenever necessary to follow up their decisions, those decisions must be their own." Then I outlined my plan: "To arrange for the regular cooperation of the states of Western Europe in the political, economic and cultural spheres, as well as that of defense, is an aim that France deems desirable, possible and practical. . . . It will entail organized, regular consultations between the governments concerned and the work of specialist bodies in each of the common domains, subordinated to those governments. It will entail periodic deliberations by an assembly made up of delegates of the national parliaments. It must also, in my view, entail as soon as possible a solemn European referendum, in order to give this new departure for Europe the popular backing which is essential to it." I concluded: "If we set out on this road . . . links will be forged, habits will be developed, and, as time does its work, it is possible that we will come to take further steps towards European unity."

. . .

6 Preamble to the Single European Act

Representatives of the twelve members of the European Community signed the Single European Act (SEA) in February 1986 and saw it implemented in July 1987. The SEA, the first major revision of the Treaty of Rome, brought together in one "single" act a treaty on European cooperation in the area of foreign policy and institutional and procedural reforms (such as the increased use of qualified majority voting) designed to facilitate the completion of the single market. The act, although not universally recognized at the time as significant, marked a milestone in the attempt by Community leaders to bury the legacy of Charles de Gaulle and "relaunch" Europe. The success of the SEA in facilitating the single market opened the way for further institutional reforms in the early 1990s.

The preamble to the SEA differs significantly from its predecessors. Gone is the vision of a united Europe important primarily as an alternative to war. In its place is a vision of an evolving "European Union" ready to act in the world as a single entity to protect the common interests of its members, promote democracy and human rights, contribute to the "preservation of international peace," and "improve the economic and social situation in Europe." The preamble assumed that the European Communities resembled a sovereign entity more than a mere collection of individual states, an evolution the signatories believed corresponded to the "wishes of the democratic peoples of Europe."

. . .

MOVED by the will to continue the work undertaken on the basis of the Treaties establishing the European Communities and to transform relations as a whole among their States into a European Union, in accordance with the Solemn Declaration of Stuttgart of 19 June 1983,

RESOLVED to implement this European Union on the basis, firstly, of the Communities operating in accordance with their own rules and, secondly, of European Cooperation among the Signatory States in the sphere of foreign policy and to invest this union with the necessary means of action,

DETERMINED to work together to promote democracy on the basis of the fundamental rights recognized in the constitutions and laws of the Member States, in the Convention for the Protection of Human Rights and Fundamental Freedoms and the European Social Charter, notably freedom, equality and social justice,

CONVINCED that the European idea, the results achieved in the fields of economic integration and political cooperation, and the need for new developments correspond to the wishes of the democratic peoples of Europe, for whom the European Parliament elected by universal suffrage, is an indispensable means of expression,

AWARE of the responsibility incumbent upon Europe to aim at speaking ever increasingly with one voice and to act with consistency and solidarity in order more effectively to protect its common interests and independence, in particular to display the principles of democracy and compliance with the law and with human rights to which they are attached, so that together they may make their own contribution to the preservation of international peace and security in accordance with the undertaking entered into by them within the framework of the United Nations Charter,

DETERMINED to improve the economic and social situation by extending common policies and pursuing new objectives, and to ensure a smoother functioning of the Communities by enabling the institutions to exercise their powers under conditions most in keeping with Community interests,

WHEREAS at their Conference in Paris from 19 to 21 October 1972 the Heads of State or of Government approved the objective of the progressive realization of Economic and Monetary Union,

HAVING REGARD to the Annex to the conclusions of the Presidency of the European Council in Bremen on 6 and 7 July 1978 and the Resolution of the European Council in Brussels on 5 December 1978 on the introduction of the European Monetary System (EMS) and related questions, and noting that in accordance with that Resolution, the Community and the Central Banks of the Member States have taken a number of measures intended to implement monetary cooperation,

HAVE DECIDED to adopt this Act.

. . .

7 A Family of Nations

Margaret Thatcher

Margaret Thatcher served as Britain's prime minister from 1979 to 1990. During her eleven years in office, she attempted to reduce the role of government in British society, particularly the economy. Her distrust of big government extended to the institutions of the European Community, which she considered a threat to prosperity in Europe and her policy successes in Britain. While prime minister, Thatcher raised the ire of most ec leaders by working tirelessly and unapologetically for Britain's particular interests and by resisting, often alone, most attempts to expand the powers of ec institutions. After her elevation to the House of Lords, she furthered her reputation as a virulent Euroskeptic by leading a small group of parliamentarians in a loud but unsuccessful fight to block Britain's ratification of the Maastricht treaty in 1993.

Prime Minister Thatcher outlined her views on European integration in a speech at the College of Europe in Bruges, Belgium, on 20 September 1988. There she placed Britain firmly in Europe but rejected the notion that "Europe" meant the absorption of Britain—and all the other member states—into a single, bureaucratized European "superstate." The European Community, she argued, would succeed only if each member state was allowed to maintain its own identity. Her vision of Europe as a "family of nations"—which mirrors de Gaulle's—represents well the traditional British approach to integration, but challenges the federalist vision of the founders and continental builders of the Community. For this reason, Margaret Thatcher's Bruges speech proved highly controversial.

Mr Chairman, you have invited me to speak on the subject of Britain and Europe. Perhaps I should congratulate you on your courage.

Reprinted with permission from Lady Thatcher.

If you believe some of the things said and written about my views on Europe, it must seem rather like inviting Genghis Khan to speak on the virtues of peaceful coexistence!

I want to start by disposing of some myths about my country, Britain, and its relationship with Europe. And to do that I must say something about the identity of Europe itself. Europe is not the creation of the Treaty of Rome. Nor is the European idea the property of any group or institution. We British are as much heirs to the legacy of European culture as any other nation. Our links to the rest of Europe, the continent of Europe, have been the dominant factor in our history. For three hundred years we were part of the Roman Empire and our maps still trace the straight lines of the roads the Romans built. Our ancestors—Celts, Saxons and Danes—came from the continent. Our nation was—in that favorite Community word—"restructured" under Norman and Angevin rule in the eleventh and twelfth centuries. This year we celebrate the three hundredth anniversary of the Glorious Revolution in which the British crown passed to Prince William of Orange and Queen Mary. Visit the great churches and cathedrals of Britain, read our literature and listen to our language: all bear witness to the cultural riches which we have drawn from Europe—and other Europeans from us.

We in Britain are rightly proud of the way in which, since Magna Carta in 1215, we have pioneered and developed representative institutions to stand as bastions of freedom. And proud too of the way in which for centuries Britain was a home for people from the rest of Europe who sought sanctuary from tyranny. But we know that without the European legacy of political ideas we could not have achieved as much as we did. From classical and medieval thought we have borrowed that concept of the rule of law which marks out a civilized society from barbarism. And on that idea of Christendom—for long synonymous with Europe—with its recognition of the unique and spiritual nature of the individual, we still base our belief in personal liberty and other human rights.

Too often the history of Europe is described as a series of interminable wars and quarrels. Yet from our perspective today surely what strikes us most is our common experience. For instance, the story of how Europeans explored and colonized and—yes, without apology—civilized much of the world is an extraordinary tale of talent, skill and courage.

We British have in a special way contributed to Europe. Over the centuries we have fought to prevent Europe from falling under the dominance of a single power. We have fought and we have died for her freedom. Only miles from here in Belgium lie the bodies of 120,000 British soldiers who died in the First World War. Had it not been for that willingness to fight and to die, Europe would have been united long before now—but not in liberty, not in justice. It was British support to resistance movements throughout the last War that helped to keep alive the flame of liberty in so many countries until the day of liberation. It was from our island fortress that the liberation of Europe itself was mounted. And still today we stand together. Nearly 70,000 British servicemen are stationed on the mainland of Europe. All these things alone are proof of our commitment to Europe's future.

The European Community is one manifestation of that European identity. But it is not the only one. We must never forget that east of the Iron Curtain peoples who once enjoyed a full share of European culture, freedom and identity have been cut off from their roots. We shall always look on Warsaw, Prague and Budapest as great European cities. Nor should we forget that European values have helped to make the United States of America into the valiant defender of freedom which she has become.

This is no arid chronicle of obscure facts from the dust-filled libraries of history. It is the record of nearly two thousand years of British involvement in Europe, cooperation with Europe and contribution to Europe, a contribution which today is as valid and as strong as ever. Yes, we have looked also to wider horizons—as have others—and thank goodness for that because Europe never would have prospered and never will prosper as a narrow-minded, inward-looking club.

The European Community belongs to all its members. It must reflect the traditions and aspirations of all its members. And let me be quite clear. Britain does not dream of some cozy isolated existence on the fringes of the European Community. Our destiny is in Europe, as part of the Community. That is not to say that our future lies only in Europe. But nor does that of France or Spain or indeed any other member.

The Community is not an end in itself. Nor is it an institutional device to be constantly modified according to the dictates of some abstract intellectual concept. Nor must it be ossified by endless regulation. The European Community is the practical means by which Europe can ensure the future prosperity and security of its people in a world in which there are many other powerful nations and groups of nations. We Europeans cannot afford to waste our energies on internal disputes or arcane institutional debates. They are no substitute for effective action. Europe has to be ready both to contribute in full measure to its own security and to compete commercially and industrially, in a world in which success goes to the countries which encourage individual initiative and enterprise, rather than to those which attempt to diminish them.

This evening I want to set out some guiding principles for the future which I believe will ensure that Europe does succeed, not just in economic and defence terms but also in the quality of life and the influence of its peoples.

My first guiding principle is this: willing and active cooperation between independent sovereign states is the best way to build a successful European Community. To try to suppress nationhood and concentrate power at the center of a European conglomerate would be highly damaging and would jeopardize the objectives we seek to achieve. Europe will be stronger precisely because it has France as France, Spain as Spain, Britain as Britain, each with its own customs, traditions and identity. It would be folly to try to fit them into some sort of identikit European personality.

Some of the founding fathers of the Community thought that the United States of America might be its model. But the whole history of America is quite different from Europe. People went there to get away from the intolerance and constraints of life in Europe. They sought liberty and opportunity; and their strong sense of purpose has, over two centuries, helped create a new unity and pride in being American—just as our pride lies in being British or Belgian or Dutch or German.

I am the first to say that on many great issues the countries of Europe should try to speak with a single voice. I want to see us work more closely on the things we can do better together than alone. Europe is stronger when we do so, whether it be in trade, in defense, or in relations with the rest of the world. But working more closely together does not require power to be centralized in Brussels or decisions to be taken by an appointed bureaucracy. Indeed, it is ironic that just when those countries such as the Soviet Union, which have tried to run everything from the center, are learning that success depends on dispersing power and decisions away from the center, some in the Community seem to want to move in the opposite direction. We have not successfully rolled back the frontiers of the state in Britain, only to see them reimposed at a European level, with a European superstate exercising a new dominance from Brussels.

Certainly we want to see Europe more united and with a greater sense of common purpose. But it must be in a way which preserves the different traditions, parliamentary powers and sense of national pride in one's own country; for these have been the source of Europe's vitality through the centuries.

My second guiding principle is this: Community policies must tackle present problems in a practical way, however difficult they may be. If we cannot reform those Community policies which are patently wrong or ineffective and which are rightly causing public disquiet, then we shall not get the public's support for the Community's future development.

. . .

My third guiding principle is the need for Community policies which encourage enterprise. If Europe is to flourish and create the jobs of the future, enterprise is the key. The basic framework is there: the treaty of Rome itself was intended as a Charter for Economic Liberty. But that is not how it has always been read, still less applied.

The lesson of the economic history of Europe in the 1970s and 1980s is that central planning and detailed control don't work, and that personal endeavor and initiative do. That a state-controlled economy is a recipe for low growth; and that free enterprise within a framework of law brings better results. The aim of a Europe open to enterprise is the moving force behind the creation of the Single European Market by 1992. By getting rid of barriers, by making it possible for companies to operate on a Europewide scale, we can best compete with the United States, Japan and the other new economic powers emerging in Asia and elsewhere. And that means action to free markets, action to widen choice, action to reduce government intervention. Our aim should not be more and more detailed regulation from the center: it should be to deregulate and to remove the constraints on trade.

. . .

My fourth guiding principle is that Europe should not be protectionist. The expansion of the world economy requires us to continue the process of removing barriers to trade, and to do so in the multilateral negotiations in the GATT [General Agreement on Tariffs and Trade]. It would be a betrayal if, while breaking down constraints on trade within Europe, the Community were to erect greater external protection. We must ensure that our approach to world trade is consistent with the liberalization we preach at home.

We have a responsibility to give a lead on this, a responsibility which is particularly directed towards the less developed countries. They need not only aid; more than anything they need improved trading opportunities if they are to gain the dignity of growing economic strength and independence.

I believe it is not enough just to talk in general terms about a European vision or ideal. If we believe in it, we must chart the way ahead and identify the next steps. That is what I tried to do this evening.

This approach does not require new documents: they are all there, the North Atlantic Treaty, the Revised Brussels Treaty, and the Treaty of Rome, texts written by far-sighted men. However far we may want to go, the truth is that we can only get there one step at a time.

What we need now is to take decisions on the next steps forward rather than let ourselves be distracted by Utopian goals. Utopia never comes, because we know we should not like it if it did. Let Europe be a family of nations, understanding each other better, appreciating each other more, doing more together but relishing our national identity no less than our common European endeavor.

Let us have a Europe which plays its full part in the wider world, which looks outward not inward, and which preserves that Atlantic Community—that Europe on both sides of the Atlantic—which is our noblest inheritance and our greatest strength.

8   A Necessary Union

JACQUES DELORS

Jacques Delors assumed the presidency of the Commission of the European Community in January 1985. Prior to his appointment to the Commission, he was elected to the European Parliament (1979) and served as minister of finance (1981–1984) in France. Delors's energetic and visionary leadership contributed significantly to the revival of the Community in the 1980s and early 1990s. Under his watch, the Community took several significant steps, including the creation of the Single Market and the European Economic Area, and the negotiation and implementation of the Single European Act and the Maastricht treaty.

On 17 October 1989, one year after Margaret Thatcher made her Bruges speech, Jacques Delors traveled to the same spot and offered an alternative vision. His purpose was to convince the Community to seize the moment afforded by history and take a dramatic leap toward federalism. World events, particularly those in the East, and global interdependence necessitated the strengthening of EC institutions and the expansion of the "joint exercise of sovereignty." But true federalism, he asserted, included the principle of subsidiarity: "Never entrust to a bigger unit anything that is best done by a smaller one." Subsidiarity, he argued in response to Margaret Thatcher, made federalism the savior of pluralism, diversity, patriotism, and national identity in Europe. Indeed, the rejection of federalism, he warned, would mean the return of ugly nationalism.

Two years later, in Maastricht, EC leaders heeded Delors's Bruges call.

Reprinted with permission from *Address by Mr. Jacques Delors, President of the Commission of the European Communities, Bruges, 17 October 1989.* Copyright 1989 by the European Communities.

I am speaking to you today at the invitation of your Rector, Professor Lukaszewski, as the College of Europe celebrates its fortieth birthday. European integration has had its up and downs over those forty years, its high seasons of hope and progress and its long winters of despondency and stagnation. But here, in Bruges, faith in the European ideal has never wavered. Your Rector affirmed this, ten years ago, in an exacting, pluralist conception of Europe. He wrote:

> Shaping European awareness, fostering attachment to Europe as a community of civilization and destiny, is totally in keeping with the great university tradition of the West.

It is a happy coincidence that this year your College has chosen to pay tribute to Denis de Rougemont, an all too little-known figure, whose lifework and writings are a precious legacy. I would like to speak in more personal terms of Denis de Rougemont, I never had the good fortune to work with him, but I would like to tell you why I think so much of him, why I draw on his intellectual and political contribution.

First of all, as a militant European, I, like many others, am carrying on the work he began in his time. He was an ardent federalist. For him federalism was a many-splendored thing; he saw it as a method, an approach to reality, a view of society. I often find myself invoking federalism as a method, with the addition of the principle of subsidiarity. I see it as a way of reconciling what for many appears to be irreconcilable: the emergence of a United Europe and loyalty to one's homeland; the need for a European power capable of tackling the problems of our age and the absolute necessity to preserve our roots in the shape of our nations and regions; and decentralization of responsibilities, so that we never entrust to a bigger unit anything that is best done by a smaller one. This is precisely what subsidiarity is about.

As a personalist, a disciple of Emmanuel Mounier, whose influence will, I am convinced, revive as Europeans become aware of the quandaries of frenzied individualism, just as, for some years now, they have been rejecting collectivism and, in its attenuated form, the benevolent State.

I am pleased therefore to pay tribute today to a man who, throughout his life, kept on tilling the fields of hope. It is significant that, at the 1948 Congress in The Hague, Denis de Rougemont was asked to help draft and then read the Message to Europeans. He declared:

> Europe's mission is to unite her peoples in accordance with their genius of diversity and with the conditions of modern community life, and to open the way towards organized freedom for which the world is seeking. . . . Human dignity is Europe's finest achievement,

freedom her true strength. Both are at stake in our struggle. The union of our continent is now needed not only for the salvation of the liberties we have won, but also for the extension of their benefits to all mankind. Upon this union depend Europe's destiny and the world's peace.

Were he with us here today, I would want to discuss two points with him which have a bearing on our common future.

Denis de Rougemont believed in what I would call working from the bottom up, rebuilding from below, from small entities rooted naturally in a solidarity of interests and a convergence of feeling. That is of course essential, but it is not enough. Others, and I am one of them, must at the same time work from the top down, viewing the paths of integration from above. Otherwise the small streams of solidarity will never converge to form a wide river.

And de Rougemont abhorred power. Let me quote him again: "My philosophy comes down to this: power is the authority one would wield over others; freedom is the authority one can wield over oneself." Although I would not deny the philosophical value of this statement, I would beg to disagree with it from a political standpoint.

Politically speaking, power is not necessarily the obverse of freedom. Neither the European Community—nor the peoples and nations that form it—will truly exist unless it is in a position to defend its values, to act on them for the benefit of all, to be generous. Let us be powerful enough to command respect and to uphold the values of freedom and solidarity. In a world like ours, there is no other way.

I would link power with the necessity I have so often invoked to promote the revitalization of European integration. Today I would like to get power working for the ideal. Where would necessity take us had we no vision of what we want to achieve? And, conversely, what impact can an ideal have without the resolve and the means to act? The time has come, I feel, to reconcile necessity and the ideal.

We can do so by drawing on our own experiences, on our national heritages, and on the strength of our institutions. Let me underline the importance of this at a time when people can appreciate the limits of any action implemented with national resources alone. Our present concerns—be it the social dimension or the new frontier represented by economic and monetary union—offer a golden opportunity for the joint exercise of sovereignty, while respecting diversity and hence the principles of pluralism and subsidiarity.

There is a need for urgency, for history does not wait. As upheavals shake the world, and the other "Europe" in particular, our reinvigorated Community must work for increased cohesion and set objectives commensurate with the challenges thrown down by history.

History is only interested in the far-sighted and those who think big, like Europe's founding fathers. They are still with us today in the inspiration they provided and the legacy they left.

By "thinking big," I mean taking account of worldwide geopolitical and economic trends, the movement of ideas and the development of the fundamental values which inspire our contemporaries. The founding fathers wanted to see an end to internecine strife in Europe. But they also sensed that Europe was losing its place as the economic and political center of the world. Their intuition was confirmed before our very eyes, to the point in the 1970s when we had to choose between survival and decline. I shocked many people at that time by constantly arguing this point. Gradually, though, the need for a quantum leap became apparent and created a climate in which a single European market by 1992 could be accepted as an objective. The same dynamism led to revision of the Treaty of Rome—the Single Act—and to what is known as the Delors package, in other words the financial reforms necessary to pay for our ambitious plans. Necessity woke Europe from its slumbers.

By "far-sighted," I mean being simultaneously capable of drawing on our historical heritage and looking to the future. Futurology has a part to play but so has a code of ethics for the individual, society and the human adventure. This, frankly, is what we most lack today. I can say, with both feet on the ground, that the theory of the bogeyman-nation has no place in the life of our Community if it wants to be a Community worthy of the name. The inevitable conflicts of interest between us must be transcended by a family feeling, a sense of shared values. These include the enhancement of personality through mutual knowledge and exchange. The younger generation is very conscious of this new horizon. It rejects isolation, it wants to experience other ideas, to explore new territory. The time has come, my friends, to revive the ideal.

To get there, however, we must take the path of necessity. At a time when the Community is being courted by some, threatened by others; at a time when there are those who, with scant regard for the mortar which already binds us, advocate a headlong dash in the name of a greater Europe, or offer us as an ultimate reference nothing more than the laws of the market; to these we must say that our Community is the fruit not only of history and necessity, but also of political will.

Let us consider necessity for a moment. Since the turn-around of 1984–85 our achievements are there for all to see. The threat of a decline is receding. Businessmen and manufacturers are more aware of this than politicians, many of whom still underestimate the way in which the gradual achievement of the single European market and common policies have supported national efforts to adapt to the new world economic order. Yet all we need to do to see how far we have come is look beyond our frontiers: Europe is once again a force to be reckoned with and is arousing interest everywhere: in America, in Asia, in Africa, in the North and in the South.

Then there is political will. I know that the term has sometimes been abused, as a sort of incantation, but it is precisely political will that led first six, then nine, ten, twelve countries to decide to unite their destiny, with their eyes wide open. The contract binding them is clear, involving both rights and obligations.

Last of all, history. The Twelve cannot control history but they are now in a position to influence it once again. They did not want Europe to be cut in two at Yalta and made a hostage in the Cold War. They did not, nor do they, close the door to other European countries willing to accept the terms of the contract in full.

The present upheavals in Eastern Europe are changing the nature of our problems. It is not merely a matter of when and how all the countries of Europe will benefit from the stimulus and the advantages of a single market. Our times are dominated by a new mercantilism and our young people expect something better of us. Are we going to turn away?

Make no mistake about it. Behind triumphant nationalism and excessive individualism, ethics are making a comeback in the wake of scientific progress. How far, for example, are we prepared to allow genetic manipulation to go? We need a code of ethics for man, we need to promote our concept of the individual and his integrity. Nature, whether pillaged or neglected, strikes back with disturbances and upheavals. So we also need a code of ethics governing the relationship between man and nature. With millions of young people knocking in vain on the door of adult society, not least to find their place in the world of work, with millions of pensioners—still in the prime of life—cut off from any real role in society, we must ask ourselves what kind of society are we building. A society in which the door is always closed?

Europe has always been the continent of doubt and questioning, seeking a humanism appropriate to its time, the cradle of ideas which ultimately encircle the globe. The time has come to return to ideals, to let them penetrate our lives. Let us continue to consider, in everything we do in the field of politics, economics and social and cultural life, what will enable every man, every woman, to achieve their full potential in an awareness not only of their rights, but also of their obligations to others and to society as a whole. We must sustain our efforts to create a humane society in which the individual can blossom through contact and cooperation with others.

Of course any reference to humanism is bound to unleash a debate among Europeans. People will hold conflicting views, but a synthesis will emerge to the benefit of democracy and Europe itself. For the Community is a concept charged with significance. "Where there is no big vision, the people perish," as Jean Monnet said, making this saying of President Roosevelt's [and Prov. 29:18] his own.

In this respect we are engaged in a unique adventure. We are creating a model, admittedly by reference to inherited principles, but in circumstances so extraordinary that the end result will be unique, without historical precedent. We owe much to the strength of our institutions because our Community is a Community based on the rule of law. And the condition for success is the joint, transparent exercise of sovereignty.

Let us consider the strength of our institutions for a moment, beginning with legitimacy. Without legitimacy—as earlier attempts to unite nations have shown—no progress, no permanence is possible. In the Community the progress of history is there for all to see. We have the Treaty duly ratified by all national parliaments, an expression of national will. The Court of Justice plays a vital role in dealing with differences of interpretation. The European Council—now institutionalized—allows Heads of State and Government to monitor progress, to pinpoint delays and failures to honor the contract that unites and binds us, to provide impetus and to make good any deficiencies. A new development is that the Commission now presents a balance sheet at each meeting of what has been accomplished and what remains to be done. The Commission takes the European Council's pronouncements very seriously and does not hesitate to remind the Twelve of undertakings given. In this way the Community is demonstrating more and more clearly that it has little in common with organizations that produce worthy resolutions that are rarely if ever acted upon.

· · ·

But effectiveness is another measure of the strength of our institutions. We must never underestimate the inspired approach of the authors of the Treaty of Rome. What demands it makes on us!

First of all on the Commission, which is responsible for seeing to it that the ground rules are observed, for ensuring that commitments are honored, for implementing Council decisions when the Council see fit to allow it to do so. From this point of view we are wide of the mark, more precisely of the targets set by the Single Act. But it is above all in exercising its right of initiative that the Commission shoulders its responsibilities. And everyone gives it credit for having defined goals and proposed ways and means of revitalizing European integration.

The Commission intends to retain this dynamic approach, assuming it can come up with new ideas and options. Let us be quite clear here.

The Commission must never get drunk on its own powers. It must be strict in applying the principle of subsidiarity. It must be aware of the conditions for a dynamic compromise between the Twelve and to that end endeavor to understand each nation and its people. It must draw conclusions from this and be tireless in the pursuit of consensus. It must have the courage to say no when there is a danger of the letter and the spirit of the Treaty being ignored. And most important of all, it must have the courage to take a back seat whenever this can serve the European cause.

The strength of the law is illustrated in turn by the European Parliament. I know that there is a debate on the democratic deficit and I have no doubt whatsoever that, before too long, the powers of the Strasbourg assembly will be strengthened further. But we cannot ignore the influence that today's Parliament has had on European integration. Let me just ask you this: do you think that it would have been possible to convene the Intergovernmental Conference that produced the Single Act had Parliament not thrown its weight behind the idea on the basis of the draft European Union Treaty which it had adopted at the initiative of that great European, Altiero Spinelli?

Many envy us our Community based on the rule of law and this explains its growing influence. What a model our institutions, which allow every country irrespective of its size to have its say and make its contribution, offer the nations of Eastern Europe. They, and many other nations besides, admire the practical, forward-looking application of pluralist democracy within our borders. In the circumstances how can anyone expect us to accept absorption into a larger, looser structure along intergovernmental lines? We would be abandoning a bird in the hand for two in the bush. It would be a tragic mistake for Europe.

Despite the success of our Community based on the rule of law, disputes about sovereignty continue. We need to face the issues squarely.

A dogmatic approach will get us nowhere. It will merely complicate the difficult discussions that lie ahead and make it even harder to remove the remaining obstacles on the road to the single European market and 1992.

The facts speak for themselves. Each nation needs to consider how much room for manoeuvre it genuinely has in today's world. The growing interdependence of our economies, the internationalization of the financial world, the present or growing influence of the main protagonists on the world stage—all point to a dual conclusion. Firstly, nations should unite if they feel close to each other in terms of geography, history, values—and also necessity. Secondly—and ideally at the same time—cooperation should develop at world level to deal with such matters as international trade, the monetary system, underdevelopment, the environment and drugs. The two are complementary rather than concurrent. Because in order to exist on a global level and to influence events, not only the trappings of power are needed, but also a strong hand—that is, a capacity for generosity which is essential to any great undertaking. Europe has little clout as yet, although, as I have said, our economic performance is impressing our partners and reassuring our own people. It is quite clear that the fault lies in the deliberately-fostered fiction of full national sovereignty and hence of the absolute effectiveness of national policies.

We are all familiar with the expression "speaking with a single voice." This is a reality rather than a formula. It is a reality that strengthens our institutions, a reality reflected in the results achieved when we do agree to the joint exercise of sovereignty. The consequences of the opposite approach proves the point. Think of the shortcomings of our common commercial policy—enshrined though it is in the Treaty—often explained by countries acting alone or failing to identify their own interests correctly. Think of our inability to make a constructive contribution to the problems of indebtedness and underdevelopment, when joint action could move mountains of egoism and hegemony. May I remind you of what Sir Geoffrey Howe said on July 19 last: "The sovereign nations of the European Community, sharing their sovereignty freely, are building for themselves a key role in the power politics of the coming century."

This brings me back to our institutions. You will all remember the decision-making debate which paralysed the Community in the 1960s and led ultimately to the pseudo-compromise reached in Luxembourg. Since the Single Act and increased recourse to majority voting, there is a new dynamic. Sometimes the Council takes a vote, sometimes it considers it wiser not to force countries into a minority position and adopts a decision without a vote. Thanks to this progress on the institutional front, the Community is advancing rapidly towards the single European market and strengthening its rules and common policies. To the advantage of some? No, to the advantage of all: in a sort of positive-sum game.

To put it another way, the old "inequality-unanimity-immobility" triangle has been replaced by a new "equality-majority-dynamism" triangle, the key to success. We will need to draw conclusions from this experiment when the time comes to make further improvements to our institutional apparatus.

And that time is not far off. By its very nature, economic and monetary union is the interface between economic integration and political integration. It is the political crowning of economic convergence. It is a perfect illustration of the joint exercise of sovereignty because a single market for capital and financial services in a world dominated by matters financial calls for a monetary policy which is sufficiently coordinated and sufficiently tight to allow us to make the most of it. Without such a policy, we would be prey to international speculation and the instability of dominant currencies.

Monetary union will be acceptable and feasible only if there is parallel progress towards increased convergence of our economies so that policies are more consistent and harnessed to agreed objectives. There is consensus on economic expansion against a background of stability, on qualitative growth to generate new jobs. In a democratic society objectives can only be defined by political authorities which have democratic legitimacy. We therefore need to combine an independent monetary authority—the guarantor of stability—with the subsidiarity which is vital if each nation is to pursue its own policies in areas which are a matter for it alone, and control by our elected representatives in the shape of the European Parliament, our governments and our national parliaments.

Let me remind you before I go any further that the decision on economic and monetary union has been taken. The report of the committee which I had the honor of chairing was recognized as an essential basis for discussion by the European Council. What we need now is an institutional framework compatible with the principles discussed above and adapted to the new tasks entrusted to the Community.

Subsidiarity is central to future discussions. The principle is clear, but we need to define how it will apply in this particular case. The committee's report is quite specific. A new monetary institution would formulate a common policy valid inside and outside the union. Its federal structure would guarantee that each central bank had a hand in the formulation of decisions and implemented joint guidelines nationally with substantial margins for manoeuvre. The Council would concentrate on the convergence of objectives and the tools of economic policy, but each nation would retain the resources necessary to finance its own policies on security at home and abroad, justice, education, health, social security, regional planning and so on.

. . .

Where does this rather cursory explanation leave those who argue that economic and monetary union will lead to excessive centralization and dirigisme? The fact of the matter is that realistic application of the principle of subsidiarity leaves them without a leg to stand on. The debate—and a debate there must be—should concentrate rather on what economic and monetary union will bring, what it will add in economic and social terms to the expected benefits of the single European market. And at a time when political leaders seem to be vacillating between further development of the Community and its absorption into a larger configuration, economic and monetary union is a necessary step which will strengthen European integration and guarantee political dynamism.

Acceptance of subsidiarity implies respect for pluralism and, by implication, diversity. This is evident not only in the discussions on economic and monetary union, but also in what we call the Community's social dimension.

The facts are clear. Our twelve countries have differing traditions in the area of industrial relations. Major disparities persist in terms of living standards, although our common policies are designed to reduce these gradually. There can be no question, therefore, of artificially forcing standards upwards, or, conversely, of provoking the export of social problems. Last but not least, our governments have differing, and in some cases opposing points of view. There are enormous problems to be overcome, then, if we are to make progress on the social dimension. But it is equally important whether our concern is regional development, town and country planning, or the need for common standards.

The social dimension permeates all our discussions and everything we do: our efforts to restore competitiveness and cooperate on macroeconomic policy to reduce unemployment and provide all young Europeans with a working future; common policies designed to promote the development of less-prosperous regions and the regeneration of regions hit by industrial change; employment policy and the concentration of efforts on helping young people to gain a foothold in the labor market and combating long-term unemployment; and the development of rural regions threatened by the decline in the number of farms, desertification and demographic imbalances. Think what a boost it would be for democracy and social justice if we could demonstrate that we are capable of working together to create a better-integrated society open to all.

. . .

In this area, as in others, the Commission has no intention of getting embroiled in insidious tactical manoeuvering designed to lead the member states in a direction they do not wish to take. Let me repeat that our Community is a community based on the rule of law, where we work by the book with complete openness. Indeed, this is the first rule for success. Everyone must acknowledge this in good faith. If I turn to the principles of federalism in a bid to find workable solutions, it is precisely because they provide all the necessary guarantees on pluralism and the efficiency of the emergent institutional machinery. Here, there are two essential rules:

1. the rule of autonomy, which preserves the identity of each member state and removes any temptation to pursue unification regardless;
2. the rule of participation, which does not allow one entity to be subordinated to another, but on the contrary, promotes cooperation and synergy, on the basis of the clear and well-defined provisions contained in the Treaty.

This is the starting point for an original experiment which resists comparison with any other models, such as the United States of America, for instance. I have always shied away from such parallels, because I know that our task is to unite old nations with strong traditions and personalities. There is no conspiracy against the nation state. Nobody is being asked to renounce legitimate patriotism. I want not only to unite people, as Jean Monnet did, but also to bring nations together. As the Community develops, as our governments emphasize the need for a people's Europe, is it heresy to hope that all Europeans could feel that they belong to a Community which they see as a second homeland? If this view is rejected, European integration will founder and the specter of nationalism will return to haunt us, because the Community will have failed to win the hearts and minds of the people, the first requirement for the success of any human venture.

The success of the Community is such that it is attracting interest from all quarters. It cannot ignore this without abandoning its claim to a universal dimension. But here again the question of "what should be done" is inseparable from the question of "how do we go about it."

History will not wait for the Single Act to work through the system. It is knocking at our door even now.

. . .

Communist Europe is exploding before our eyes. Gorbachev has launched Perestroika and Glasnost. Poland and Hungary are carrying out political reforms, ushering in an era of greater freedom and democracy. East Germany totters as tens of thousands of its people flee to the West. The virus of freedom has reached Leipzig and East Berlin.

As early as 1984 François Mitterrand, in a speech to the European Parliament, voiced his presentiment of a radical new departure in Europe. "It is clear," he said, "that we are moving away from the time when Europe's sole destiny was to be shared out and divided up by others. The two words 'European independence' now sound different.

This is a fact that our century, which is nearing its end, will, I am sure, remember."

As many European leaders have already stressed, it is our Community, a Community based on the rule of law, a democratic entity and a buoyant economy, that has served as the model and the catalyst for these developments. The West is not drifting eastward, it is the East that is being drawn towards the West. Will the Community prove equal to the challenges of the future? This is the question we should ask ourselves today, whether we mean helping the countries of Eastern Europe to modernize their economies—a precondition for the success of political reforms—or getting to grips with the German question when the time comes—in other words, extending the right of self-determination to everyone.

I have no doubt that if we refuse to face up to these new challenges, not only will we be shirking our responsibilities but the Community will disintegrate, stopped in its tracks by the weight of unresolved contradictions. When I look around me now, as these events unfold, I see too much despondency, too much defeatist thinking, too much willingness paralyzed by passive acquiescence. Let me remind these pessimists of a statement by Hans-Dietrich Genscher which goes to the heart of the German question:

> The German people. In the heart of Europe, must never be seen as an obstacle to the prosperity of the people of Europe. On the contrary. It should behave in such a way that its existence is seen as a piece of good fortune, or indeed a necessity, for the whole. That is the best possible guarantee of its survival.

How are we to find a solution except by strengthening the federalist features of the Community which, to paraphrase Hans-Dietrich Genscher, offer the best possible guarantee of survival to all concerned? There, I am quite sure, lies the only acceptable and satisfactory solution to the German question.

How are we to shoulder our international responsibilities and at the same time pave the way for the emergence of a greater Europe, except by pressing ahead with European integration? Only a strong, self-confident Community, a Community which is united and determined, can truly hope to control that process.

The pace of change is gathering momentum and we must try to keep up. If our institutions are to adapt to the new situation, we cannot afford to shilly-shally about economic and monetary union. There is no question of shortening the time we need to test wide-ranging cooperation and move on to successive stages. That would be unrealistic. But time is running out for the political decision which will generate the dynamism necessary for success and lead to the creation of institutions with the capacity to face up to the demands imposed by our international responsibilities.

. . .

I have always favored the step-by-step approach—as the experiment we are embarked upon shows. But today I am moving away from it precisely because time is short. We need a radical change in the way we think of the Community and in the way we act on the world stage. We need to overcome whatever resistance we encounter. If only to adapt the instruments we already have, so that we can, for example, inject more substance into the Lomé Convention or make a success of our aid program for Poland and Hungary. We need to give countries that depend on exports for survival more access to our markets to prevent them plunging deeper into debt. We need financial instruments which will help these countries to adapt and modernize their economies.

I am concerned that we will never achieve all this with our present decision-making procedures. Thanks to the Single Act, the Council, Parliament and the Commission are a more efficient institutional troika than they were a few years ago. But this is not enough to enable us to keep pace with events.

For the honor of your generation and mine, I hope that in two years' time we will be able to repeat the very words which another great European, Paul-Henri Spaak, spoke at the signing of the Treaty of Rome: "This time the people of the West have not lacked daring and have not acted too late."

It is time, then, for a new political initiative. The Commission is ready for it and will play its full part in pointing the way. It will propose answers to the questions raised by another quantum leap: who takes the decisions; how do the various levels of decisionmaking intermesh (subsidiarity again!); who puts decisions into practice; what resources will be available; what will it mean in terms of democracy?

There is no doubt that we are living in exciting times, but they are dangerous times too. The Community is faced with the challenge of making a telling contribution to the next phase of our history.

As I stand before a predominantly young audience, I find myself dreaming of a Europe which has thrown off the chains of Yalta, a Europe which tends its immense cultural heritage so that it bears fruit, a Europe which imprints the mark of solidarity on a world which is far too hard and too forgetful of its underdeveloped regions.

I say to these young people: If we can achieve this Europe you will be able to stretch yourselves to the utmost, you will have all the space you need to achieve your full potential. For you are being invited to play your part in a unique venture, one which brings peoples and nations together for the better, not for the worse. It will bring you back to your philosophical and cultural roots, to the perennial values of Europe. But you will need to give of yourselves and insist that those who govern you display boldness tempered with caution, a fertile imagination and a clear commitment to making the Community a necessity for survival and an ideal towards which to work.

9 Preamble to the Treaty on European Union (The Maastricht Treaty)

● *Several factors, including the success of the Single Market program and the collapse of communism, increased momentum for integration as the European Community entered the 1990s. In December 1990, the member states opened negotiations to complete economic and monetary union, reform EC institutions, and expand Community competence in foreign and security policy. Final negotiations took place in December 1991 in Maastricht, The Netherlands, and the Maastricht treaty was signed there on 7 February 1992. Ratification seemed certain until Danish voters rejected the treaty on 2 June 1992 and opened a debate in Europe over the merits of integration. Public dissatisfaction with the complex treaty combined with a currency crisis and a severe economic recession to sap popular and elite enthusiasm for the European project. Nevertheless, all twelve countries finally ratified the treaty, which came into force in late 1993.*

The preamble to the Maastricht treaty reflects the essence of Jacques Delors's thinking. The need to construct a new Europe out of a formerly divided continent requires a leap to a new stage of integration through the creation of a European Union. The institutions of the Union will have responsibility for issue areas previously reserved for national governments. But respect for Europe's core values, increased accountability, and faithful application of the principle of subsidiarity will, according to the treaty, preserve democracy and diversity within the new Europe.

Reprinted with permission from *Treaty on European Union* (Office for Official Publications of the European Communities, 1992). Copyright 1992 by the European Communities.

. . .

RESOLVED to mark a new stage in the process of European integration undertaken with the establishment of the European Communities,

RECALLING the historic importance of the ending of the division of the European continent and the need to create firm bases for the construction of the future Europe,

CONFIRMING their attachment to the principles of liberty, democracy and respect for human rights and fundamental freedoms and the rule of law,

DESIRING to deepen the solidarity between their peoples while respecting their history, their culture and their traditions,

DESIRING to enhance further the democratic and efficient functioning of the institutions so as to enable them better to carry out, within a single institutional framework, the tasks entrusted to them,

RESOLVED to achieve the strengthening and the convergence of their economies and to establish an economic and monetary union including, in accordance with the provisions of this Treaty, a single and stable currency,

DETERMINED to promote economic and social progress for their peoples, within the context of the accomplishment of the internal market and of reinforced cohesion and environmental protection, and to implement policies ensuring that advances in economic integration are accompanied by parallel progress in other fields,

RESOLVED to establish a citizenship common to nationals of their countries,

RESOLVED to implement a common foreign and security policy including the eventual framing of a common defence policy, which might in time lead to a common defence, thereby reinforcing the European identity and its independence in order to promote peace, security and progress in Europe and in the world,

REAFFIRMING their objective to facilitate the free movement of persons, while ensuring the safety and the security of their peoples, by including provisions on justice and home affairs in this Treaty,

RESOLVED to continue the process of creating an ever closer union among the peoples of Europe, in which decisions are taken as closely as possible to the citizen in accordance with the principle of subsidiarity,

IN VIEW of further steps to be taken in order to advance European integration,

HAVE DECIDED to establish a European Union.

. . .

PART 2

Early Currents in Integration Theory

⑩ Altiero Spinelli and the Strategy for the United States of Europe

Sergio Pistone

Integration theory describes and explains the process of unifying sepa-
rate nation states. Early theories of integration also contained a strong
prescriptive element. Thus, Altiero Spinelli (1907–1986), the Italian
resistance leader, leader of the European Federalist Movement, member
of the Italian parliament, European Commissioner, member of the
European Parliament, and ardent federalist was dedicated not just to
understanding the integration process, but even more so to the actual
uniting of Europe. During his lifetime, Spinelli contributed to several
important documents that called for a federal Europe, including the
Ventotene Manifesto (1941), the Geneva Document (1944), and the
Draft Treaty on European Union (1984).

Spinelli's ideas, here summarized by Sergio Pistone, represent
unadulterated federalism. His goal was a new European state composed
of individual states that had ceded their sovereignty to common demo-
cratic institutions. Overcoming resistance from national governments
required a popular pan-European movement that demanded a U.S.-style
constitutional convention. This constituent assembly would command
such democratic legitimacy that national governments would have to
concede to its wishes and ratify the new European constitution. Spinelli
believed that only a dramatic leap to federalism would succeed in
unifying Europe; functionalism's step-by-step approach would never
create institutions strong enough to solve major problems and demo-

Reprinted with permission from *Altiero Spinelli and Federalism in Europe and the World*, ed. Lucio Levi (Franco Angeli, 1990). Copyright 1990 by Franco Angeli. Notes omitted.

cratic enough to respond to the people. For Spinelli, European union was an all-or-nothing proposition.

What distinguishes Spinelli's approach to European federalism from that of its former supporters is his commitment to turn it into an active movement with a political program. That is why his ideas about a campaign strategy for the United States of Europe, which he had always considered as a first stage in the process of unifying the whole world, are amongst the most important, if not the most important contribution to federalism. To illustrate the essential elements of these ideas is, in my view, a contribution to a clearer understanding of the problems of the struggle for European unification (still in progress), but also to help in the fight for world unity (now in its initial stages).

For the purposes of synthesis, my case will follow a logical rather than chronological course. In other words I will not trace the origins of Spinelli's strategic concepts, but the basic theses that emerged from his ideas and actions. In my view these boil down to three:

1. The autonomous nature of the movement for the European federation;
2. The European Constituent Assembly;
3. The exploitation of the contradictions of the functional approach to European unification.

The arguments in favor of the autonomy of the movement for the European federation stem from the belief that the national democratic governments are, simultaneously, the means and the obstacles to European unification.

They are the means because unification can only be achieved as a result of freely arrived at decisions by democratic governments. This implies the rejection of two other ways forward. Spinelli rejects any attempts to unite Europe by force, as Hitler tried, and against which European federalists fought in the Resistance during the Second World War. As a matter of principle he also rejects unification by illegal and violent means from below, because the federalist struggle takes place in Western Europe within democratic political systems which provide legal means for even the most radical change. Moreover such unification stems from the historical development of European democracy.

Whilst European unification can only be achieved by the free decisions of democratic national governments, by their very nature they represent obstacles to its attainment. As a direct consequence of the Second World War, which led to the collapse of the European nation states, they are obliged to face the alternative of "either unite or perish."

Yet, at the same time, they are inclined to reject a genuine European federation involving the irreversible transfer of substantial parts of their sovereignty to a supranational authority.

With regard to this obstacle one must clarify Spinelli's important distinction between the permanent agents of executive power, such as diplomats, civil servants and the military, and those who wield political power temporarily, such as heads of governments and their ministers. The strongest opposition to the transfer of sovereignty usually comes from the former because they would suffer immediate and substantial loss of power and status. After all, the permanent agents of executive power, were originally created to put into effect the unfettered sovereignty of the state, and they thus became the natural defenders of nationalist traditions. For the latter, wielders of temporary power, the situation is rather more complex for three reasons: (1) without permanent positions of power they have much greater opportunities of playing a role within a wider European political framework; (2) they represent democratic parties with international programs which usually include support for a European federation; (3) they are in direct touch with public opinion which, in countries suffering from the decline and crisis of the nation state, is generally favorable to European unification. This distinction is of great importance, as we shall see later, in considering procedures for the creation of institutions for European unity. Nevertheless, there remains the fact that democratic national governments, by the very nature of their structures, are unfavorably inclined towards federal unification. In the absence of ulterior reasons they are only likely to favor the type of unification which does not involve the irrevocable transfer of power.

A direct consequence springs from these structural problems: namely, that an essential condition for exercising pressure on governments and political parties in favor of genuine federal unification is the existence of an independent movement for a European federation, which is able to persuade them in favor of action they would not, otherwise, take readily on their own.

According to Spinelli, the basic features of such a movement must be:

1. it should not be a political party, but an organization aimed at uniting all supporters of a European federation, irrespective of their political beliefs or social background. This is because a political party seeking national power to achieve European unification would be fatally weakened by intending to transfer to supranational institutions substantial parts of the national power for which it would be competing;

2. it has to be a supranational organization uniting all federal-

ists beyond their national allegiance, so as to imbue them
with a supranational loyalty and enable them to organize
political action at European level;

3. it must seek to establish direct influence on public opinion,
outside national electoral campaigns, which would help it to
exert effective pressure on the European policies of governments. One should remember that these have been the
guiding principles of the Italian European Federalist Movement from its inception in 1943, even when Spinelli ceased
to be its leader and continued to cooperate with the MFE
[European Federalist Movement] as an ordinary member,
while working in the European Commission or Parliament.

The existence of a European federal movement with these characteristics represents for Spinelli merely a subjective condition for effective
federalist action. There is, however, also need for objective conditions
for a successful struggle, such as those provided by crises within national
political systems.

During periods of relative stability of national political systems,
when governments appear able to deal with the principal political,
economic or social problems, the movement for a European federation
is unable to influence national governments effectively, because public
opinion tends to support the latter and their policies. Only at times of
acute crisis, when governments are unable to cope and this fact is
generally evident, will public opinion be able to share the federalist point
of view. At such times the federalist movement ought to be able to
mobilize support for federal solutions and persuade governments in
favor of them. Spinelli was always convinced that such crises were
bound to arise because we are living during a historically critical stage
for nation states which, after periods of relative and apparent stability,
will be subject to intense crises of their political systems. And this is also
true for policies of European unification based on the maintenance of
absolute national sovereignty, because intergovernmental cooperation
does not provide adequate means for facing such crises, which stem from
an irreversible decline of national power of European states.

I will now deal with second main theme of Spinelli's strategy—the
concept of a European constituent assembly.

The fact that national governments are simultaneously the means
and the obstacles to the federal unification of Europe carries important
implications for the procedure needed to establish European institutions: if one wants federal institutions then one must proceed by way of
a constituent assembly and not by the use of intergovernmental or
diplomatic conferences.

In other words, Spinelli was always convinced that the creation of European institutions, being entrusted to representatives of national governments, and diplomats in particular, or if they have the last word over the constituent procedure, cannot bring about federal solutions, because the tendency of all such diplomatic negotiations will be the maintenance of absolute national sovereignty at the expense of effective unification. In contrast, in a constituent assembly, composed of people representing public opinion, a favorable attitude towards federal institutions is likely to be incomparably stronger than nationalist tendencies. This is for a number of reasons: (1) the great majority of public opinion (especially in countries first committed to European unification) is in favor of genuine unification and its representatives have to take account of this; (2) the parties and the principal democratic political trends have an international orientation which, by its very nature, would be favorable to a European federation, and would, therefore, back the creation of transnational groups within a European assembly working to strengthen pro-European attitudes; (3) those representing public opinion, unlike the diplomats, do not hold positions of power which are directly dependent on the maintenance of absolute national sovereignty.

Thus, in the event of a critical situation, the pre-eminent task of the movement for a European federation will be to persuade governments (which, at such moments, are susceptible to persuasion by the federalists) to initiate a constituent democratic procedure under which the ultimate responsibility for proposing the nature of the European institutions will be entrusted to the representatives of public opinion, and whose draft of the European constitution will then be directly submitted for ratification to the appropriate constitution organs of the member states, without being subjected to prior diplomatic negotiations.

The concept of a constituent European assembly was patterned by Spinelli on the way the first federal constitution in history was drawn up, namely that of the American constitution, worked out by the Philadelphia Convention in 1787. The example of Philadelphia which, according to him, should provide the model for a European constituent procedure contains three essential elements:

1. governments of individual states have the basic responsibility for initiating the process by conferring the constituent mandate upon the convention, but refrain from interfering in its deliberations;
2. the convention acts by majority votes in drawing up the constitution;
3. the ratification of the constitution is entrusted to the appropriate constitutional organs of individual states, and it

comes into force once ratified by a majority of them (in the
American case it required ratification by 9 out of the 13
states).

Throughout his federalist campaign Spinelli never ceased to press
for the adoption of a constituent procedure on these lines. One needs to
stress that for him the essence lay not in the form but the substance of
the procedure, namely to give the last word on the constitutional project
to a parliamentary assembly. During the various stages of his campaign
he proposed various forms of political action, each adapted to prevailing
circumstances, to advance the constituent procedure:

1. a constituent assembly elected by universal suffrage with the
   sole mandate of drawing up a European constitution;
2. the transformation of the consultative parliamentary assembly into a constituent one, either by its own action or by
   mandate conferred upon it by national governments;
3. by the direct election of a European parliament with a
   specific constituent mandate;
4. by a popular referendum which would confer the constituent
   mandate upon the European parliament.

But the substance remained unchanged.

Spinelli's constituent concept stemmed from his belief that the
functional approach to European unification will not achieve profound
and irreversible unity. He never shared the conviction of the supporters
of the functional approach that one can integrate selected sectors of
national activity without a federalist constitutional framework from the
very start. And this for two fundamental reasons:

1. by refusing to start with a supranational authority of a
   democratic character the principle of the national veto is
   retained (even with a formal acceptance of majority voting).
   This would deprive European institutions of the capacity to
   overcome special interests that arise from the exercise of
   unfettered national sovereignty, and to ensure the supremacy
   of the common European interest;
2. the chaos and inefficiency which results from the lack of
   common management of the interdependent economies of
   modern states and of their foreign and defense policies.

One needs to recognize, however, that Spinelli accepted that
unification could start with effective supranational powers being first

confined to economic issues, while postponing their immediate adoption in matters of foreign and security policies (as provided in the draft treaty for European Union). And this from the consideration that convergence in the latter sectors was already being influenced by American leadership. But he always stressed the need for genuine federal institutions which would ensure the ultimate extension of supranational powers from economic to defence and foreign policies. That is why he never ceased to insist on the constitutional approach, in place of the functional one, by calling for a federal constitution from the start, obtained by a democratic constituent procedure.

Spinelli's criticism of the functional method was not confined to a dialectical and doctrinaire preference for the constitutional approach. First he was clearly aware that the functional approach stemmed largely from the contradictory nature of the attitudes of national governments to European unification. As objective historical circumstances force them to face the need for supranational unification, whilst they resist giving up their sovereignty, it is natural that they prefer an approach that postpones indefinitely the establishment of an authentic supranational authority. At the same time he recognized that the functional approach could assist the constitutional process by exposing, due to its inadequacy, the contradictions of the former, that could be exploited in the course of the federalist struggle.

These contradictions boil down to two. The first stems from the precariousness and inefficiency of functional unification. Functional institutions established by the unanimous decisions of national governments have shown themselves to be weak and incapable of acting decisively at critical moments when particularly grave problems face them. As a consequence, positive results obtained in more favorable circumstances tend to be compromised or abandoned in time of crisis. This leads to the disappointment of expectations in the development of European integration and can lead to support for federal solutions. The second contradiction stems from the democratic deficit which arises when important responsibilities and powers are transferred to the supranational level without subjecting them to effective democratic control. This causes uneasiness among political parties and to democratically sensitive public opinion which can be thus influenced to favor the concept of supranational democracy. Spinelli's federalist campaign had always aimed at exploiting these contradictions in order to initiate the democratic constituent procedure.

. . .

11 A Working Peace System

DAVID MITRANY

David Mitrany (1888–1975) was a Romanian-born academic who spent most of his adult life in Britain and the United States. During World War II, Professor Mitrany thought seriously about the shape of the postwar world and how to prevent future wars. The result of his reflection was a pamphlet entitled A Working Peace System, *which he published in London in the summer of 1943, still two years before the end of the war. In this pamphlet, Mitrany argued for a transformation of the way people think about international relations, particularly the prevention of war. His "functional alternative" aimed at world, not European, unity. Nevertheless, it had a profound effect on European activists, such as Jean Monnet (see Chapter 4), and later integration theorists, especially the neofunctionalists (see Chapter 12).*

Mitrany saw the division of the world into "competing political units" as the root of international conflict. A world federal government, he argued, would eliminate these divisions but would be impossible to establish given the modern "disregard for constitutions and pacts" and continuing nationalism. Mitrany called, instead, for a functional approach that would "overlay political divisions with a spreading web of international activities and agencies, in which and through which the interests and life of all the nations would be gradually integrated." Functional integration would be pragmatic, technocratic, and flexible; it would deliberately blur distinctions between national and international, public and private, and political and nonpolitical. As functional agencies were formed and joined, national divisions would become less and less important. Ultimately, a central authority might coordinate the various agencies, but such a government would not be necessary for

Reprinted from *A Working Peace System* (Quadrangle Books, 1966). Copyright 1966 by The Society for a World Service Federation. Notes omitted.

*successful international relations and might not be desirable. Here
Mitrany parted with many other functionalists (such as Monnet) and the
neofunctionalists, who believed federal institutions were essential to the
success of functional integration.*

• THE GENERAL PROBLEM

The need for some new kind of international system was being widely
canvassed before the Second World War, in the measure in which the
League of Nations found itself frustrated in its attempts to prevent
aggression and to organize peace. Some blamed this failure on the
irresponsibility of small states; others rather the egoism of the Great
Powers. Still others imputed the League's failure more directly to
weaknesses in its own constitution and machinery: the proper ingredi-
ents were there, but the political dosage was inadequate. It was especially among those who held this view that the idea of a wide international federation began to be embraced as a new hope.

Federation seemed indeed the only alternative to a League tried so
far for linking together a number of political units by democratic
methods. It would mean an association much closer than was the
League, and its advocacy therefore takes it for granted that the League
failed because it did not go far enough. In what way would federation
go further? Federation would be a more intensive union of a less
extensive group; the constitutional ties would be closer. Second, certain
activities would be more definitely and actively tied together. More
definite common action is clearly the end; the formal arrangements
which the federalists put in the forefront would be merely a necessary
adjunct, to ensure the reliable working of the federal undertakings. And
that is as it should be for, leaving formal arguments aside, it is plain that
the League failed not from overstrain but from inanition. It might have
done more about sanctions, but that would not have been enough. Even
if the League's action for "security" had been more fearless that would
not by itself have sufficed to give vitality to an international system that
was to last and grow. To achieve that end, such a system must in some
important respects take over and coordinate activities hitherto controlled by the national state, just as the state increasingly has to take over
activities which until now have been carried on by local bodies; and like
the state, any new international authority could under present conditions not be merely a police authority.

We realize now that the League failed because, whatever the
reasons, it could not further that process of continuous adjustment and
settlement which students of international affairs call "peaceful change."

But they themselves, taking the form for the substance, all too often thought of it mainly as a matter of changing frontiers. We shall have to speak of this again, but what peaceful change should mean, what the modern world, so closely interrelated, must have for its peaceful development, is some system that would make possible automatic and continuous social action, continually adapted to changing needs and conditions, in the same sense and of the same general nature as any other system of government. Its character would be the same for certain purposes; only the range would be new. It is in that sense that the League's work has in truth been inadequate and ineffective, as one may readily see if one reflects whether a change of frontiers now and then would really have led to a peaceful and cooperative international society.

A close federation is supposed to do just what the League proved unable to do, and in a set and solid way. But to begin with, can we take a system which has worked well in one field and simply transplant it to another, so much wider and more complex? Federations have still been national federations; the jump from national states to international organization is infinitely more hazardous than was the jump from provincial units to national federations. None of the elements of neighborhood, of kinship, of history are there to serve as steps. The British Empire is bound closely by old ties of kinship and history, but no one would suggest that there is among its parts much will for federation. Yet apart from this matter of whether the federal idea has any great prospects, there is the more important question whether it would have any great virtues in the international sphere. If the evil of conflict and war springs from the division of the world into detached and competing political units, will it be exorcised simply by changing or reducing the lines of division? Any political reorganization into separate units must sooner or later produce the same effects; any international system that is to usher in a new world must produce the opposite effect of subduing political division. As far as one can see, there are only two ways of achieving that end. One would be through a world state which would wipe out political divisions forcibly; the other is the way discussed in these pages, which would rather overlay political divisions with a spreading web of international activities and agencies, in which and through which the interests and life of all the nations would be gradually integrated. That is the fundamental change to which any effective international system must aspire and contribute: to make international government coextensive with international activities. A League would be too loose to be able to do it; a number of sectional federations would, on the contrary, be too tight to be welded into something like it. Therefore when the need is so great and pressing, we must have the vision to break away from traditional political ideas, which in modern times have always linked authority to a given territory, and try some new way that might take us without violence toward that goal. The beginnings cannot be anything but experimental; a new international system will need, even more than national systems, a wide freedom of continuous adaptation in the light of experience. It must care as much as possible for common needs that are evident, while presuming as little as possible upon a global unity which is still only latent and unrecognized. As the late John Winant well said in a lecture at Leeds in October 1942: "We must be absolute about our principal ends (justice and equality of opportunity and freedom), relative and pragmatic about the mechanical means used to serve those ends."

The need for a pragmatic approach is all the greater because we are so clearly in a period of historical transition. When the state itself, whatever its form and constitution, is everywhere undergoing a deep social and political sea-change, it is good statesmanship not to force the new international experiments into some set familiar form, which may be less relevant the more respectable it seems, but to see above all that these experiments go with and fit into the general trend of the time.

When one examines the general shape of the tasks that are facing us one is, to begin with, led to question whether order could be brought into them by the device of formal written pacts. Why did written constitutions, declarations of rights, and other basic charters play such a great role during the nineteenth century? The task of that time, following the autocratic period, was to work out a new division of the sphere of authority, to determine new relationships between the individual and the state, to protect the new democracy. These relationships were meant to be fixed and final, and they had to rest on general principles, largely of a negative character. It was natural and proper that all that should be laid down in formal rules, meant to remain untouched and permanent. In much the same way the new nation state was in world society what the new citizen was in municipal society; and with the increase in their number, the liberal growth in international trade and cultural and social intercourse, the resulting international rules and a host of written treaties and pacts sought, like the national constitutions, to fix the formal relationship between the sovereign individual states and their collectivity; which in this case also was expected to be fixed and final, with international law as a gradually emerging constitution for that political cosmos.

Viewed in this light, the Covenant of the League is seen to have continued that nineteenth-century tradition. It was concerned above all with fixing in a definite way the formal relationship of the member states and in a measure also of non-members, and only in a very secondary way with initiating positive common activities and action. The great expectation, security, was a vital action, but a negative one; its end was not to promote the active regular life of the peoples but only to protect it against being disturbed. Broadly one might say that the Covenant was an attempt to universalize and codify the rules of international conduct, gradually evolved through political treaties and pacts, and to give them general and permanent validity. It was neither unnatural nor unreasonable to follow up that nineteenth-century trend and try to steady international relations by bringing them within the framework of a written pact, one provided with set rules for its working. But when it came to going beyond that, the League could not be more or do more than what its leading members were ready to be and do, and they were ready to do but little in a positive way. It was indeed characteristic of the post-Armistice period 1918–19 that even the victors hastened to undo their common economic and other machinery, such as the Allied Shipping Control, which had grown and served them well during the war. And that was at a time when within each country government action and control were spreading fast, causing many a private international activity also to be cut down or cut off. In other words, the incipient common functions, as well as many old connections, were disbanded in the international sphere at the very time when a common constitution was being laid down for it. It was that divorce between life and form that doomed the League from the outset, and not any inadequacy in its written rules.

Hence it is pertinent to ask: Would another written pact, if only more elaborate and stringent, come to grips more closely with the problems of our time? Let us by way of a preliminary answer note two things: First, the lusty disregard for constitutions and pacts, for settled rules and traditional rights, is a striking mark of the times. In the pressure for social change no such formal ties are allowed to stand in the way, either within the several countries or between them. It is a typical revolutionary mood and practice. If it does not always take the outward form of revolution that is because the governments themselves act as spearheads of the trend, and not only in countries ruled by dictatorships. Those who lead in this rush for social change pride themselves indeed on their disregard for forms and formalities. The appeal which communism, fascism, and nazism had for youth in particular and for the masses in general lies in no small degree in that political iconoclasm. At the turn of the nineteenth century the radical masses were demanding settled rules and rights, and Napoleon could play the trump card of constitutional nationalism against the autocratic rulers. Now the masses demand social action without regard to established "rights," and the totalitarian leaders have been playing the strong card of pragmatic socialism against constitutional democracy.

That universal pressure for social reform, in the second place, has utterly changed the relation of nationalism to internationalism, in a way that could be promising if rightly used. In constitution-making there was a parallel between the two spheres, but nothing more, for they belonged politically to different categories. The nineteenth-century nationalism rested mainly on cultural and other differential factors, and the creation of the nation state meant inevitably a breaking up of world unity. A cosmopolitan outlook spread rapidly, but the nations at the same time balked at international political organization and control, and they could justify that refusal by seemingly good principle. At present the new nationalism rests essentially on social factors; these are not only alike in the various countries, thus paradoxically creating a bond even between totalitarian groups, but often cannot make progress in isolation. At many points the life of the nation state is overflowing back into that common world which existed before the rise of modern nationalism. At present the lines of national and international evolution are not parallel but converging, and the two spheres now belong to the same category and differ only in dimensions.

In brief, the function of the nineteenth-century was to restrain the powers of authority; that led to the creation of the "political man" and likewise of the "political nation," and to the definition through constitutional pacts of their relation to the wider political group. The Covenant (and the Locarno and Kellogg pacts) was still of that species essentially, with the characteristic predominance of rules of the "thou shall not" kind. The function of our time is rather to develop and coordinate the social scope of authority, and that cannot be so defined or divided. Internationally it is no longer a question of defining relations between states but of merging them—the workday sense of the vague talk about the need to surrender some part of sovereignty. A constitutional pact could do little more than lay down certain elementary rights and duties for the members of the new community. The community itself will acquire a living body not through a written act of faith but through active organic development. Yet there is in this no fundamental dispute as to general principles and ultimate aims. The only question is, which is the more immediately practicable and promising way: whether a general political framework should be provided formally in advance, on some theoretical pattern, or left to grow branch by branch from action and experience and so find its natural bent.

• THE FUNCTIONAL ALTERNATIVE

Can these vital objections be met, and the needs of peace and social advance be satisfied, through some other way of associating the nations for common action? The whole trend of modern government indicates such a way. That trend is to organize government along the lines of specific ends and needs, and according to the conditions of their time and place, in lieu of the traditional organization on the basis of a set constitutional division of jurisdiction and of rights and powers. In national government the definition of authority and the scope of public action are now in a continuous flux, and are determined less by constitutional norms than by practical requirements. The instances are too many and well known to need mentioning; one might note only that while generally the trend has been toward greater centralization of services, and therefore of authority, under certain conditions the reverse has also occurred, powers and duties being handed over to regional and other authorities for the better performance of certain communal needs. The same trend is powerfully at work in the several federations, in Canada and Australia, and especially in the United States, and in these cases it is all the more striking because the division of authority rests on written constitutions which are still in being and nominally valid in full. Internationally, too, while a body of law had grown slowly and insecurely through rules and conventions, some common activities were organized through ad hoc functional arrangements and have worked well. The rise of such specific administrative agencies and laws is the peculiar trait, and indeed the foundation, of modern government.

A question which might properly be asked at the outset in considering the fitness of that method for international purposes is this: Could such functions be organized internationally without a comprehensive political framework? Let it be said, first, that the functional method as such is neither incompatible with a general constitutional framework nor precludes its coming into being. It only follows Burke's warning to the sheriffs of Bristol that "government is a practical thing" and that one should beware of elaborating constitutional forms "for the gratification of visionaries." In national states and federations the functional development is going ahead without much regard to, and sometimes in spite of, the old constitutional divisions. If in these cases the constitution is most conveniently left aside, may not the method prove workable internationally without any immediate and comprehensive constitutional framework? If, to cite Burke again, it is "always dangerous to meddle with foundations," it is doubly dangerous now. Our political problems are obscure, while the political passions of the time are blinding. One of the misfortunes of the League experiment was that a new institution was devised on what have proved to be outworn premises. We might also recollect that of the constitutional changes introduced in Europe after the First World War, fine and wise though they may have been, none has survived even a generation. How much greater will that risk of futility be in Europe after the Second World War, when the split within and between nations will be much worse than in 1919? We know now even less about the dark historical forces which have been stirred up by the war, while in the meantime the problems of our common society have been distorted by fierce ideologies which we could not try to bring to an issue without provoking an irreconcilable dogmatic conflict. Even if an action were to be to some extent handicapped without a formal political framework, the fact is that no obvious sentiment exists, and none is likely to crystallize for some years, for a common constitutional bond.

In such conditions any pre-arranged constitutional framework would be taken wholly out of the air. We do not know what, if anything, will be in common—except a desperate craving for peace and for the conditions of a tolerable normal life. The peoples may applaud declarations of rights, but they will call for the satisfaction of needs. That demand for action could be turned into a historic opportunity. Again we might take to heart what happened to the U.S. in 1932–33 and think of what chances the Roosevelt administration would have to have had to achieve unity, or indeed to survive, if instead of taking immediate remedial action it had begun by offering constitutional reforms— though a common system was already in being. A timid statesman might still have tried to walk in the old constitutional grooves; Mr. Roosevelt stepped over them. He grasped both the need and opportunity for centralized practical action. Unemployment, the banking collapse, flood control, and a hundred other problems had to be dealt with by national means if they were to be dealt with effectively and with lasting results.

The significant point in that emergency action was that each and every problem was tackled as a practical issue in itself. No attempt was made to relate it to a general theory or system of government. Every function was left to generate others gradually, like the functional subdivision of organic cells; and in every case the appropriate authority was left to grow and develop out of actual performance. Yet the new functions and the new organs, taken together, have revolutionized the American political system. The federal government has become a national government, and Washington for the first time is really the capital of America. In the process, many improvements in the personnel and machinery of government have come about, and many restrictive state regulations have melted away. More recently there has been heard the significant complaint that the ties between cities and their states are becoming looser, while those with the national government become ever stronger. No one has worked to bring this about, and no written act has either prescribed it or confirmed it. A great constitutional transformation has thus taken place without any changes in the Constitution. There have been complaints, but the matter-of-course acceptance has been overwhelming. People have gladly accepted the service when they might have questioned the theory. The one attempt at direct constitutional revision, to increase and liberalize the membership of the Supreme Court, was bitterly disputed and defeated. Yet that proposal involved in effect much less of a constitutional revolution than has the experiment of the Tennessee Valley Authority. The first would not have ensured any lasting change in the working of the American government, whereas the second has really introduced into the political structure of the United States a new regional dimension unknown to the Constitution.

In many of its essential aspects—the urgency of the material needs, the inadequacy of the old arrangements, the bewilderment in outlook— the situation at the end of the Second World War will resemble that in America in 1933, though on a wider and deeper scale. And for the same reasons the path pursued by Mr. Roosevelt in 1933 offers the best, perhaps the only, chance for getting a new international life going. It will be said inevitably that in the United States it was relatively easy to follow that line of action because it was in fact one country, with an established Constitution. Functional arrangements could be accepted, that is, because in many fields the federal states had grown in the habit of working together. That is no doubt true, but not the most significant point of the American experiment; for that line was followed not because the functional way was so easy but because the constitutional way would have been so difficult. Hence the lesson for unfederated parts of the world would seem to be this: If the constitutional path had to be avoided for the sake of effective action even in a federation which already was a working political system, how much less promising must it be as a starting mode when it is a matter of bringing together for the first time a number of varied, and sometimes antagonistic, countries? But if the constitutional approach, by its very circumspectness, would hold up the start of a working international system, bold initiative during the period of emergency at the end of the war might set going lasting instruments and habits of a common international life. And though it may appear rather brittle, that functional approach would in fact be more solid and definite than a formal one. It need not meddle with foundations; old institutions and ways may to some extent hamper reconstruction, but reconstruction could begin by a common effort

without a fight over established ways. Reconstruction may in this field
also prove a surer and less costly way than revolution. As to the new
ideologies, since we could not prevent them we must try to circumvent
them, leaving it to the growth of new habits and interests to dilute them
in time. Our aim must be to call forth to the highest possible degree the
active forces and opportunities for cooperation, while touching as little
as possible the latent or active points of difference and opposition.

There is one other aspect of the post-war period which has been
much discussed and has a bearing on this point, and which helps to bring
out the difference in outlook between the two methods contrasted here.
Much has been heard of a suggestion that when the war ends we must
have first a period of convalescence and that the task of permanent
reorganization will only come after that. It is a useful suggestion, insofar
as it may help to clear up certain practical problems. But it could also
be misleading and even dangerous if the distinction were taken to justify
either putting off the work of international government or differentiat-
ing between the agencies by which the new international activities are
to be organized, into nurses for convalescence and mentors for the new
life. A clean division in time between two such periods in any case is not
possible, for the period of convalescence will be different for different
activities and ends; but, above all, except for such direct and exceptional
consequences of the war as demobilization and the rebuilding of
damaged areas, the needs of society will be the same at once after the war
as later on. The only difference will be the practical one of a priority of
needs, the kind of difference which might be brought about by any social
disturbance—an epidemic or an earthquake or an economic crisis—and
the urgency of taking action. For the rest, one action and period will
merge into the other, according to circumstances. Seed and implements
will be as urgent for ensuring the food supply of Europe and Asia as the
actual distribution of relief, and indeed more urgent if the war should
end after a harvest. Again, both relief and reconstruction will depend
greatly on the speedy reorganization and proper use of transport, and
so on.

Both circumstances point again to the advantage of a functional
practice and to the disadvantage, if not the impossibility, of a comprehensive attempt at political organization. To obtain sufficient agreement for some formal general scheme would, at best, not be possible
without delay; at the same time, action for relief and reconstruction will
have to start within the hour after the ceasefire. The alternatives would
be, if a comprehensive constitutional arrangement is desired and waited
for, either to put the immediate work in the hands of temporary
international agencies or to leave it to the individual states. The one, in
fact, would prepare for the other. Except in matters of relief—the

distribution of food, fuel, and clothing and also medical help—*ad hoc* temporary agencies could have no adequate authority or influence; all of what one might call the society-building activities, involving probably considerable planning and reorganization within and between the several countries, would fall upon the individual states again, as in 1919, when they competed and interfered rather than cooperated with each other, to the loss of them all. Yet it is vital that international activity should be from the outset in the same hands and move in the same direction after the war as later; otherwise the chances of building up an international system would be gravely prejudiced. It is certain that one of the chief reasons for the failure of the League was that it was given a formal authority and promissory tasks for the future, while the immediate, urgent, and most welcome tasks of social reconstruction and reform were left to be attended to by national agencies. Later efforts to retrieve that mistake only led to a series of barren economic conferences, as by that time the policy of each country was set hard in its own mold. It is inevitable with any scheme of formal organization that the national states should have to re-start on their own, and natural therefore that refuge should be sought in the idea of a period of convalescence while the full-fledged scheme is worked out and adopted. But functional authorities would not need such political hospitalization, with its arbitrary and dangerous division of stages; they would merely vary, like any other agency anywhere and at any time, the emphasis of their work in accordance with the changing condition of their task, continuing to control and organize transport, for instance, after they had rebuilt it, and in the same way taking each task in hand with a plan and authority for continuing it. The simple fact is that all the re-starting of agriculture and industry and transport will either be done on some pre-arranged common program or it will have to be done, for it could not wait, on disjointed local plans; it will be done either by pre-established international agencies or it will have to be done by local national agencies—and the agencies which will act in the supposed convalescence period will also be those to gather authority and acceptance unto themselves.

. . .

○ *The Broad Lines of Functional Organization*

The problem of our generation, put very broadly, is how to weld together the common interests of all without interfering unduly with the particular ways of each. It is a parallel problem to that which faces us in national society, and which in both spheres challenges us to find an alternative to the totalitarian pattern. A measure of centralized planning and control, for both production and distribution, is no longer to be avoided, no matter what the form of the state or the doctrine of its constitution. Through all that variety of political forms there is a growing approximation in the working of government, with differences merely of degree and of detail. Liberal democracy needs a re-definition of the public and private spheres of action. But as the line of separation is always shifting under the pressure of fresh social needs and demands, it must be left free to move with those needs and demands and cannot be fixed through a constitutional re-instatement. The only possible principle of democratic confirmation is that public action should be undertaken only where and when and insofar as the need for common action becomes evident and is accepted for the sake of the common good. In that way controlled democracy could yet be made the golden mean whereby social needs might be satisfied as largely and justly as possible, while still leaving as wide a residue as possible for the free choice of the individual.

That is fully as true for the international sphere. It is indeed the only way to combine, as well as may be, international organization with national freedom. We have already suggested that not all interests are common to all, and that the common interests do not concern all countries in the same degree. A territorial union would bind together some interests which are not of common concern to the group, while it would inevitably cut asunder some interests of common concern to the group and those outside it. The only way to avoid that twice-arbitrary surgery is to proceed by means of a natural selection, binding together those interests which are common, where they are common, and to the extent to which they are common. That functional selection and organization of international needs would extend, and in a way resume, an international development which has been gathering strength since the latter part of the nineteenth century. The work of organizing international public services and activities was taken a step further by the League, in its health and drug-control work, in its work for refugees, in the experiments with the transfer of minorities and the important innovations of the League loan system, and still more through the whole activity of the ILO [International Labour Organisation]. But many other activities and interests in the past had been organized internationally by private agencies—in finance and trade and production, etc., not to speak of scientific and cultural activities. In recent years some of these activities have been brought under public national control in various countries; in totalitarian countries indeed all of them. In a measure, therefore, the present situation represents a retrogression from the recent past: the new turn toward self-sufficiency has spread from economics to the things of the mind; and while flying and wireless were opening up the world, many old links forged by private effort have been forcibly severed. It is unlikely that most of them could be resumed now except through public action, and if they are to operate as freely as they did in private hands they cannot be organized otherwise than on a non-discriminating functional basis.

What would be the broad lines of such a functional organization of international activities? The essential principle is that activities would be selected specifically and organized separately—each according to its nature, to the conditions under which it has to operate, and to the needs of the moment. It would allow, therefore, all freedom for practical variation in the organization of the several functions, as well as in the working of a particular function as needs and conditions alter. Let us take as an example the group of functions which fall under communications, on which the success of post-war reconstruction will depend greatly. What is the proper basis for the international organization of *railway* systems? Clearly it must be European, or rather *continental*, North American, and so on, as that gives the logical administrative limit of coordination. A division of the Continent into separate democratic and totalitarian unions would not achieve the practical end, as political division would obstruct that necessary coordination; while British and American participation would make the organization more cumbersome without any added profit to the function. As regards shipping, the line of effective organization which at once suggests itself is *international*, or inter-continental, but not universal. A European union could not solve the problem of maritime coordination without the cooperation of America and of certain other overseas states. *Aviation* and *broadcasting*, a third example in the same group, could be organized effectively only on a *universal* scale, with perhaps subsidiary regional arrangements for more local services. Such subsidiary regional arrangements could in fact be inserted at any time and at any stage where that might prove useful for any part of a function. Devolution according to need would be as easy and natural as centralization, whereas if the basis of organization were political every such change in dimension would involve an elaborate constitutional re-arrangement. Similarly, it could be left safely to be determined by practical considerations whether at the points where functions cross each other—such as rail and river transport in Europe and America—the two activities should be merely coordinated or put under one control.

These are relatively simple examples. The functional coordination of production, trade, and distribution evidently would be more complex, especially as they have been built up on a competitive basis. But the experience with international cartels, with the re-organization of the shipping, cotton, and steel industries in England, not to speak of the even wider and more relevant experience with economic coordination in the two world wars—all shows that the thing can be done and that it has always been done on such functional lines. No fixed rule is needed, and no rigid pattern is desirable for the organization of these working functional strata.

A certain degree of fixity would not be out of place, however, in regard to more *negative* functions, especially those related to law and order, but also to any others of a more formal nature which are likely to remain fairly static. Security, for instance, could be organized on an interlocking regional basis, and the judicial function likewise, with a hierarchy of courts, as the need may arise—the wider acting as courts of appeal from the more local courts. Yet, even in regard to security, and in addition to regional arrangements, the elasticity inherent in functional organization may prove practicable and desirable, if only in the period of transition. Anglo-American naval cooperation for the policing of the seas may prove acceptable for a time, and it would cut across physical regions. Agreement on a mineral sanction would of necessity mean common action by those countries which control the main sources; and other such combinations might be found useful for any particular task in hand. That is security only for defense; security arrangements were conceived usually on a geographical basis because they were meant to prevent violence, and that would still be the task of sanctions, etc., based on some regional devolution. But in addition there is a growing functional devolution in the field of social security in connection with health, with the drug and white slave traffic, with crime, etc. In all that important field of social policing it has been found that coordination and cooperation with the police of other countries on functional lines, varying with each task, was both indispensable and practicable. There is no talk and no attempt in all this to encroach upon sovereignty, but only a detached functional association which works smoothly and is already accepted without question.

However that may be, in the field of more *positive* active functions—economic, social, cultural—which are varied and ever changing in structure and purpose, any devolution must, like the main organization, follow functional lines. Land transport on the Continent would need a different organization and agencies should the railways after a time be displaced by roads; and a Channel tunnel would draw England into an arrangement in which she does not at present belong, with a corresponding change in the governing organ.

Here we discover a cardinal virtue of the functional method— what one might call the virtue of technical self-determination. The functional *dimensions*, as we have seen, determine its appropriate *organs*. It also reveals through practice the nature of the action required under given conditions, and in that way the *powers* needed by the respective authority. The function, one might say, determines the executive instrument suitable for its proper activity, and by the same process provides a need for the reform of the instrument at every stage. This would allow the widest latitude for variation between functions, and also in the dimension or organization of the same function as needs and conditions change. Not only is there in all this no need for any fixed constitutional division of authority and power, prescribed in advance, but anything beyond the original formal definition of scope and purpose might embarrass the working of the practical arrangements.

o   The Question of Wider Coordination

The question will be asked, however, in what manner and to what degree the various functional agencies that may thus grow up would have to be linked to each other and articulated as parts of a more comprehensive organization. It should be clear that each agency could work by itself, but that does not exclude the possibility of some of them or all being bound in some way together, if it should be found needful or useful to do so. That indeed is the test. As the whole sense of this particular method is to let activities be organized as the need for joint action arises and is accepted, it would be out of place to lay down in advance some formal plan for the coordination of various functions. Coordination, too, would in that sense have to come about functionally. Yet certain needs and possibilities can be foreseen already now, though some are probable and others only likely, and it may help to round off the picture if we look into this aspect briefly.

1. *Within the same group* of functions probably there would have to be coordination either simply for technical purposes or for wider functional ends, and this would be the first stage toward a wider integration. To take again the group concerned with communications— rail, road, and air transport in Europe would need *technical* coordination in regard to timetables, connections, etc. They may need also a wider *functional* coordination if there is to be some distribution of passenger and freight traffic for the most economic performance— whether that is done by a superior executive agency or by some arbitral body, perhaps on the lines of the Federal Commerce Commission in America. Sea and air traffic across the Atlantic or elsewhere, though separately organized, probably would also benefit from a similar type of coordination. Again, various mineral controls, if they should be organized separately, would need some coordination, though this arbitrary grouping of "minerals" would be less to the point that the

coordination of specific minerals and other products with possible substitutes—of crude oil with synthetic oil, of crude rubber with synthetic rubber, and so on.

2. The next degree or stage might be, if found desirable, the coordination of *several groups* of functional agencies. For instance, the communications agencies may not only work out some means of acting together in the distribution of orders for rolling stock, ships, etc., but they could or should work in this through any agencies that may have come into being for controlling materials and production, or through some intermediary agency as a clearinghouse. There is no need to prescribe any pattern in advance, or that the pattern adopted in one case should be followed in all the others.

3. The coordination of such working functional agencies with any *international planning* agencies would present a third stage, and one that brings out some interesting possibilities, should the ideas for an international investment board or an international development commission, as an advisory organ, come to fruition. One can see how such a development commission might help to guide the growth of functional agencies into the most desirable channels, and could watch their inter-relations and their repercussions. And an investment board could guide, for instance, the distribution of orders for ships, materials, etc., not only according to the best economic use but also for the purpose of ironing out cyclical trends. It could use, according to its nature, its authority or its influence to make of such orders a means additional to international public works, etc., for dealing with periods or pockets of unemployment. Coordination of such a general kind may in some cases amount almost to arbitration of differences between functional agencies; regional boards or councils like those of the Pan-American Union might be used to adjust or arbitrate regional differences.

4. Beyond this there remains the habitual assumption, as we have already said, that international action must have some overall *political authority* above it. Besides the fact that such a comprehensive authority is not now a practical possibility, it is the central view of the functional approach that such an authority is not essential for our greatest and real immediate needs. The several functions could be organized through the agreement, given specifically in each case, of the national governments chiefly interested, with the grant of the requisite powers and resources; whereas it is clear, to emphasize the previous point, that they could not allow such organizations simply to be prescribed by some universal authority, even if it existed. For an authority which had the title to do so would in effect be hardly less than a world government; and such a strong central organism would inevitably tend to take unto itself rather more authority than that originally allotted to it, this calling in turn for

the checks and balances which are used in federal systems, but which would be difficult to provide in any loose way. If issues should arise in any functional system which would call either for some new departure or for the re-consideration of existing arrangements, that could be done only in council by all the governments concerned. Insofar as it may be desired to keep alive some general view of our problems, and perhaps a general watch over the policies of the several joint agencies, some body of a representative kind, like the League Assembly or the governing body of the ILO, could meet periodically, perhaps elected by proportional representation from the assemblies of the member states. Such an assembly, in which all the states would have a voice, could discuss and ventilate general policies, as an expression of the mind and will of public opinion; but it could not actually prescribe policy, as this might turn out to be at odds with the policy of governments. Any line of action recommended by such an assembly would have to be pressed and secured through the policy-making machinery of the various countries themselves.

These, then, are the several types and grades of coordination which might develop with the growth of functional activities. But there is, finally, in the political field also the problem of security, admittedly a crucial problem, for on its being solved effectively the successful working of the other activities will depend. At the same time, the general discussion of functional organization will have served to bring out the true place and proportion of security, as something indispensable but also as something incapable by itself of achieving the peaceful growth of an international society. It is in fact a separate function like the others, not something that stands in stern isolation, overriding all the others. Looking at it in this way, as a practical function, should also make it clear that we would not achieve much if we handled it as a one-sided, limited problem—at present too often summed up in "German aggression." German aggression was a particularly vicious outgrowth of a bad general system, and only a radical and general change of the system itself will provide continuous security for all. In this case also it would be useful to lay down some formal pledges and principles as a guiding line, but the practical organization would have to follow functional, perhaps combined with regional, lines. That is all the more necessary as we know better now how many elements besides the purely military enter into the making of security. The various functional agencies might, in fact, play an important role in that wide aspect of security; they could both watch over and check such things as the building of strategic railways or the accumulation of strategic stocks in metals or grains. Possibly they could even be used, very properly and effectively, as a first line of action against threatening aggression, by their withholding services from those who are causing the trouble. They could apply such preventive sanctions more effectively than if this were to wait upon the agreement and action of a number of separate governments; and they could do so as part of their practical duties, and therefore with less of the political reactions caused by political action.

○   *Representation in Controls*

One aspect likely to be closely examined is that of the structure of the functional controls, and here again the initial difficulty will be that we shall have to break away from attractive traditional ideas if we are to work out the issue on its merits. It is not in the nature of the method that representation on the controlling bodies should be democratic in a political sense, full and equal for all. Ideally it may seem that all functions should be organized on a worldwide scale and that all states should have a voice in control. Yet the weight of reality is on the side of making the jurisdiction of the various agencies no wider than the most effective working limits of the function; and while it is understandable that all countries might wish to have a voice in control, that would be really to hark back to the outlook of political sovereignty. In no functional organization so far have the parties interested had a share in control as "by right" of their separate existence—neither the various local authorities in the London Transport Board, nor the seven states concerned in the TVA [Tennessee Valley Authority]. An in any case, in the transition from power politics to a functional order we could be well satisfied if the control of the new international organs answered to some of the merits of each case, leaving it to experience and to the maturing of a new outlook to provide in time the necessary correctives.

. . .

●   **THROUGH FUNCTIONAL ACTION
TO INTERNATIONAL SOCIETY**

○   *The Way of Natural Selection*

One cannot insist too much that such gradual functional developments would not create a new system, however strange they might appear in the light of our habitual search for a unified formal order. They would merely rationalize and develop what is already there. In all countries social activities, in the widest sense of the term, are organized and reorganized continually in that way. But because of the legalistic structure of the state and of our political outlook, which treat national and international society as two different worlds, social nature, so to speak, has not had a chance so far to take its course. Our social activities are cut off arbitrarily at the limit of the state and, if at all, are allowed to be linked to the same activities across the border only by means of uncertain and cramping political ligatures. What is here proposed is simply that these political amputations should cease. Whenever useful or necessary the several activities would be released to function as one unit throughout the length of their natural course. National problems would then appear, and would be treated, as what they are—the local segments of general problems.

. . .

○ *Epilogue*

Peace will not be secured if we organize the world by what divides it. But in the measure in which such peace-building activities develop and succeed, one might hope that the mere prevention of conflict, crucial as that may be, would in time fall to a subordinate place in the scheme of international things, while we would turn to what are the real tasks of our common society—the conquest of poverty and of disease and of ignorance. The stays of political federation were needed when life was more local and international activities still loose. But now our social interdependence is all-pervasive and all-embracing, and if it be so organized the political side will also grow as part of it. The elements of a functional system could begin to work without a general political authority, but a political authority without active social functions would remain an empty temple. Society will develop by our living it, not by policing it. Nor would any political agreement survive long under economic competition, but economic unification would build up the foundation for political agreement, even if it did not make it superfluous. In any case, as things are, the political way is too ambitious. We cannot start from an ideal plane but must be prepared to make many attempts from many points, and build things and mend things as we go along. The essential thing is that we should be going together, in the same direction, and that we get into step now.

. . .

Cooperation for the common good is the task, both for the sake of peace and of a better life, and for that it is essential that certain interests and activities should be taken out of the mood of competition and worked together. But it is not essential to make that cooperation fast to a territorial authority, and indeed it would be senseless to do so when the number of those activities is limited, while their range is the world.

"Economic areas do not always run with political areas," wrote the *New York Times* (February 26, 1943) in commenting on the Alaska Highway scheme, and such cross-country cooperation would simply make frontiers less important. "Apply this principle to certain European areas and the possibilities are dazzling." If it be said that all that may be possible in war but hardly in peace, that can only mean that practically the thing is possible but that we doubt whether in normal times there would be the political will to do it. Now, apart from everything else, the functional method stands out as a solid touchstone in that respect. Promissory covenants and charters may remain a headstone to unfulfilled good intentions, but the functional way is action itself and therefore an inescapable test of where we stand and how far we are willing to go in building up a new international society. It is not a promise to act in a crisis, but itself the action that will avoid the crisis. Every activity organized in that way would be a layer of peaceful life; and a sufficient addition of them would create increasingly deep and wide strata of peace—not the forbidding peace of an alliance, but one that would suffuse the world with a fertile mingling of common endeavor and achievement.

This is not an argument against any ideal of formal union, if that should prove a possible ultimate goal. It is, above all, a plea for the creation now of the elements of an active international society. Amidst the tragedy of war one can glimpse also the promise of a broader outlook, of a much deeper understanding of the issues than in 1918. It is because the peoples are ready for action that they cannot wait. We have no means and no standing to work out some fine constitution and try to impose it in time upon the world. But we do have the standing and the means to prepare for immediate practical action. We do not know what will be the sentiments of the peoples of Europe and of other continents at the end of the war, but we do know what their needs will be. *Any* political scheme would start a disputation; *any* working arrangement would raise a hope and make for confidence and patience.

The functional way may seem a spiritless solution—and so it is, in the sense that it detaches from the spirit the things which are of the body. No advantage has accrued to anyone when economic and other social activities are wedded to fascist or communist or other political ideologies; their progeny has always been confusion and conflict. Let these things appear quite starkly for what they are, practical household tasks, and it will be more difficult to make them into the household idols of "national interest" and "national honor." The ideological movements of our time, because of their indiscriminate zeal, have sometimes been compared to religious movements. They may be, but at their core was not a promise of life hereafter. The things which are truly of the spirit—

and therefore personal to the individual and to the nation—will not be less winged for being freed in their turn from that worldly ballast. Hence the argument that opposes democracy to totalitarianism does not call the real issue. It is much too simple. Society is everywhere in travail because it is everywhere in transition. Its problem after a century of laissez faire philosophy is to sift anew, in the light of new economic possibilities and of new social aspirations, what is private from what has to be public; and in the latter sphere what is local and national from what is wider. And for that task of broad social refinement a more discriminating instrument is needed than the old political sieve. In the words of a statement by the American National Policy Committee, "Part of the daring required is the daring to find new forms and to adopt them. We are lost if we dogmatically assume that the procedures of the past constitute the only true expression of democracy."

12 Political Integration: Definitions and Hypotheses

LEON N. LINDBERG

Functionalism failed as theory for several reasons, but one stands out: it contained no theory of politics. It assumed that economic problems could be solved by technical experts apart from the political process. Without some understanding of politics, however, it could not explain why certain choices were made. From the late 1950s to the mid-1970s, a group predominantly composed of U.S. social scientists, led by Ernst Haas at the University of California–Berkeley, sought to explain the development of the European Community by addressing the deficiencies of functionalism. Neofunctionalists, as the new theorists were called, drew on democratic theory, systems theory, group theory, and a host of other approaches to produce a scientifically,rigorous explanation for European integration that they also believed held predictive power.

Leon Lindberg (University of Wisconsin–Madison), one of Haas's students at Berkeley, helped define and advance neofunctionalism with the publication of three books in the 1960s and early 1970s. In the first chapter of The Political Dynamics of European Economic Integration *(1963), Lindberg illustrates early neofunctionalism's systematic approach to explaining integration, as well as its enthusiasm for a European project that promised to "move beyond the nation state as a basic framework for action." Lindberg first draws on Haas to define "political integration," then goes on to identify conditions for integration. The central roles played by political actors are key to Lir.dberg's view of the integration process. New central institutions, for instance, help "precipitate unity;" political groups "restructure their expectations and activi-*

*ties" in response to integration; and member states must possess "the will
to proceed" if integration is to continue. Also important is the role of
"spillover," which propels integration forward as cooperation in one
area spills over into other areas. Lindberg does not argue that spillover
is inevitable (and thus integration, once started, will proceed indefinitely), but he does display a faith in its power that is not yet tempered
by Charles de Gaulle and the Luxembourg compromise.*

    The Europe that gave birth to the idea of the nation state appears
to be well on the way to rejecting it in practice. The Treaty establishing
the European Economic Community (EEC), signed in Rome on 25 March
1957, represents the latest in a series of steps designed to break down the
bastions of European national separatism. Its six signatories, France,
Germany, Italy, Belgium, the Netherlands, and Luxembourg, were
already members of the European Coal and Steel Community (ECSC),
whose foundation in 1952 had created a common market restricted to
coal and steel. The experience with this first effort at sector integration
led ultimately to the creation of the EEC as well as the European Atomic
Energy Community (EURATOM):

> It soon became evident that integration by sectors could only yield
> limited results. Its restricted scope, unconnected with the other
> parts of the economic and financial system, ruled out any large-
> scale activities and made it impossible to achieve an over-all
> equilibrium. To sweep away from Europe protectionism and
> economic nationalism with their resulting high production costs,
> high costs of living and economic stagnation, a different approach
> was required, a wide attack in more than one dimension as it were;
> it must have the depth of integration and the wide scope of a freeing
> of trade. This approach was provided first by the Beyen Plan and
> then by the Spaak Report, which marked the first step towards the
> Common Market.

    The EEC has as its primary goal the creation of an area in which
goods, people, services, and capital will be able to circulate freely. To
achieve this, a customs union is created, but a customs union in which
attention is devoted not only to barriers between states, but to economic,
financial, and social reactions that may take place in the member states.
The main purpose is the abolition of trade barriers, tariffs, and quotas,
which is to be accomplished more or less automatically during a twelve-
to fifteen-year transition period, divided into three four-year stages. A
series of targets is assigned to each stage, and these relate not only to
progress in removal of trade barriers, but also to parallel measures of
economic and social alignment. This process is to be accompanied by the

establishment of a common external tariff, within which an alignment of the several economies is to go on in order to adjust differences in price and working conditions, and in productive resources. Advancement from one stage to another is dependent upon achieving these respective targets. All this is to be supervised by institutions specially set up by the Treaty.

The economic and social significance of these developments is certainly far-reaching—one need only read the newspapers to confirm this. For the political scientist, too, they are of consuming interest, for here he can observe the actual processes whereby political actors move beyond the nation state as a basic framework for action, appearing finally to realize the oft-proclaimed "fact" of the international interdependence of nations. Forces are at work in Western Europe that may alter the nature of international relations, as well as offer promise of a fuller and more prosperous life for the inhabitants of the region.

The stated goal of the EEC is the creation of a customs union and ultimately the achievement of a significant measure of economic integration. The fundamental motivation is political. It is, in the words of the Treaty, to establish "an ever closer union among the European peoples." Our concern will be with the political *consequences* of economic integration. We shall try to measure the extent to which the creation of the EEC and the activities which take place in its framework give rise to the phenomenon of political integration. Whereas in terms of commercial policy the establishment of the EEC is "already the most important event of this century," its vast political significance is still only a potential.

• POLITICAL INTEGRATION

What, then, do we mean by political integration? Some writers define it as a *condition,* and others as a *process.* In the works of Karl W. Deutsch, integration refers to the probability that conflicts will be resolved without violence. The central concept is that of a "security-community," which is "a group of people which has become integrated:" that is, they have attained "within a territory . . . a 'sense of community' and . . . institutions and practices strong enough and widespread enough to assure, for a 'long' time, dependable expectations of 'peaceful change' among its population." Integration may come about through several types of security-communities, "amalgamated" or "pluralistic," implying respectively either the presence or the absence of any real central decision-making institutions or delegations of national autonomy. In either case, integration is achieved when the states concerned cease to prepare for war against each other.

Similarly, North, Koch, and Zinnes list six criteria in terms of which one can consider integration: the probability of violence given a conflict situation (same as Deutsch); the frequency of conflicts between any given number of organizations in a given span of time; the number of compatible policy conditions; the degree of interdependency between n given organizations; the number and significance of interlocking communications systems or structures; and the extent to which membership overlaps.

Such conceptualizations of political integration as a *condition* have been criticized on the grounds that they permit only a general discussion of the environmental factors influencing integration, and that they fail to provide us with the tools needed to make a clear distinction between the situation prior to integration and the situation prevailing during the process, thus obscuring the role of social change. For these reasons, Haas insists that we should look at political integration as a *process:* "Political integration is the process whereby political actors in several distinct national settings are persuaded to shift their loyalties, expectations and political activities toward a new center, whose institutions possess or demand jurisdiction over the preexisting national states. The end result of a process of political integration is a new political community, superimposed over the pre-existing ones."

In Haas's work, this definition is rigorously tied to an ideal-type analysis in which the institutions of the ECSC are compared to those of an ideal federal-type system. This kind of heuristic device is certainly above reproach and did in fact yield extremely valuable results. My own investigations, however, have led me to adopt a more cautious conception of political integration, one limited to the development of devices and processes for arriving at collective decisions by means other than autonomous action by national governments. It seems to me that it is logically and empirically possible that collective decision-making procedures involving a significant amount of political integration can be achieved without moving toward a "political community" as defined by Haas. In fact, use of this type of ideal, or model, analysis may well direct the researcher to a different set of questions and a different interpretation of the data collected:

> European integration is developing, and may continue so for a long time, in the direction of different units. . . . We can only speculate about the outcome, but a forecast of the emergence of a pluralistic political structure, hitherto unknown, might not be wholly errone-ous. Such a structure might very well permit to a great extent the participating nations to retain their identity while yet joined in the organizations that transcend nationality.

For the purpose of this study, political integration will be defined as a *process*, but without reference to an end point. In specific terms, political integration is (1) the process whereby nations forgo the desire and ability to conduct foreign and key domestic policies independently of each other, seeking instead to make *joint decisions* or to *delegate* the decision-making process to new central organs; and (2) the process whereby political actors in several distinct settings are persuaded to shift their expectations and political activities to a new center.

Although this dual definition lacks the analytical clarity and precision of model analysis, it is, I believe, appropriate to the problem at hand. Not only does it provide us with a set of interrelated indicators by means of which to judge the experience of the EEC, but it specifies what I take to be the process of political integration. The first part of the definition refers to two modes of decisionmaking which are, in my opinion, intimately related, the existence of delegated decisionmaking being a basic precondition for progress in shared decisionmaking. The processes of *sharing* and of *delegating* decisionmaking are likely to affect the governmental structure in each state involved, creating new internal problems of coordination and policy direction, especially between Ministries of Foreign Affairs and such specialized ministries as Economic Affairs, Agriculture, and Labor that are accustomed to regarding their spheres as wholly or primarily of domestic concern. States with traditions of representative and parliamentary government are also faced with the problem created by the development of decision-making centers whose authority derives from an international, rather than a national, consensus.

The second part of the definition refers to the patterns of behavior shown by high policy makers, civil servants, parliamentarians, interest-group leaders, and other elites. Here our attention is directed to the perceptions and resulting behavior of the political actors in each of the states involved. The relationship between this set of indicators and those referring to governmental decisionmaking is very close. By the nature of the process, government policy-makers and civil servants are involved increasingly in the new system of decisionmaking: they attend meetings of experts, draft plans, and participate in an over-all joint decision-making pattern. Similarly, as the locus of decisionmaking changes, so will the tactics of groups and individuals seeking to influence the decision-making process. They may oppose the change, but once made they will have to adjust to it by changing their tactics, or their organization, or both, to accommodate to the new situation. In Haas's words: "Conceived not as a condition but as a *process,* the conceptualization [of political integration] relies on the perception of interests . . . by the actors participating in the process. Integration takes place when these perceptions fall into a certain pattern and fails to take place when they do not." Moreover, "as the process of integration proceeds, it is assumed . . . that interests will be redefined in terms of regional rather than a purely national orientation."

So much for defining the concept of political integration. The problem now is to try to spell out how it can be made to occur in actual life. Since there have been numerous efforts at transnational organization and cooperation that have not had political results of this kind, political scientists have tried to identify constant background, or environmental, factors or conditions upon which political integration is contingent. Thus Deutsch isolates the following conditions as essential or helpful for a pluralistic or amalgamated security-community: initially compatible value systems, mutually responsive elites, adequate communications channels, a commitment to a "new way of life," and the existence of a "core area." Similarly, Haas calls for a pluralistic social structure, a high level of economic and industrial development, and a modicum of ideological homogeneity.

But the examination of background factors or conditions does not help us account completely for the *process* of political integration, nor does it permit differentiation between the situation prior to integration and the situation prevailing during the process. Accordingly, it is necessary to try to identify some additional variable factors to specify *how* political integration occurs. On the basis of Haas's researches and my own experiences in Western Europe, I suggest that the process of political integration requires the following conditions: (1) Central institutions and central policies must develop. (2) The tasks assigned to these institutions must be important enough and specific enough to activate socioeconomic processes to which conventional international organizations have no access. (3) These tasks must be inherently expansive. (4) The member states must continue to see their interests as consistent with the enterprise.

• CENTRAL INSTITUTIONAL DEVELOPMENT

Central institutions are required in order to *represent* the common interests which have brought the member states together, and in order to *accommodate* such conflicts of interest as will inevitably arise. In discussing the institutions of the EEC, I prefer to avoid the concept of "supranationality" and to focus instead on the extent to which the Community institutions are enabled to deal directly with fields of activity, rather than merely influencing the actions of individual governments in respect of these fields. There are four main aspects to be considered:

1. North, Koch, and Zinnes seek to distinguish between compromise and "true integration," both seen as ways of dealing with conflict. Both depend upon *reducing the intensity* of the conflict by uncovering its sources, and by taking the demands of both sides and breaking them into their constituent parts. Each party to the conflict is forced to reexamine and reevaluate its own desires against those of the other party and against the implications of the total situation. True integration is achieved when a solution has been found in which "both desires have found a place," in which the interests of the parties "fit into each other." I suggest that the central institutions of the EEC, by isolating issues and identifying common interests, may play a crucial role here in "precipitating unity."

2. The integrative impact of the central institutions will depend in part upon the *competencies* and *roles* assigned to them. Much, however, depends upon whether or not the institutions make full use of their competencies and upon *how they define their role*. The literature on organizational decisionmaking suggests some relevant questions in this context. What formal and informal decisionmaking and relational patterns will develop? What patterns of commitment will be enforced by organizational imperatives, by the social character of the personnel, by "institutionalization," by the social and cultural environment, and by centers of interest generated in the course of action and decision? I suggest that the early years of the existence of these institutions will be significant in determining their long-range competence, that patterns of internal differentiation and conflicting values will develop, that organizational behavior will be conditioned by the necessity of adjusting to the environment, and that cooptation will be used as a tactic to head off opposition.

3. Central institutions lacking real competency to affect policymaking directly may develop a *consensus* that will influence those national or international decision makers who do determine policy.

4. Finally, the patterns of interaction engendered by the central institutions may affect *the overall system* in which they operate; in other words, these institutions may have latent effects that contribute to political integration. Participants in the activities of central institutions may develop multiple perspectives, personal friendships, a comraderie of expertise, all of which may reflect back upon the national governments and affect future national policymaking. Such latent effects, however, are significant only if the individuals concerned are influential at the national level, *and* if their activities in the central institutions involve significant policymaking.

• ELITE ACTIVATION

Thanks to the efforts of the so-called "group theorists," political scientists today know that any analysis of the political process must give a central place to the phenomena of group conflict, to the beliefs, attitudes, and ideologies of groups participating in the process of policy formation. If political integration, as we have defined it, is going on, then we would expect to find a change in the behavior of the participants. Consequently we must identify the aims and motives of the relevant political groups, the conditions of their emergence, and the means by which they seek and attain access to centers of political power.

One of the main obstacles to political integration has been the fact that international organizations lack direct access to individuals and groups in the national communities involved. "Short of such access, the organization continues to be no more than a forum of intergovernmental consultation and cooperation."

Actors with political power in the national community will restructure their expectations and activities only if the tasks granted to the new institutions are of immediate concern to them, and only if they involve a significant change in the conditions of the actors' environment. Several patterns of reaction may be expected:

1. Individual firms may undertake measures of self-protection or adjustment in the form of cartels to limit competition, the conclusion of agreements, and so on.
2. Groups may change their political organization and tactics in order to gain access to, and to influence, such new central decision-making centers as may be developing.
3. These activities may act back upon the central institutions and the member states by creating situations that cannot be dealt with except by further central institutional development and new central policies. An example would be a developing need for antitrust legislation in response to an evolving network of agreements between firms in several countries.
4. Such activities may also have latent effects of the kind already described, operative under the same conditions.

• INHERENTLY EXPANSIVE TASKS

Here is a problem of central importance because changes in the policy needs of the member states create definite phases in the life of international organizations. To remedy this, the task assigned to the institutions must be inherently expansive and thus capable of overcoming what Haas calls "the built-in autonomy of functional contexts."

> Lessons about integrative processes associated with one phase do not generally carry over into the next because the specific policy context . . . determines what is desired by governments and tolerated by them in terms of integrative accommodations. . . . There is no dependable, cumulative process of precedent formation leading to ever more community-oriented organizational behavior, unless the task assigned to the institutions is inherently expansive, thus capable of overcoming the built-in autonomy of functional contexts and of surviving changes in the policy aims of member states.

This is the principle involved in the concept of "spillover." In its most general formulation, "spillover" refers to a situation in which a given action, related to a specific goal, creates a situation in which the original goal can be assured only by taking further actions, which in turn create a further condition and a need for more action, and so forth. The concept has been used by Haas to show that integrating one sector of the economy—for example, coal and steel—will inevitably lead to the integration of other economic and political activities. We shall formulate it as follows: the initial task and grant of power to the central institutions creates a situation or series of situations that can be dealt with only by further expanding the task and the grant of power. Spillover implies that a situation has developed in which the ability of a member state to achieve a policy goal may depend upon the attainment by another member state of one of its policy goals. The situation may show various features:

1. The dynamics of spillover are dependent upon the fact that support for any given step in integration is the result of a convergence of goals and expectations. These often competing goals give rise to competing activities and demands, which may be the basis of further convergence leading to further integration.
2. Lack of agreement between governments may lead to an expanded role for the central institutions; in other words, member states may delegate difficult problems.
3. At the level of elite groupings, demands and expectations for further actions may be expressed as a result of partial actions taken by the central institutions.
4. The activities of the central institutions and nonofficial elites may *create situations* that cannot be dealt with except by

further central institutional development and new central policies.

5. Far-reaching economic integration, involving all sectors of the economy, as in the EEC, may offer great scope for spillover *between* sectors. Conflicts over further integration in a given sector, involving disparate national interests, may be resolved by bargains between such sectors (e.g., agriculture and energy).

6. Participation in a customs union will probably elicit reactions from nonmember states, a situation which may create problems that can be resolved only by further integration or by expanding the role of the central institutions.

• CONTINUITY OF NATIONAL POLICY AIMS

"Spillover" assumes the continued commitment of the member states to the undertaking. The Treaty of Rome was the result of a creative compromise, a convergence of national aspirations. Political and economic integration cannot be expected to succeed in the absence of a will to proceed on the part of the member states. Granted that it would be difficult for a state to withdraw from the EEC, it must be stressed that little could be done to move beyond minimal obligations if one or several states were to maintain a determined resistance. It seems likely, however, that with the operation of the other integrative factors, the alternatives open to any member state will gradually be limited so as to reduce dependence upon this factor. For the will to proceed need not have a positive content. Given only a general reluctance to be charged with obstruction, or to see the enterprise fail, the stimulus to action can be provided by the central institutions or by other member states.

The way in which decisions are made, in which conflicts of interest among the member states are resolved, will be of definitive importance for political integration, because the kind of accommodation that prevails will indicate the nature of the positive convergence of pro-integration aims, and of the extent to which the alternatives open to national decision makers may have been limited by participation in the enterprise. In this connection we may ask the question, under what conditions does conflict produce a stronger bond between the parties than that which existed before? Moreover, as already mentioned, the mode of accommodation is directly correlated to the developmental potential of the central institutions.

Conflicts between states may be resolved on the basis of "the minimum common denominator," by "splitting the difference," or by "upgrading common interests." The "minimum common denominator" type, characteristic of classical diplomatic negotiations, involves relatively equal bargainers who exchange equal concessions while never going beyond what the least cooperative among them is willing to concede. Accommodation by "splitting the difference" involves a similar exchange of concessions, but conflicts are ultimately resolved somewhere between the final bargaining positions, usually because of the mediatory role performed by a secretariat or expert study groups, or out of deference to third-party pressure such as might be institutionalized in "parliamentary diplomacy." This implies "the existence of a continuing organization with a broad frame of reference, public debate, rules of procedure governing the debate, and the statement of conclusions arrived at by some kind of majority vote." Although such mediating organs may not be able to define the terms of agreement, they do participate in setting limits within which the ultimate accommodation is reached. Accommodation on the basis of "upgrading common interests," whether deliberately or inadvertently, depends on the participation of institutions or individuals with an autonomous role that permits them to participate in actually defining the terms of the agreement. It implies greater progress toward political integration, for it shows that

> the parties succeeded in so redefining their conflict so as to work out a solution at a higher level, which almost invariably implies the expansion of the mandate or task of an international or national governmental agency. In terms of results, this mode of accommodation maximizes . . . the "spillover" effect of international decisions: policies made pursuant to an initial task and grant of power can be made real only if the task itself is expanded, as reflected in the compromises among the states interested in the task.

This last type comes closest to what North, Koch, and Zinnes call "true integration."

We now have a set of definitions, variable factors, indicators, and hypotheses with which to assess the extent to which the EEC is contributing to the process of political integration. We are concerned above all with determining the impact of the EEC on official and nonofficial decision-making patterns in the "Europe of the Six," and with analyzing the structure and content of such central decisionmaking as may develop.

. . .

13 Neofunctionalism: A Case of Mistaken Identity

A. J. R. GROOM

Neofunctionalism proved fertile and flexible in the 1960s and early 1970s. Numerous scholars in international relations and comparative politics, most of them very young U.S. citizens, applied their considerable energies to dissecting the integration process. Several empirical and theoretical problems cropped up along the way, but creative thinkers modified neofunctionalism to settle most of the issues. By 1970, the theory was rigorously specified but very complex—hardly the elegant model of the early 1960s. Problems with the theory continued to mount in the early 1970s, and in 1975 Ernst Haas declared regional integration theory (read neofunctionalism) "obsolescent." Most neofunctionalists took Haas's hint and moved on to other theories of international political economy such as interdependence theory and regime theory.

This 1978 article by Professor A. J. R. Groom (University of Kent, Canterbury, England) illustrates the skeptical approach to neofunctionalism taken by scholars in the late 1970s. In it, Groom first describes the underlying currents that informed neofunctionalism and the hypotheses that it yielded. He then identifies the key criticism of neofunctionalist theory: that it does not adequately explain "empirical reality" in its only important case, Western Europe. Task expansion, spillover, and engrenage did not occur as predicted; pluralistic interest groups did not drive integration forward; masses did not follow elites; and national governments remained politically powerful. This failure to explain and predict the course of European integration cast doubt on the mainly U.S. concepts used in formulating the theory and opened to

Reprinted with permission from *Political Science*, 30(1)(1978): 15-28. Copyright 1978 by Victoria University Press. Notes omitted.

scrutiny its normative bias in favor of powerful supranational institutions. From Groom's functionalist perspective, neofunctionalism's normative bias toward state building put it at odds with traditional functionalism but at ease with the central goals of federalism.

The words "functionalism" and "functional" bid fair to rival "power" or "power politics" as two of the most frequently used but confusing terms in the social scientist's lexicon. The term "neofunctionalism" only compounds this confusion since it is an approach which has characteristics that, far from being near to functionalism, are in fact antithetical to it. The term "functional" and its derivatives are widely used in sociology, anthropology, psychology, environmental studies and fine arts as well as political science and international relations. It is with their use in political science and international relations that this article is concerned since, while neofunctionalism is being questioned as explanation and prediction by its founding fathers, not sufficient attention has been focused on the fundamental differences between neofunctionalism and the functionalist notions from which it was originally derived. Indeed, the questioning of neofunctionalism has concentrated on some of those very aspects where it deviated from the basic tenets of functionalism.

. . .

• NEOFUNCTIONALISM—A STATEMENT

Neofunctionalism has several noteworthy peculiarities. Its genesis owes much to the process of Western European integration in the postwar period as conceptualized by scholars in the United States on the basis of models initially conceived in the context of the political system of that country. Moreover, although this conceptualization is dubbed neofunctionalism, it is, in both spirit and fact, far from the tenets of functionalism. While neofunctionalism was concocted in an attempt to explain the extraordinary phenomenon of integration in Western Europe based on the reconciliation of two erstwhile traditional enemies—France and Germany—it has since been used as the conceptual basis for the analysis of integration processes in other parts of the world. Indeed, it has now reached the status of a conceptual framework independent of a particular empirical setting and forms part of a repertoire of approaches to integration from which a student can choose, modify and amend to suit his analytical purpose. Yet it would be foolish not to acknowledge neofunctionalism's European genesis, since the early experience of the European communities provides a clear exemplification of the theory—one that we shall not ignore.

This European experience suggests a further aspect of neofunctionalism that it is both a conceptual framework and a plan of action. In the former guise it purported to describe what was happening, while in the latter role it pointed to what should be done to further that process. Those Europeans committed to some form of federalism, but who realized that a federal United States of Europe was unlikely to be constructed out of the rubble of the Second World War and the glowing embers of the Cold War, saw the construction of their goal in terms of the incremental transfer of competencies from the integrating state governments to a new supranational authority. Functions were to be transferred to a new central authority in relatively painless installments which would frighten no one, since in each instance they would not be enough singly to blast away the foundations of state sovereignty. Yet there was the hope that a momentum would be created whereby the transfer of some competencies would facilitate the transfer of other competencies on the pragmatic grounds that they go together and cannot be properly managed apart—the functional imperative. In addition the successful achievement of the transfer of some would enhance the acceptability of further transfers.

To the Western European elite seeking to create their conception of a united Western Europe—liberal and democratic, Christian and neo-capitalist, and free from the dictates of Soviet power externally and the scourge of Muscovite communist parties internally as well as from the tutelage of the United States—"neofunctionalism" offered a means to an end. It would be wrong to suggest that the theory came first and the action followed: rather, a strategy evolved out of the conjuncture of an ideologically defined goal and the pragmatic considerations of the day. Only later was it conceptualized in an academic formulation.

This conceptualization was undertaken by a number of scholars in the United States. While their colleagues in Europe were primarily concerned with purely descriptive legal or economic analyses, the United States scholars made an analogy and an innovation. The analogy was with the process of integration within the United States, and the innovation was the application of new methodology to the study of international integration in Europe. At the time the United States was viewed as an ideal for which to aim—free, rich, stable and secure—in contrast to Europe, which could not hope for any of those attributes with any great degree of surety. To achieve the American goal, the American way of democratic pluralism in a variety of domains and economic *laissez-faire* was advocated. The intellectual baggage of pluralism, which was the dominant explanation of American society, could be applied to Europe both to assess progress and to point the way.

At the same time, social science as a whole was becoming much more behavioral and scientific in aspiration and orientation in the

United States. There was a highly meritorious attempt to be precise in the formulation of hypotheses, to be ruthless in the control of values, to be exact in the observation of data and to be rigorous in their analysis. But a conceptual framework suitable for the European context was still necessary and one was at hand—functionalism. Functionalism had the merit of being compatible with the American experience of pluralism and liberalism and of being sufficiently flexible that it could be applied in the context of regional integration in Europe. However, when made precise so that it could be used empirically to describe and analyze the European phenomenon, "functionalism" became, in reality, not *neo-*functionalism but anti-functionalism except for one key and highly controversial area, namely, the learning process—a point to which we shall return later. Nevertheless, this sustained intellectual effort by scholars in the United States to elaborate and test neofunctionalism has been one of the major achievements in the study of international relations since the war. It is one of the principal reasons why integration theory has been a growth area in the discipline. As we shall see, the model is a good explanation of the Western European integration process of the fifties and early sixties, but it is less applicable to the more recent experience in Europe and elsewhere. However, hypotheses can be and have been reformulated, and the intellectual and explanatory mileage to be obtained from neofunctionalism has not yet been exhausted.

Neofunctionalism shares with other integration theories which seek to transcend the existing state structure the notion of a set of background conditions which are likely to be propitious for such a process to take place. These conditions include a degree of homogeneity in both levels of development (social, economic and political) and basic values, a network of transactions which give rise to mutual knowledge and a sense of mutual relevance, compatible decision-making processes, compatible expectations, and especially a belief both that future problems can be met in a mutually acceptable manner and that integration will enhance the satisfaction of felt needs to a degree not otherwise possible. Such conditions may give rise to a process of integration which, in its neofunctionalist mode, involves the incremental transfer of competencies to a new supranational authority within a defined geographical area which can be characterized as *Gesellschaft* integration. What is more, it is a teleological process with an end in mind—namely, the creation of a new political entity incorporating the previously independent units as subunits of the new polity.

Although the process is in terms of particular functions such as agriculture, the unit of analysis remains the traditional one of the territorially-based state system (in dramatic opposition to that of the functionalist which is based on a territorial systems of transactions with no fixed conception of a final goal). For the neofunctionalist the goal is the creation of a new state out of the integration of several states: neofunctionalism reinforces the state system in aspiring to beget more viable "regional" states. There is no attempt to transcend the state system as in classical or traditional functionalism. The neofunctionalist strategy is merely a stratagem to give a new lease of life to the state system, not a device for its demise.

While the goal is fundamentally political, the means are initially nonpolitical. Clearly the creation of a new "regional" state is a political task. Moreover, as functions are transferred to the new supranational decision-making center there is an attempt to politicize the process in the sense that interest groups are encouraged to direct their activities to the new center and the civil servants and political figures associated with it "go out and look for business." As their activities expand they seek political relevance and legitimacy so that their activities may expand still further. However, such a strategy has its dangers since, if pursued too soon, too vigorously, and to too great an extent, then political actors, interest groups and civil servants associated with the old independent decision-making centers may act to retard or stop the process of integration, as in the case of the European Defence Community. Thus the initial stages may be essentially nonpolitical, and nonpolitical in two senses.

First, the process of integration depends greatly on a perceived convergence of economic interest. This building block of the neofunctionalist's edifice may owe its origin to the approach's elaboration in the context of Western European economic integration starting with the Marshall Plan and reaching its apogee in the EEC. It also provided a link with functionalism, since there too the satisfaction of "nonpolitical" welfare (economic and social) needs is deemed to be a crucial element in forging a "working peace system." But both the functionalists and neofunctionalists have been roundly and rightly criticized for assuming that economic integration is "nonpolitical," and therefore in some sense the easy road to integration, and for suggesting that task expansion and spillover in the economic sphere will have a great deal of automaticity. In the light of these criticisms based on empirical research, the neofunctionalist hypothesis has been reformulated to acknowledge the politicization of economic integration and the extent to which progress depends upon an act of will. Integration is not like Topsy—it has not "just growed."

The second reason why the process of neofunctionalist integration was thought to be nonpolitical lies in the pluralistic character of the states involved in the process. The *force motrice* of integration is generated by economic actors, both state and nonstate, who have developed convergent goals which grow ever stronger as the process develops. Transnational interest groups arise for whom the furtherance of this process is a vested interest. Thus interest groups of a nonpolitical character are the prime carriers of integration and they demand appropriate state action to further integration. These demands are not the traditional "high politics" or "power politics," but are made in the framework of a consensus of values derived from the process of integration to further economic goals. There is an end to ideology: politics is about giving people what they want, which is crudely interpreted as an increase in goods and services, and the means to achieve this is further integration. Consensus on values is assumed, and so high politics or power politics which deals with dissensus is not relevant.

To a degree this neofunctionalist requirement was an empirical reality in Western Europe in the fifties and the early sixties, but a consensus once attained needs to be maintained in a changing environment. The discovery that high politics was not dead and that the age of ideology had not ended but was merely in abeyance, so that economic interest groups and supranational technocratic bureaucrats did not have free run, led to further reformulations of the neofunctionalist hypothesis. In short, as the goal was highly political in nature, a degree of success in achieving it led to the politicization of the means used: such means had political implications despite their nonpolitical pretensions.

The reason for this lies in the *Gesellschaftliche* nature of neofunctionalist integration. The neofunctionalists assumed that as competencies were transferred to a new decision-making center this center would, through the fulfillment of felt needs, gradually accrete authority and legitimacy. Thus a new sense of community would grow giving rise to a *Gemeinschaft*, first at the elite level and later at the mass level. In reality, while competencies have been transferred, loyalties have not altered to the same extent. At the community level, Western Europe is a *Gesellschaft* highly vulnerable to any lack of success since it has no cushion of legitimacy at the mass level, and to a lesser extent at the elite level, to buttress it in hard times. Such attempts to curry legitimacy as the perversion of a universal masterpiece, Beethoven's Choral Symphony, for a "national" anthem, or the pathetic "European" passport, are distasteful and probably counter-productive.

At the heart of these observed failings of the neofunctionalist model to explain the events in Western Europe and elsewhere and the model's subsequent reformulation lies the learning process. Through the learning process a politically inspired common market would give rise to economic union which in turn would lead to political union. There was a functional imperative that lent this process a high degree of automaticity. This functional imperative had three components: task expansion, spillover, and *engrenage*. These components are not mutually exclusive, nor are they always clearly defined, but we can take task expansion to refer to increased cooperation in the same area, spillover to mean cooperation in a new area often of a more salient political character arising out of existing cooperation, and *engrenage* to indicate a locking-in process.

The learning process occurs when successful cooperation in a joint endeavor gives rise to a willingness on the part of the actors, and especially the bureaucratic and political elite, to contemplate closer cooperation in that area especially when the initial cooperation will be greatly facilitated and enhanced by further cooperation. Thus the common task is expanded. It might also spill over into an adjacent domain, as for example in the coordination of transport systems to increase the flow of goods which has been stimulated by a reduction in tariffs or, more grandly, to move from economic integration to political integration. But the process as a whole needs to take place in a compatible framework so that the maximum benefits from task expansion and spillover can be realized: the bringing together of disparate elements for the achievement of greater integration involves a sort of *engrenage*. In early neofunctionalist writings it was asserted that task expansion and spillover would be automatic. This was thought to be due to the satisfaction of felt needs through cooperation which would inspire further cooperation, and the subsequent belief that integration would lead to the maximization first of compatible self-interest and then of common interests. As with the functionalists, it was held that the successful endeavor to satisfy interests in common would lead to a growth of common interests. Thus, as crises arose, they would be resolved not by deadlock or splitting the difference, but by upgrading the common interest to the evident benefit of all.

The neofunctionalists felt the economic domain to be particularly propitious for these phenomena to occur since it was a nonpoliticized domain in which supranational actors and interest groups could extract the maximum amount of integration without state actors interfering. Then, when it was "too late," after economic union had been achieved, political union would inevitably follow since it would be made necessary by the need to manage the economic union which could not be dispensed with because of its success in providing benefits for all.

• **NEOFUNCTIONALISM—A COMMENT**

So much for the hypotheses: empirical reality was very different in the context of Western Europe (and elsewhere) except for the period of the fifties and early sixties. Functional integration was often precise, with limited potentiality for task expansion or spillover; it was not oriented towards a common goal and therefore *engrenage* was difficult; it was based on temporary pragmatic considerations rather than on a long-term notion of common interest, so there was little spillover. As Schmitter has pointed out, there is a "functionalist paradox." "The narrower, more separable, and hence more technical, the scope of 'integrated policymaking,' the easier it may be to get initial agreement but the less significant is likely to be the subsequent impact upon national structures/values and, indirectly, regional processes."

Equally, Hansen has commented that "there was too little recognition of the fact that policy coordination among member states of the European Community could substitute for greater supranational control. While economic integration does require that many economic policies be coordinated, it does not require formal political or quasi-political institutions to undertake that coordination." Moreover, a pluralistic environment had some drawbacks in that each issue required the construction of a new and different majority coalition among the interest groups and other actors concerned. This meant that integration was often uncoordinated and even incompatible from area to area, and thus *engrenage* was difficult to achieve. Furthermore, with state actors willing and able to intervene, the neofunctionalists' learning process will only act through the functional imperative if there is a prior political consensus; otherwise the state "gatekeepers" will lock and bar the gates.

In the pluralistic model of the United States the situation is different, since in the domestic realm there are no gatekeepers of the order of independent state governments, and so learning can take place and the functional imperative can more easily hold sway as the neofunctionalist hypothesis suggests. However, in international integration the potential effects of politicization, not of the permissive kind that was sought after but of a negative character from the point of view of integration, are of much greater significance, and the neofunctionalists failed to realize that political *disagreement* can come from economic success and that spillback, or disintegration, can occur from political and military disagreements between states. Thus we need to consider the role and effect of politicization in the integration process in a neofunctionalist mode.

Joseph Nye has aptly summarized the way in which successful progress towards integration, by its very success, stirs up political factors.

> More groups become involved through the effects of rising trans-actions, inherent linkages, or deliberate coalition formation. The larger the number, the more likely the possible divergent interpre-

tations of the common interest in integration. The growth of the powers of the central institutions not only makes them more visible to mass opinion but may also stimulate action by groups opposed to integration, including national bureaucrats jealous of incursion into their powers. The growth of ideological-identitive appeal and the involvement of external actors makes the integration process more salient both to mass opinion and to the dramatic-political decision makers. At the same time costs are likely to rise or become more visible as the effects of integration begin to work themselves out. The greater the politicization of subjects the less amenable they are to the quiet technocratic decision-making style. . . . This does not necessarily mean that further integration is impossible. It does mean, however, that reaching decisions may be more difficult and involve a wider range of forces.

More generally, while formal or informal unanimity decision-making processes prevail, governments will maintain a gatekeeping role. Indeed, in the neofunctionalist mode of integration this role is bound to be a highly political one since the goal is the creation of a new state. Unlike neofunctionalism, traditional functionalism does not have the goal of the creation of a new state, but rather there is a transfer of competencies to a new "functional authority" in different domains, the forms of which may range from the nebulous to the formal and which are, in any case, not coterminous in extent. Thus the process is less traumatic than in neofunctionalism, and so the likelihood of the political gatekeeper intervening is lessened and integration, diverse and diffuse, can more easily proceed because of the multiplicity and diversity of different decision-making centers. Nevertheless, there is one aspect of high politics—overt war—from the scourge of which we might expect neofunctionalism to have delivered us. This is happily true in Europe, but elsewhere, in Central America and East Africa, war between integrating units either has happened (the football war) or has been near (Uganda and its neighbors).

The role of technocratic-bureaucratic decision makers in supranational, national and interest group settings is important in neofunctionalism because such elites are considered to be imbued with the urgency of practical integration. At the supranational level they seek to shield the integration process from the negative taint of high politics and power politics by the maximization of the potential for task expansion, spillover and *engrenage* whenever possible. They nevertheless are political actors seeking to create a propitious climate for greater integration. This involves a conscious attempt to penetrate national bureaucracies and to ally with and organize interest groups.

To a considerable degree they have been successful, but not wholly so, since the dead hand of national standard operating procedures and bureaucratic politics blunts the impact of measures for integration at the level of implementation. Moreover, in the European case the Commission itself has become ponderous in the extreme. Gone are the halcyon days of enthusiastic and talented "political" civil servants: the "satisficing" career man has taken over. In addition, it was assumed that if the elite led, the mass would follow. In most cases of regional integration in a neofunctionalist style this has not occurred. Western Europe is an exception, but not to the extent that there is great enthusiasm, especially in Britain. However, this is not any great moment at present since general mass attitudes are not important. It is elite attitudes and activities that are significant, as has been shown by the undemocratic nature of the European Communities. The Commission, the European Council and the Council of Ministers and the interest groups, national bureaucracies and governments that deal with them are the locus of power, interest and activity, not the European Parliament. Neofunctionalist integration is led from the top and can proceed far with only grudging mass support. Since elites are important as generators of integration, it is not surprising that neofunctionalists give considerable importance to decisionmaking.

Neofunctionalists have been concerned to discover the degree to which the locus of decisionmaking is transferred, both formally and informally, to the supranational authority. However, while this may well indicate the extent to which a new polity is emerging, it need not correlate with the degree of integration. There is, for example, little supranationality in Scandinavia but a great deal of integration. Nevertheless, given the goal of the neofunctionalist—political union—it is hardly surprising that detailed analyses of the decision-making process have been undertaken.

Lindberg has suggested that we consider whether collective decisionmaking encompasses few or many issue areas and bear in mind their importance for integration. He also raises the questions of whether collective decisionmaking operates throughout the process from pre-decisional stages to implementation, whether it is marginal or decisive in determining outcome, the degree to which it is used, the resources available, the extent to which leadership is given and the degree to which the common interest is maximized and with which there is compliance with decisions. But an institution with administrative functions and regulatory powers, such as the Commission of the European Communities, that lacks a popular legitimizing base can, in the context of a unit-veto system, expand its role only within the narrow limits of consultation, advice, persuasion, mediation and conciliation. Moreover, central institutions will only become a focus of aspirations when they play a significant role in decisions to which individual member actors may object but which they accept as binding because they have consented to the procedures through which they were evolved. The failure to meet these exacting requirements indicates why several "neofunctionalist" enterprises have not achieved their goals. But an alternative to persuasion in a legitimized framework is coercion.

Of the three forms of integrative power often cited—attitudinal, utilitarian and coercive—the neofunctionalists usually stress utilitarian measures which they hope will generate a change in attitudes so that loyalties are transferred to the new decision-making center. Integration comes not from preexisting mass attitudes but from the ideological commitment of an elite which promotes utilitarian measures of integration, such as a common market, and the satisfactions which arise from these measures generate a supportive change in elite and mass attitudes for further integration. Nowhere is coercion important, either internally or externally. Indeed, coercive integration would be a negation of the neofunctionalist (and functionalist) ethic.

In the European Communities the judgement of the Court of Justice is avoided as much as possible, although the initial processes to secure a judgement may be embarked upon in order to provide a context for settlement. Problems are, however, usually resolved in other ways. Furthermore, even though there is no provision for withdrawal from the Treaty of Rome, the possibility of British withdrawal did not raise the specter of coercive measures of a serious, violent nature. Nor does integration in response to an external threat feature very strongly in the neofunctionalist literature as a motive force. In this respect it is instructive to compare Atlantic integration, which in the early years clearly owed much to a perceived threat, with the European Community process, which is much more dependent on endogenous factors. Interestingly, federalist writers, who have so much in common with the neofunctionalists, differ in this respect, for they lay great emphasis on the importance of a common perception of an external threat as a motive for integration. While for the neofunctionalist integration may arise out of the upgrading of the common interest in order to resolve a conflict or crisis within a community, such a common interest cannot rest on a coercive basis. It is a characteristic that he shares with the functionalist and one which renders many ostensibly functionalist links between the developed and developing worlds—such as the activities of some multinationals—anathema to functionalists.

• A CONCLUDING COMPARISON

While sharing this basic ethic with the functionalists, the neofunctionalists differ in that their unit of analysis is the state and not the system of transactions, and their approach is teleological—a single decisionmaking center for a newly integrated territorially-based unit. Functionalists abhor such regional integration unless it is based on coterminal systems of transactions, which in Europe and elsewhere are not the case. Thus, while the interest of both may coincide when restricted to a single functional dimension, such as the European Coal and Steel Community, they diverge radically in multi-dimensional analysis. The neofunctionalist, as we have seen, was inspired by the pluralistic model and values embedded in the federalist political thought and tradition of the United States, while the functionalist owes more to the tradition of utopian, anarchistic and progressive-radical thought, which seeks to reconcile diversity, complexity, participation, welfare and efficiency, and whose roots lie deep in the European and especially the East and Central European experience.

Although the neofunctionalists have been adventurous methodologically, and praiseworthy in their empirical rigor, the functionalists, in contrast, have not exhibited such virtues even though their approach is in part amenable to rigorous empirical examination, as the transactionalist school has demonstrated.

Having chided the functionalists for their lack of initiative in empirical research, we can return to that point which they have most in common with neofunctionalists—the learning process. It was the learning process or the functional imperative which attracted the zealots of Western European integration as a tactic for the achievement of their federalist goal "by installments." It was the functional imperative in a pluralist setting that provided the neofunctionalist academics with a framework for the analysis of such a process. For practitioner and academic alike it has been found wanting, since the neofunctionalist goal of a "regional" state has nowhere been achieved, nor is its attainment highly probable.

The traditional functionalist sees the learning process in a somewhat different light. It is not the means to a specific end, but to a diffuse working peace system the characteristics of which are only generally specified. It is a world in which legitimized relationships are expanding but one in which neither specific goals nor time limits are set. Indeed, the functionalist can give no guidance for the appropriate time span for testing functionalism. Is it a year? A decade? A century? Traditional functionalism is, in this sense, difficult to test as there is little specific to test since it is as much a set of values and a way of thinking as a definite plan of action. Its prescriptions, while clear, are general and thus difficult to pin down in quantitative empirical research. Neofunctionalism, on the other hand, has set goals and a plan of action to achieve those goals. That the goal of federalism by functional installments, the concentration on the state, integrating and regional, and its rigorous methodology differentiate it so much from traditional functionalism, despite the concern of both with a learning process based on a functional imperative, is sufficient to constitute a case of mistaken identity: neofunctionalism owes far more to its "federal" goal than it does to its "functionalist" means.

14 The Theory of Economic Integration: An Introduction

BELA BALASSA

Federalists, functionalists, and neofunctionalists in the postwar period were largely concerned with the political results of integration, even if some of them paid little attention to the political dimension of the integration process. They were, after all, chiefly interested in the peaceful resolution of international conflict. Postwar economists were also interested in the integration process in Europe, but for different reasons. They were engaged in describing the process of economic integration and its impact on welfare. As war among Western European nations became unthinkable in the years immediately following World War II, the economic gains of integration became the chief motive for continuing the process. Thus, the work of the economists took center stage.

Bela Balassa (Johns Hopkins University, Baltimore, Maryland) has been one of the most prolific students of economic integration. Drawing on the work of Jacob Viner and others, Balassa made a major contribution to our understanding of the effects of integration on trade and other economic activities in the 1960s and 1970s. In this introductory chapter to his important work The Theory of Economic Integration, *Balassa defines economic integration, identifies its stages, discusses political and ideological aspects of the integration process, and specifies what he means by "economic welfare." Finally, Balassa argues that functional integration, though perhaps politically expedient, is not as economically defensible as "the simultaneous integration of all sectors."*

• THE CONCEPT AND FORMS OF INTEGRATION

In everyday usage the word "integration" denotes the bringing together of parts into a whole. In the economic literature the term "economic integration" does not have such a clear-cut meaning. Some authors include social integration in the concept, others subsume different forms of international cooperation under this heading, and the argument has also been advanced that the mere existence of trade relations between independent national economies is a sign of integration. We propose to define economic integration as a process and as a state of affairs. Regarded as a process, it encompasses measures designed to abolish discrimination between economic units belonging to different national states; viewed as a state of affairs, it can be represented by the absence of various forms of discrimination between national economies.

In interpreting our definition, distinction should be made between integration and cooperation. The difference is qualitative as well as quantitative. Whereas cooperation includes actions aimed at lessening discrimination, the process of economic integration comprises measures that entail the suppression of some forms of discrimination. For example international agreements on trade policies belong to the area of international cooperation, while the removal of trade barriers is an act of economic integration. Distinguishing between cooperation and integration, we put the main characteristics of the latter—the abolition of discrimination within an area—into clearer focus and give the concept definite meaning without unnecessarily diluting it by the inclusion of diverse actions in the field of international cooperation.

Economic integration, as defined here, can take several forms that represent varying degrees of integration. These are a free-trade area, a customs union, a common market, an economic union, and complete economic integration. In a free-trade area, tariffs (and quantitative restrictions) between the participating countries are abolished, but each country retains its own tariffs against nonmembers. Establishing a customs union involves, besides the suppression of discrimination in the field if commodity movements within the union, the equalization of tariffs in trade with nonmember countries. A higher form of economic integration is attained in a common market, where not only trade restrictions but also restrictions on factor movements are abolished. An economic union, as distinct from a common market, combines the suppression of restrictions on commodity and factor policies, in order to remove discrimination that was due to disparities in these policies. Finally, total economic integration presupposes the unification of monetary, fiscal, social, and countercyclical policies and requires the setting-up of a supra-national authority whose decisions are binding for the member states.

Adopting the definition given above, the theory of economic integration will be concerned with the economic effects of integration in its various forms and with problems that arise from divergences in national monetary, fiscal, and other policies. The theory of economic integration can be regarded as a part of international economics, but it also enlarges the field of international trade theory by exploring the impact of a fusion of national markets on growth and examining the need for the coordination of economic policies in a union. Finally, the theory of economic integration should incorporate elements of location theory, too. The integration of adjacent countries amounts to the removal of artificial barriers that obstruct continuous economic activity through national frontiers, and the ensuing relocation of production and regional agglomerative and deglomerative tendencies cannot be adequately discussed without making use of the tools of locational analysis.

• THE RECENT INTEREST IN ECONOMIC INTEGRATION

In the twentieth century no significant customs unions were formed until the end of the Second World War, although several attempts had been made to integrate the economies of various European countries. Without going into a detailed analysis, political obstacles can be singled out as the main causes for the failure of these projects to materialize. A certain degree of integration was achieved during the Second World War via a different route, when—as part of the German *Grossraum* policy— the Hitlerites endeavored to integrate economically the satellite countries and the occupied territories with Germany. In the latter case, economic integration appeared as a form of imperialist expansion.

The post–Second World War period has seen an enormous increase in the interest in problems of economic integration. In Europe the customs union and later the economic union of the Benelux countries, the European Coal and Steel Community, the European Economic Community (Common Market), and the European Free Trade Association (the "Outer Seven") are manifestations of this movement. Plans have also been made for the establishment of a free-trade area encompassing the countries of the Common Market and the Outer Seven, but negotiations in the years 1957–60 did not meet with success. However, concessions offered in early 1961 by the United Kingdom with regard to the harmonization of tariffs on non-agricultural commodities give promise for the future enlargement of the Common Market in some modified form.

· · ·

The interwar period has witnessed a considerable degree of disintegration of the European and the world economy. On the European scene the mounting trade-and-payments restrictions since 1913 deserve attention. Ingvar Svennilson has shown that, as a result of the increase in trade impediments, the import trade of the advanced industrial countries of Europe shifted from the developed to the less developed economies of this area, which did not specialize in manufactured products. This shift implies a decline in competition between the industrial products of the more advanced economies and a decrease in specialization among these countries. But lessening of specialization was characteristic not only among the more advanced European economies but also of the European economy as a whole. This development can be demonstrated by trade and production figures for the period of 1913–38. While the volume of commodity production in Europe increased by 32 per cent during those years, intra-European trade increased by 10 per cent. The formation of a European union can be regarded, then, as a possible solution for the reintegration of European economies.

Another factor responsible for the disintegration of the European economy has been the stepping-up of state intervention in economic affairs in order to counteract cyclical fluctuations, sustain full employment, correct income distribution, and influence growth. Plans for economic integration are designed partly to counteract the element of discrimination inherent in the increased scope of state intervention.

A related argument regards the establishment of customs unions as desirable for mitigating cyclical fluctuations transmitted through foreign-trade relations. The foreign-trade dependence of the European Common Market countries decreases, for example, by about 35 per cent if trade among the six countries is regarded as internal trade. The memory of the depression in the 1930s gives added weight to this argument. Note, however, that for this proposition to be valid, there is need for some degree of coordination in counter-cyclical policies among the participating countries.

Last but not least, it is expected that integration will foster the growth of the European economies. This outcome is assumed to be the result of various dynamic factors, such as large-scale economies on a wider market, lessening of uncertainty in intra-area trade, and a faster rate of technological change. In this regard, the increased interest in economic growth has further contributed to the attention given to possibilities of economic integration.

. . .

To summarize, economic integration in Europe serves to avoid discrimination caused by trade-and-payments restrictions and increased state intervention, and it is designed to mitigate cyclical fluctuations and to increase the growth of national income.

. . .

• INTEGRATION AND POLITICS

In examining the recent interest in economic integration, we have yet to comment on the role of political factors. There is no doubt that—especially in the case of Europe—political objectives are of great consequence. The avoidance of future wars between France and Germany, the creation of a third force in world politics, and the re-establishment of Western Europe as a world power are frequently mentioned as political goals that would be served by economic integration. Many regard these as primary objectives and relegate economic considerations to second place. No attempt will be made here to evaluate the relative importance of political economic considerations. This position is taken, partly because this relationship is not quantifiable, partly because a considerable degree of interdependence exists between these factors. Political motives may prompt the first step in economic integration, but economic integration also reacts on the political sphere; similarly, if the initial motives are economic, the need for political unity can arise at a later stage.

From the economic point of view, the basic question is not whether economic or political considerations gave the first impetus to the integration movement, but what the economic effects of integration are likely to be. In some political circles the economic aspects are deliberately minimized and the plan for economic integration is regarded merely as a pawn in the play of political forces. Such a view unduly neglects the economic expediency of the proposal. Even if political motives did have primary importance, this would not mean that the economist could not examine the relevant economic problems without investigating elusive political issues. By way of comparison, although the formation of the United States was primarily the result of political considerations, nobody would deny the economic importance of its establishment.

We shall not disregard the political factors, however. Political *ends* will not be considered, but at certain points of the argument we shall examine various economic problems the solution of which is connected with political *means* and political processes. We shall explore, for example, how the objective of exploiting the potential benefits of economic integration affects the decision-making process. Changes in the decision-making process, on the other hand, become a political problem. Nevertheless, we shall go no further than to state the need for coordinated action in certain fields and will leave it for the political scientist to determine the political implications of such developments.

- ## THE "LIBERALIST" AND THE "DIRIGIST" IDEAL OF ECONOMIC INTEGRATION

The recent interest in economic integration has prompted various proposals concerning the means and objectives of integration. Two extreme views—an all-out liberalist and a dirigist solution—will be contrasted here. The champions of economic liberalism regard regional integration as a return to the free-trade ideals of the pre–First World War period within the area in question and anticipate the relegation of national economic policy to its pre-1914 dimensions. If this approach is followed, integration simply means the abolition of impediments to commodity movements. At the other extreme, integration could also be achieved through state trading and through the coordination of national economic plans without the lifting of trade barriers. This alternative discards the use of market methods and relies solely on administrative, nonmarket means. It can be found in the integration projects of Soviet-type economies; the operation of the Council of Mutual Economic Assistance, comprising the Soviet Union and her European satellites, is based on the coordination of long-range plans and bilateral trade agreements. A similar method, but one which put more reliance on market means, was used by Germany during the last war. In this study we shall examine problems of economic integration in market economies and shall not deal with Nazi Germany and Soviet-type economies. Nevertheless, we shall see that dirigistic tendencies appear in the writings of some Western authors, too.

Among the proponents of the liberalist solution, Allais, Röpke, and Heilperin may be cited. They regard economic integration as identical with trade (and payments) liberalization. Allais asserts that "practically, the only mutually acceptable rule for close economic cooperation between democratic societies is the rule of the free market." Röpke is of the opinion that European economic integration is nothing else than an attempt to remedy the disintegration of the post-1914 period that destroyed the previous integration of national economies. A less extreme position is taken by Heilperin, who rejects the consideration of regional development plans and subsidies to industries for reconversion purposes but accepts state responsibility for investment decisions in certain areas. To the majority of observers, however, the liberalist ideal of integration is a relic from the past, and its application to present-day economic life appears rather anachronistic. As Jean Weiller put it, "It would be a great error to believe that the decision to create a regional union would re-establish the conditions of an economic liberalism, extirpating with one stroke all so-called dirigistic policies."

It can rightly be said that considerations such as the avoidance of depressions, the maintenance of full employment, the problems of regional development, the regulation of cartels and monopolies, and so forth, require state intervention in economic life, and any attempts to integrate national economies would necessarily lead to harmonization in various policy areas. This idea is not new. The need for the coordination of fiscal, monetary, social, and countercyclical policies was stressed in the League of Nations study on customs unions published immediately after the end of the Second World War. In fact, the question is not whether government intervention is needed or not in an integrated area, but whether economic integration results in a more intensive participation of the state in economic affairs or in a more intensive reliance on market methods.

Some authors advocate an intensification of state intervention in economic affairs. The need for economic planning in a union is emphasized, for example, by André Philip and by other French Socialists. In Philip's opinion, "there is no alternative to a directed economy," since "the market can be extended not by liberalizing but by organizing." Although not an advocate of centralized planning, the stepping-up of state intervention is also recommended by Maurice Bye, who contrasts his "integration theory" with Heilperin's "market theory." Considering the pronouncements of French economists and industrialists, it can be said that, by and large, the French view of economic integration contains more dirigistic elements than, for example, that of most German economists and entrepreneurs.

The defenders of dirigistic tendencies fail to consider, however, the lessening of planning and government intervention—and the beneficial effects thereof—in Europe since the end of the Second World War. Although this change does not indicate a return to the pre-1914 situation, it brought about an increased use of the market mechanism and contributed to the spectacular growth of the European economy during the 1950's. It appears, then, that a reintroduction of dirigistic methods would slow down, rather than accelerate, future growth. State intervention may be stepped up in some areas, such as regional development planning, and will also be required to deal with transitional problems, but it is expected that an enlargement of the economic area will intensify competition and lead to less interference with productive activities at the firm level. Therefore, those who regard the European Common Market as a *marché institué* err in the opposite direction from the holders of old-fashioned liberalist views.

· · ·

• ECONOMIC INTEGRATION AND WELFARE

It can be said that the ultimate objective of economic activity is an increase in welfare. Thus, in order to assess the desirability of integration, its contribution to welfare needs to be considered. But the concept of welfare is fraught with much obscurity. First, the noneconomic aspects present some ambiguity; second, even restricting the meaning of the concept to "economic welfare" in the Pigovian tradition, we are confronted with the well-known difficulties of interpersonal comparisons if we try to say anything over and above the Pareto condition: an increase in one man's welfare leads to an increase in social welfare only if there is no reduction in the welfare of any other members of the group. In the case of integration, economic welfare will be affected by (a) a change in the quantity of commodities produced, (b) a change in the degree of discrimination between domestic and foreign goods, (c) a redistribution of income between the nationals of different countries, and (d) income redistribution within individual countries. Accordingly, distinction is made between a real-income component and a distributional component of economic welfare. The former denotes a change in potential welfare (efficiency); the latter refers to the welfare effects of income redistribution (equity).

With regard to potential welfare, separate treatment is allotted to changes in the quantity of goods produced and changes in their distribution. First, there is an increase (decrease) in potential welfare if— owing to the reallocation of resources consequent upon integration— the quantity of goods and services produced with given inputs increases (decreases) or, alternatively, if the production of the same quantity of goods and services requires a smaller (larger) quantity of inputs. If we regard inputs as negative outputs, we may say that a rise in net output leads to an increase in potential welfare. A higher net output entails an increase in potential welfare in the sense that a larger quantity of goods and services can now be distributed among individuals so as to make some people better off without making others worse off. Second, potential welfare is also affected through the impact of economic integration on consumer's choice. Restrictions on commodity movements imply discrimination between domestic and foreign commodities; a tariff causes consumers to buy more of lower-valued domestic and less of higher-valued foreign goods. The removal of intra-union tariffs will do away with discrimination between the commodities of the member countries but will discriminate against foreign goods in favor of the commodities of partner countries. In short, economic efficiency means efficiency in production and efficiency in exchange, and an improvement in one or both constitutes an increase in potential welfare.

Given a change in potential welfare (the real-income component), we also have to consider the distributional component in order to determine changes in economic welfare. It can easily be seen that an evaluation of changes in income distribution would require interpersonal comparisons of welfare. The new welfare economics, however, does not admit the possibility of making interpersonal comparisons. As a possible solution, it has then been suggested that changes in welfare could be determined in terms of potential welfare; that is, the *possibility* of making everybody better off (or, at least, no one worse off) would be taken as equivalent to an increase in economic welfare. This proposition can be criticized primarily on the grounds that the hypothetical situation *after* compensation is irrelevant if compensation actually does not take place. Nevertheless, changes in the real-income component give a good approximation of changes in welfare *within a country,* since compensation is politically feasible, and in case of integration this would actually be carried out to some degree in the form of assistance to relocating workers or reconverting firms. In addition, a nation can be regarded as an entity, where a redistribution of income accompanying an increase in real income can be accepted—provided that the redistribution does not run counter to generally accepted ideals of equity.

The distribution component cannot be neglected if economic integration redistributes income between countries, especially between the member states of a union, on the one hand, and the non-participating economies, on the other. It is not possible to claim an increase in world welfare in every case when the increase in real income in the participating countries will be greater than the loss to third countries. This proposition would hold true only if international comparisons of welfare could be made or if we disregarded differences in the marginal utility of income between countries. The first possibility was ruled out above, and the equality of the marginal utility of income is no less implausible. According to some, the marginal utility of income in an underdeveloped economy might be two or three times as high as in the rest of the world. If such a view were accepted, a union of developed economies which would register gains in the real-income component might still reduce world welfare by redistributing income from "poor" to "rich" countries.

In the preceding discussion we have followed the customary exposition of welfare economics in using the concept of potential welfare in a static sense. Thus an increase in potential welfare was taken as equivalent to an improvement in the allocation of resources at a point of time. Static efficiency, however, is only one of the possible success criteria that can be used to appraise the effects of economic integration. Instead of limiting our investigation to a discussion of efficiency in resource allocation under static assumptions, greater attention should be paid to the impact of integration on dynamic efficiency. I have elsewhere defined dynamic efficiency as the hypothetical growth rate of national income achievable with given resource use and saving ratio. In technical terms, whereas static efficiency would require that the economy operate on its production-possibility frontier, dynamic efficiency can be represented by the movement of this frontier in the northeast direction. The concept of dynamic efficiency can be used in intercountry comparisons to indicate which economy is capable of faster growth under identical conditions with regard to resources and saving, or, alternatively, it can be applied for comparing the growth potentialities of an economy at different points of time. In the present context, we wish to compare the hypothetical growth rate attainable *before* and *after* integration, under the assumption of given initial resources and saving ratio.

Given the static efficiency of an economy, the main factors affecting its dynamic efficiency are technological progress, the allocation of investment, dynamic interindustry relationships in production and investment, and uncertainty and inconsistency in economic decisions. In addition to these factors, the actual growth of national income would also be affected by an increase in the proportion of national income saved and/or by interference with the individual's choice between work and leisure. Changes in the latter variables will be disregarded here, partly because we assume that they are but rarely affected by economic integration, partly because their effects cannot be evaluated in welfare terms, given the disutility of increased saving and/or work. Under these assumptions an increase in the rate of growth can be considered as equivalent to an improvement in dynamic efficiency and represents a rise in potential welfare.

In evaluating the effects of economic integration, we shall use dynamic efficiency as the primary success indicator, taking into account both changes in the efficiency of resource allocation in the static sense and the dynamic effects of integration. In addition, attention will be paid to the impact of integration on income distribution, on the regional pattern of production and income, and on the stability of the participating economies.

. . .

- **THE SECTORAL APPROACH TO INTEGRATION**

In this chapter, distinction has been made between various forms of economic integration. All these forms require concerted action in the entire field of economic activity, be it the abolition of customs barriers or the coordination of fiscal policies. Another approach to economic integration would be to move from sector to sector, integrating various industries successively. The application of this method had already been commended in the interwar period, and it found many champions in the period following the Second World War. Proposals were made to integrate various sectors such as the iron and steel industry, transportation, and agriculture. The Stikker Plan advocated the integration of national economies by removing barriers, industry by industry. Supporters of this view contended that national governments were more inclined to make limited commitments with reasonably clear implications than to integrate all sectors at the same time. The flexibility of this method was also extolled, and it was hoped that integration in one sector would encourage integration on a larger scale.

From the theoretical point of view, various objections can be raised against the sectoral approach. Whereas the simultaneous integration of all sectors allows for compensating changes, integration in one sector will lead to readjustment in this sector alone, the reallocation of resources in other sectors being impeded by the continued existence of tariffs and other trade barriers—hence the losses suffered by countries whose productive activity in the newly integrated sector contracts will not be compensated for until the next phase. More generally, under the sectoral approach every step in integration results in a new and temporary equilibrium of prices, costs, and resource allocation, and this "equilibrium" is disturbed at every further step. Production decisions will then be made on the basis of prices that are relevant only in a certain phase of integration, and shifts in resource allocation will take place which may later prove to be inappropriate. On the other hand, the adjustment of relative prices and the reallocation of resources proceed more smoothly if all sectors are integrated at the same time, since some industries are expanding, others contracting, and unnecessary resource shifts do not take place.

Integration sector by sector puts an additional burden on the external balance also. At various steps, pressures will be imposed on the balance of payments of countries where the newly integrated sector is a high-cost producer. In the absence of exchange-rate flexibility, this process unnecessarily burdens exchange reserves in some, and inflates reserves in other, participating countries. If, on the other hand, exchange rates are left to fluctuate freely, temporary variations in rates of exchange will bring about transitional and unnecessary changes in the international division of labor.

In addition, lack of coordination in monetary, fiscal, and other policies is likely to cause difficulties under the sectoral approach, since differences in economic policies can lead to perverse movements of commodities and factors. For example, if inflationary policies are followed in one country while deflationary policies are pursued in another, an overadjustment will take place in the integrated sector (or sectors), while trade barriers restrict adjustments in other industries. Finally, any joint decisions made with respect to the integrated sector will affect all other branches of the participating economies.

A noneconomic objection of considerable importance should also be mentioned here. The sectoral approach is bound to bring about a conflict between producer and user interests in individual countries. In countries with relatively high production costs, for example, users will welcome integration because of its price-reducing effect; high-cost producers, however, will object to it. Experience suggests that producer interests have greater influence on governmental decisionmaking; hence these pressures are likely to have a restrictive effect on integration if the sectoral approach is followed. The interests of exporting and importing countries being opposed, there can be no "give and take"—the necessary pre-condition for intercountry agreements in most practical instances.

These theoretical objections suggest the inadvisability of integration sector by sector. This conclusion does not mean, however, that integration in one sector may not be beneficial if political obstacles hinder integration in all areas. The European Coal and Steel Community is a case in point. At the time of its inception, the realization of a European Common Market was not yet possible, but the governments of the participating countries were prepared to accept a limited measure of integration. The establishment of the Coal and Steel Community has been conducive to the expansion of production and trade in the partaking industries, and the Community demonstrated the possibility of integration in Europe, thereby contributing to the establishment of the Common Market.

It has also been argued that the difficulties of adjustment in production and trade in the Coal and Steel Community have been less than expected because the considerable increase in the national incomes of every participating country has made adjustment easier. This does not, however, rule out the possibility of maladjustments in other industries which will not be corrected until trade barriers are removed in all sectors. In addition, the Coal and Steel Community has encountered serious difficulties with respect to transportation policies, fiscal and social problems, etc., which have been due—to a great degree—to the fact that integration extends over only one sector.

PART 3

Theory Emerging from Practice

15 Domestic Politics and European Community Policy Making

SIMON BULMER

The apparent stagnation of the European Community in the 1970s and early 1980s and the consequent abandonment of neofunctionalism after 1975 had a chilling effect on integration theory. Most scholars (at least in the United States) migrated to other areas; those who remained interested in the EC (primarily Europeans) focused on how the Community actually worked, steering far clear of grand theory. Studies of EC decisionmaking proliferated as scholars tried to understand how the Community functioned in practice. These studies often relied on the theoretical concepts developed during the halcyon days of neofunctionalism and quietly laid the groundwork for later theoretical advances.

During the stagnant years of the 1970s and early 1980s, students of the EC emphasized the intergovernmental nature of the organization. Member governments, pursuing their own national interests, were the "central actors" in the EC policymaking process. Simon Bulmer (University of Manchester, England), therefore argued in 1983 that a "domestic politics" approach to Community decisionmaking would yield the best explanations of EC policies, and even the process of integration itself. If you want to explain what happens at the Community level, he contends, you must look first to the domestic political processes in each member state. This bottom-up approach directly confronts the neofunctionalist emphasis on supranational integrative processes that bypasses the national governments.

Reprinted with permission from *Journal of Common Market Studies*, 21(4)(1983):349–363. Copyright 1983 by Blackwell Publishers. Notes omitted.

As the pace of European integration slowed during the 1970s and the early 1980s, so the production and development of integration theories also slackened. Attention has been diverted to examining Community policymaking, particularly through case study analyses. Two influential studies of EC policymaking reflected this shift in attention and came to similar conclusions, namely that policy-making patterns differ according to the policy area concerned. The study edited by Wallace, Wallace and Webb identified in particular the importance of national governments in European Community (EC) policymaking. Yet, because of the concentration on the Community level, the linkages between the domestic and EC tiers were not fully explored. Indeed, the supranationalism-versus-intergovernmentalism debate overshadowed some of the equally important findings concerning policymaking in the member states.

Many writers take the view that EC policymaking is characterized by intergovernmentalism. This view perceives national governments as the central actors in EC policymaking in a confederalist phase of integration. The governments' importance is institutionalized in the Council of Ministers, the European Council and the explicitly intergovernmental machinery of political cooperation. However, there is another dimension to the centrality of national governments, as William Wallace has noted.

> National governments have been relatively successful at retaining control of the processes of Community policymaking, in most areas, and at maintaining their position therefore as the most important intermediaries, the continuing focus for national lobbying and national debate in Community issues.

This article examines the links between domestic politics and the European Community and seeks to explain how the former may have a vital impact on the policy-making output of the EC. There are two dimensions to these links; one concerns the domestic policy-making *structures* which are involved; the other concerns the *attitudes* held within the member states regarding the EC. The objectives of examining the relationships between domestic politics and EC policymaking is to synthesize these two dimensions with a view to illuminating the behavior of individual member states in the Community.

Helen Wallace has argued that studies of member states' interrelationships with the EC are inadequate and that, "there is no accepted framework for evaluating these findings." This is a particularly surprising state of affairs in view of the widely-shared view that the EC is characterized by intergovernmentalism. A framework for analyzing the behavior of member states is thus required.

Such a framework could make several important contributions to the study of the European Community. Firstly, at a specific, case-study level, it should be able to explain why national governments adopt particular policy positions in the Council of Ministers. Beyond its use for examining specific case studies, there is a broader, second contribution which the study of the domestic politics–EC politics linkage could make. This relates to putting together a composite picture of a member state's behavior in the EC, to examining the continuing sensitivities of individual member states towards Community activity.

. . .

Existing policy-making theories, especially supranationalism (or the "Community method") and intergovernmentalism, are focused on the characteristics of the EC as an international organization. Examining domestic European policymaking does precisely the opposite because it recognizes that the same political organizations—political parties, interest groups, parliaments—are involved as in national politics. The methodological implication of this is that EC policymaking should be examined in the same way as domestic politics. Thus electioneering may play an important part in a member state's behavior in the EC, as was seen during the British government's renegotiation of the terms of entry during 1974–5. Alternatively interest groups may be able to "capture" a national ministry with resultant impact on European policy. This is arguably the case in the client relationships which exist between several farmers' organizations and their national agriculture ministry. Equally, parliament may have a key role in EC policymaking, as the evidence indicates for the Danish *Folketing*.

• NATIONAL POLICY STYLES IN THE EUROPEAN COMMUNITY

An important ingredient of the national negotiating positions adopted and presented in the intergovernmental institutions of the EC (the Committee of Permanent Representatives—COREPER, the Council of Ministers and the European Council) is the manner in which the positions are formulated. To examine the national policy-making process we may adopt the term "policy style," a concept which has recently been employed in a comparative analysis of national politics in Western Europe. Policy style has been defined as, "the interaction between (a) the government's approach to policymaking and (b) the relationship between government and other actors in the policy process." In this case the "other actors" are those in the domestic political system.

The exact features of the policy style concept for the purpose of examining European policy in the member states will be outlined below. However, at a crude level, it is possible to identify whether a member state has a coherent single policy style in connection with the disparate areas of EC activity.

. . .

• WHY DOMESTIC POLITICS?

Before making any further empirical references in connection with the concept of policy style or with illustrating the importance of domestic politics, the analytical framework and its objectives must be set out. Firstly, the term *domestic politics* is used to explain how EC policymaking is affected by behavior within the nation state. Clearly, the very term "domestic politics" emphasizes the lower of the two tiers involved in EC policymaking. Too much literature has concentrated on the upper tier— the formal institutional framework of the Communities—without examining the domestic sources of national negotiating positions. We may think of the European Community in the manner adopted by Stanley Hoffmann for defining the term "international system."

> An international system is a pattern of relations between the basic units of world politics. . . . This pattern is largely determined by the structure of the world, the nature of the forces which operate across or within the major units, and the capabilities, pattern of power, and political culture of those units.

These basic units are the nation states.

The term "domestic politics" also underlies the fact that the lower decisional tier of the EC is rooted in policy environments which differ between member states and within them, according to the policy area concerned. For the purpose of illustrating the different environments, the concept of "policy style" is utilized as an analytical framework. Apart from its value in examining national policymaking, it remains neutral as regards integration theories. Supranationalism and the "Community method" are inextricably linked with a neofunctionalist view of integration. However, it should be clear—without resorting to concepts such as "spillback"—that the policy-making process does not follow the logic of integration but rather that integration follows the logic of decision-making processes. These processes have their roots in the power structures of the nation states.

A third dimension to the domestic politics approach concerns the nation state's position in the interdependent world of today. International monetary instability, oil supply and pricing matters are, as the transnationalist school of thought indicates, phenomena which are outside the control of individual EC member states or interests. These states do, however, have the ability to decide at which level to defend their interests: at the national level, the EC level or in other international regimes. The domestic political tier thus has an important function in determining whether the EC is an appropriate forum for responding to international economic uncertainty.

• ASSUMPTIONS OF THE DOMESTIC POLITICS APPROACH

These are five assumptions in the domestic politics approach.

1. The national polity is the basic unit in the European Community. It is the level at which governments, interest groups, parliamentary bodies and political parties derive their legitimacy, their power and at which they may be called to account.

2. Each national polity has a different set of social and economic conditions that shapes its national interests and policy content. Each state has different ideological cleavages which determine the extent of consensus. In more structural terms, policy instruments differ as does the extent of centralization in the state. Finally, each state's relationship to the outside world differs (reflecting Haas' idea of "differential enmeshment of the member states in the world economy").

3. European policy only represents one facet of a national polity's activity. It is somewhat artificial to separate a member state's European policy from its other domestic behavior. Not only are national EC policy-making environments similar to those obtaining for domestic policy decisions but the subject matter is overwhelmingly similar, too. Thus the EC's concern with regional, agricultural and monetary affairs is in tandem with the nation states' domestic policies. Katzenstein and others have explored the relationships between domestic economic and political structures, on the one hand, and foreign economic policy strategies, on the other. Thus an adaptation of this approach to European policy should be possible.

4. In formal terms the national governments hold a key position at the junction of national politics and Community politics. Whether the governments are really as powerful as the intergovernmentalists would have us believe must depend on specific examination. Governments may be "captured" by domestic interests and by the transnational forces inherent in an interdependent world. This would restrict their maneuverability greatly. On the other hand, national governments may have

considerable powers to impose a policy on affected domestic interests so that they can derive power both from their formally authoritative position in domestic politics and from their important position in the Council of Ministers.

5. The concept of policy style is employed to analyze the relationships between government and other domestic political forces vis-à-vis European policy.

These assumptions can now be examined in more detail, in particular to highlight the distinctions from the more familiar EC policymaking models of supranationalism and intergovernmentalism.

• NATIONAL POLITIES AS THE BASIC UNITS OF THE EC

Protagonists of the intergovernmental interpretation of EC policymaking may wonder what is new about the assertion that the nation states are central to the EC. Before discussing that point, however, it is worth pointing out how the failings of neofunctionalism relate to this assertion. Firstly, neofunctionalism placed too much emphasis on the role of interest groups and other elites in maintaining the momentum of integration. Harrison refers to the failing of the neofunctionalist momentum as being the product of "the mesmeric effect of behavioralism taken to the point of neglect of the authoritative element in decisionmaking." Apart from the failure of spillover, the neofunctionalist approach has also suffered from its "regional" assumptions.

The states of Western Europe belong to numerous international bodies, such as NATO, the United Nations and OECD[Organization for Economic Cooperation and Development]. During the 1970s there was a further proliferation of international regimes or conferences of varying degrees of permanency. The International Energy Agency, the Conference on Security and Cooperation in Europe, the Western economic summits, various commodity and "managed trade" agreements were amongst the developments which, in many cases, were at the expense of the European Community's status. As Hagger has noted, "other international institutions may serve Europeans as well or better than Brussels as a means of solving their interdependence problems." These developments have called into question the credentials of theories which concentrate upon regional integration. In the face of international economic and political uncertainty it is at the national level where the decisions are taken as to which forum is the most appropriate for the state's interests. Thus the policy-making model of supranationalism (or the "Community method") is undermined through being derived from a theory whose assumptions have not stood up to developments in the real world.

This is not the case with the intergovernmental approach to EC policymaking which is a much looser model. On the face of it, it ought to offer a framework for examining member states' behavior in the Community, especially since it is based much more on actual developments than on theoretical predictions. Its main postulate is that national governments have successfully retained power despite neofunctionalists' assumptions. On the one hand, intergovernmentalism is presented as showing that the European Community is not distinctive as compared to other international organizations. On the other hand, there is the picture of "governments holding the gates between the Commission and their domestic politics." Thus intergovernmentalism brings together arguments from international relations and national politics into an assertion of the resilience of national governments. Nonetheless, little seems to be offered for the purposes of analyzing member states' attitudes towards the EC, although their centrality is recognized. A particular problem of intergovernmentalism is the tendency to view national governments as omnipotent, monolithic structures when no evidence is presented to support this assumption.

. . .

One of the objectives of the domestic politics approach is to establish why a member state sees the EC as the most appropriate level of action on some issues, whilst, on other issues, the nation state or other international organizations are seen as most appropriate. Why, for example, did Helmut Schmidt come to the conclusion that a European framework was most appropriate for international monetary and, thus, trading stability? Ludlow offers the following solution:

> . . . Mr. Schmidt turned to the European Community as a framework of action because of the disorders that had emerged in the Atlantic Community and the threat that these disorders represented to his own country. It was his preoccupation with the dollar crisis, his resentment and anxiety about the growing pressure on the Federal Republic to reflate and, more generally, his unease about what seemed to him to be the fallibility of the new Carter administration in Washington that served as the principal motors of his monetary initiative.

Ludlow also notes that Schmidt's domestic political fortunes had enhanced his freedom of manoeuvre in launching EMS [European Monetary System] with the French President, Giscard d'Estaing.

Overall, therefore, a European initiative was born of international economic instability. West Germany's domestic economic and political structure represented an important agent in the EMS initiative. The West German economy's "open" nature—i.e., its dependence on stable trading relations—meant that some response to the uncertainties in the international monetary system was necessary. The EC, as an organization containing Germany's closest trading partners, represented an appropriate framework for such a response. Schmidt's activities on the European stage thus derived from his domestic context.

Indepth analysis along these lines offers considerable insight into the nature of EC policymaking in the European institutions, for example, to establish whether and why a member state vetoes Commission proposals. Such an approach may also be used to examine the behavior of national interest groups at the European level.

• DIFFERING NATIONAL POLICY ENVIRONMENTS

The second and third assumptions of a domestic politics approach together state the fairly obvious point that economic and social structures differ between EC member states. This is reflected in their varying relationships with the international economy. The national political instruments for deciding upon EC policy also differ. Indeed, these differences are increased by virtue of the economic and social issues which the EC tackles. Thus EC policy is formulated differently within member states, depending on the subject area involved. This type of differentiation is frequently overlooked in analyses of EC policymaking that focus on the specifically "European" institutions. In doing this, the national policy-making substructures are omitted, which creates the danger of superficiality.

The domestic politics approach postulates that the pattern of negotiations in each national policy substructure sets the key in which the relevant national minister (and interest groups) will behave in the upper decisional tier. Thus, using the upper tier as a medium, the pattern of negotiations on EC issues at the domestic level of the member states determines the progress on individual policy issues and on integration in general. Negotiations at the Community level are between ten *dependent* variables and not between independent ones: the European Communities do not have "an autonomous political system." Clearly, the role of national governments, as the central links between the two policy-making tiers, must now be examined.

• THE ROLE OF NATIONAL GOVERNMENTS

For those commentators who adopt an intergovernmental interpretation of policymaking it is scarcely necessary to present a case arguing that national governments are important. For them it is the orthodoxy to identify the Council of Ministers and, more recently, the European Council as intergovernmental agencies *par excellence*.

The important distinction between formal institutional structures and actual patterns of behavior is very pronounced in connection with the role of national governments in EC decisionmaking. Thus, according to the Treaty of Rome, the Council of Ministers should take its decisions by majority vote, but the 1966 Luxembourg compromise, a gentleman's agreement with no constitutional validity, has ensured that all important decisions are taken by unanimity. However, even this unwritten law was temporarily challenged by the May 1982 decision of the Council of Agriculture Ministers to vote through agricultural price rises, while ignoring the opposition—for different domestic political reasons—of Britain, Denmark and Greece. With one significant exception, namely decisions over the EC's annual budget, the practice of unanimous voting is widespread. Why is this the case?

The most important development was de Gaulle's boycott of the community in 1965. The French insistence on being able to invoke a veto in matters affecting vital national interests signalled an escape clause for national governments finding it difficult to accept a particular EC proposal. From a Community-level perspective this was seen all too clearly as undermining the distinctive nature of the EC's structures. From a domestic politics perspective the introduction of the loose, undefined concept of "vital national interests" served notice on all sectional interests that they could aspire to being vital. Thus if European integration should threaten a particular socioeconomic group, the relevant groups would respond by putting pressure on the national government through the methods available in the respective domestic policy community. In other words, such pressure as is applied to encourage the government to employ its veto, is employed in a similar manner, and using similar instruments, as in respect of contentious proposals for national legislation.

The emergence of summitry, later formalized in the European Council, represents a further chapter in the increasing share of national governments in Community decisions. Whilst the Five initially regarded France's insistence on unanimous voting as a temporary setback, the establishment of an explicitly intergovernmental body, the European Council, reflected the rather different, and still changing, environment of the 1970s. The decision in 1974 to establish the European Council recognized the structural-functional deficiencies of the existing Community system, structural changes in the international system, the greater involvement of government heads in EC affairs along with the experience gained from earlier *ad hoc* summits. An attempt to resist extra-community forces and to assert national governments' political will in the domestic context represent aspects of the European Council that intergovernmentalism frequently obscures, however.

A third development—not exclusive to the countries of the Community—enhanced the role of national governments. The economic recession resulted in member states having fewer assets to invest in the process of European integration. National governments consequently became more conscious of "ensuring that (the) national balance sheet contains more credit than debit." European-mindedness could be sacrificed, or restricted to rhetoric, and the appropriate tier of action—the nation state, the EC or other international agencies—could be sought on a more materialist basis.

This situation is closely related to other factors which necessitated greater involvement on the part of national governments. On the one hand, progress from negative to positive *economic* integration requires an explicit *political* commitment. On the other hand, this political commitment is less likely under a unanimous voting system in which member states are able to use a national veto. Implementing new policies, such as the European Regional Development Fund or the Common Fisheries Policy, was rendered more difficult, especially for national governments whose domestic political strength was weak. The Danish case in connection with fisheries is pertinent here. Even where positive integration was achieved, in the CAP [Common Agricultural Policy] for example, domestic political considerations may be pandered to at the cost of an integrated policy: witness the tactical use of realigning green currency rates.

Economic divergence is a further symptom of national governments' close control over their individual economic destinies. As "fair-weather conditions" broke down, the different national economic and political environments (identified in the previous section) became more manifest. French President Mitterrand's emphasis until June 1982 on reducing unemployment, despite the impact of increased public spending on the inflation rate, was diametrically opposed to the (historically based) anti-inflationary policies of the German government and Federal Bank along with the (more ideological) policies of the British Thatcher government. The Thatcher and Mitterrand governments' economic policies were rather different from their predecessors', Callaghan and Giscard d'Estaing respectively. Both have had a major impact on the EC:

in the case of Mitterrand, through the impact of his policies on the French exchange rate (EMS realignments); in the case of Thatcher, by reinforcing her desire to reduce British contributions to the EC Budget for domestic budgeting reasons. This shows that government changes can provide a dynamic nature to national European policies, although the change of coalition in Germany has had less impact. Economic divergence is thus a product of differing national economic structures. The lack of integration is a product of the different political standpoints that have resulted.

All the factors outlined here suggest that national governments are strong veto groups in EC policymaking. However, an investigation below the surface suggests that national governments are in many cases prisoners of domestic and international circumstances. Indeed, one only has to consider the British Labour Party's desire to leave the EC for evidence that the problem is perceived in those terms. National governments have sought to retain their formal powers through unanimous voting and the European Council. As "bankers" of economic and social peace in their country, member governments have sought to further tighten their control of European policy during the recession.

- **"POLICY STYLES" AND DOMESTIC POLITICS**

The final element of a domestic politics approach concerns providing an analytical framework. The purpose of using the concept of policy style is to provide a means for structuring the examination of a member state's behavior in the EC.

Helen Wallace has set out a grid which disaggregates the political, administrative and economic attributes of an EC member state. These three are then broken down further into the member state's "capacity and resources," its "domestic constraints," its "extra-national constraints" and its "goals and strategies" in each of the three strands. The useful table which emerges reveals the complex factors which may be at work in a member state's European policy. Using the policy style framework, these numerous factors can be orientated towards the formulation of national European policy.

Firstly, we may ask whether a national government develops policy through consensus building or through imposition. The answer to this depends on the national political culture, the government's strength and effectiveness (which varies with the technical policy area concerned) along with the strength of interest groups, parliamentary bodies, political parties and subnational government. Secondly, we may ask whether policy is pursued in an active or a reactive manner. Active policymaking requires political will, good policy coordination and a rational approach. Reactive policymaking tends to witness issues being processed through "standard operating procedures" in the government bureaucracy and, in the case of European policy, is associated with the framing of responses to Commission initiatives. The predominance of such administrative procedures tends to encourage sectorized policy.

                                    .   .   .

• CONCLUSION

The above examination of the domestic politics approach suggests an approach for examining member states' attitudes and interests in the EC. It is not bound up with integration theory which makes it more neutral, although less dynamic. Its complexity, however, makes it somewhat unwieldy for applications to policymaking from an overall EC perspective.

It corresponds most closely to the transnationalist approach of international relations theories. It looks at the power structures within member states in a general manner similar to the transnationalist study of the international political economy. There is thus a certain congruence between the two approaches that perhaps deserves further investigation than is possible here.

The domestic politics approach might be accused of having somewhat mixed intellectual parentage but is arguably more embracing and/or more realistic as a device explaining Community negotiations than the alternatives on offer. There is scope for further elaboration, too. The welfare economist may be able to append a public choice model on to the assumptions made. However, whether the language of economics can best express a political process is only answerable on the basis of evidence. In whatever way the domestic politics approach is developed or applied, it surely indicates that the study of EC policymaking— perhaps unlike that of integration theory—is not obsolescent until the Community itself is.

16 Political Elites, Popular Indifference and Community Building

MARTIN SLATER

Early integration theorists viewed the mass public as a useful tool of integration. Federalists, functionalists, and neofunctionalists, in different ways, believed the people would back European integration, exert strong pressure on recalcitrant governments, and legitimate supranational institutions through their support. In the 1970s, a few scholars began to examine the attitudes of the European mass public toward integration. They found evidence of general support but little indication that the public was willing to play a major role in pushing the integration process forward.

Martin Slater, in this 1982 article, examines the role of elites and the mass public on the building of the European Community. Looking back to the early days of European integration, Slater finds a positive attitude toward European unity within the mass public, but little knowledge of, or interest in, the EC. In the absence of strong involvement by the mass public, elites had free reign to build a new Europe. National political interests, however, divided European elites, who fought their battles without regard for popular opinion. "Real public involvement" in the EC issue developed only in new member states where an opposition elite emerged to challenge EC membership. In places where genuine debate occurred, the public displayed much less enthusiasm for further integration. Thus, Slater's findings, which describe the Community before the Single European Act, may help explain the increased negative attitudes of the public in several member countries toward the post-Maastricht European Union.

Reprinted with permission from *Journal of Common Market Studies*, 21(1,2)(1982): 69–87. Copyright 1982 by Blackwell Publishers. Notes omitted.

• INTRODUCTION

What influence have elites and mass public had in the building of the European Community? Is the Community, as many observers would argue, a construct only of political elites? Has the mass public remained largely indifferent to the various institutional arrangements, playing a negligible role in the development of the Community? Or has the reverse been the case, with political elites being pushed reluctantly towards European unification by an eager public? Certainly, this latter view has also received widespread currency, particularly in the earlier years of the Community's development. Walter Hallstein, for example, the first President of the Commission, argued strongly in the 1960s that political elites had held back further European integration. He claimed that "the decisions that have been taken lag far behind public opinion in Europe."

While this latter view had not been so popular in recent years, there still are, as we can see, alternative and conflicting interpretations of the roles played by political elites and the mass public. At this point, one might well question whether it matters which view, if any, is correct. Why, in fact, should anyone bother to explore the relationship between elites and public in the formation of the European Community? There are two main reasons which spring to mind. First, an investigation of this kind can help us understand some of the issues associated with the working of Community institutions. These issues—they might from some perspectives be called problems—concern, for instance, the ability of the European Parliament to mount effective opposition to the Council of Ministers, and also the perceived inertia within the Community's decision-making structures. Other issues could be mentioned. What they have in common is that they can all be related in some fashion to the relationship between and among elites and masses in the Community. In particular, they might also be related to the changes which Europe's political elites and mass publics have experienced over the past twenty-five years. Their social composition has changed. Their orientations and values have changed. So, too, have elite-mass relationships. In the case of the mass public, these changes have manifested themselves in, for instance, regime changes (e.g., Fifth Republic France); changes in government; and the enlargement of the Community, which has brought in new political elites. In the case of the political elites, the changes have included increased political consciousness; changing political loyalties; and changing values. A number of questions can be asked about these changes. How have they affected the working of Community institutions? How might they be related to some of the perceived problems in the functioning of these institutions? What strains have they placed upon the Community's decision-making structures and practices? How have the various institutions adapted? What adaptations or developments are likely in the future? These questions focus on one of the main themes of this paper.

A second reason for looking more closely at elite-mass relationships concerns the broader question of the viability of any political community. One of the central issues in integration theory is that of the popular legitimacy of political institutions. Almost by definition, the building of a political community means the creation of a sense of community or solidarity among the people of a given region. It is this sense of solidarity which gives legitimacy to the Community's institutions. A viable political community needs the allegiance of its mass public as well as that of elites. In the case of the European Community, a lack of public commitment to Europe tends to be seen as a major threat to the existence of the Community.

Before proceeding with an analysis of elite-mass relationships and their effect on the legitimacy and working of European Community institutions, some points should be made about the nature of political legitimacy. As we saw, for integration theorists, the importance of "public commitment" to Europe is rarely questioned. It should, however, be seen in proper context. First, it is only since the development of mass political participation that the allegiance of the masses has been regarded as a prerequisite for the viability of a political community and its institutions. Historically, the non-allegiance of large segments of the population has been no barrier to the survival of a political community, provided they have not formed rival allegiances. Most nation states came into existence with full citizenship limited to a privileged few. Nineteenth century nationalism largely excluded the masses. With the dawn of mass political participation in the late nineteenth and early twentieth centuries, the survival of nation states depended upon their success in integrating new, and possibly rival, groups into the political system. This process of national integration has been far from smooth. In the cases of Austria-Hungary, Sweden and Norway, and Britain and Ireland it resulted in national disintegration. Indeed, in Belgium today, many observers would claim that the same process of national disintegration is at work. There is, then, no iron law of integration. Europe, and many nation states within it, remain extremely heterogeneous.

The case of Belgium brings us to a second point which concerns the conditions of stable democracy, or put another way, the conditions under which governments can retain legitimacy. During the 1960s, a number of influential political theorists argued that social homogeneity with its consequent political consensus was one of the most important conditions of stable democratic development. The Anglo-Saxon nations and much of Scandinavia were seen as socially homogeneous and

therefore stable. Other European countries were seen as socially heterogeneous and therefore inherently unstable in terms of their political
institutions.

One of the problems with this research on political stability was
that it had largely ignored the experiences of the smaller continental
democracies (Belgium, Holland, Austria, and Switzerland). Work on
these countries by scholars showed that the theories of political stability
needed considerable revision. The smaller democracies were culturally
segmented in the extreme, yet they nonetheless showed the same
patterns of political stability enjoyed by the more socially homogeneous
societies of Britain and Scandinavia. The main explanations put forward
focused on the patterns of decision-making. In the small democracies,
society might be culturally divided, but cooperation among elites
prevented political disintegration. This pattern of decision-making was
given a variety of labels—consociationalism; consensus; amicable agreement; and even, quite simply, accommodation. The important point was
that unlike countries such as Britain, the principle of majority rule was
not implemented. Strict rules of representation in government were
applied to protect the interests of all social groups. There were no big
winners, but nor were there any big losers. Everyone benefitted from
stable government.

Consociationalism has not survived intact into the 1980s. Changing political values, increased cultural and political consciousness,
higher expectations about what governments can do, and also the
greater complexities of government have brought the mass public into
a new relationship with the political establishment. New and rival
political elites have emerged. The result has been, if not a breakdown,
at least a deterioration in the consociational model. This deterioration
has been most apparent in Belgium, where, with changing economic and
political circumstances, the public has become increasingly conscious of
linguistic and regional divisions. As the public has become politicized to
different ideas and values, the consociational model has broken down.

What has happened in Europe's smaller democracies is directly
relevant to the European Community. Take the consociational model.
There can be no dispute that the Community is culturally segmented.
Thus, it is hardly surprising that the pattern of decision-making which
has evolved corresponds to the consociationalism of countries like
Holland and Belgium. (Incidentally, an interesting paradox is that these
latter countries are the very ones that have pressed most strongly for
majority rule within the Council of Ministers. On the other hand,
countries such as Britain which favor majority rule at home are
happy to see the European Community operate on the basis of
consociationalism.) Take also the increasing politicization of recent

years. As expectations and demands on governments have increased, and as the problems of government have become more varied and intractable, so too has there been a breakdown within the Council of Ministers of consensus-style decision-making. The resulting inertia has put severe strain on the institutions of the Community. Under these circumstances, a crisis of legitimacy has loomed larger. We can see, then, how the relationship between elites and public, and particularly the way in which it is mediated through the decision-making structures, has an important effect on the viability of a political community.

The founders of the European Community were far-sighted enough to see that the long-term survival of the Community in a democratic age would depend on its finding legitimacy with the general public. Perhaps a solely economic community could rely for a time on the support of elites. Indeed, the "Acceleration Agreement" of 1960, pushed by business interests, suggests the strong and early allegiance of an economic elite. A political community, however, would require wider public support. For the functionalist school of integration, public legitimacy would gradually develop as people became aware of the tangible benefits of Community membership. Community loyalties would slowly replace national loyalties. The neofunctionalists saw this process being mediated through interest groups. Though the European Economic Community had started with quite limited economic functions, the logic of spillover, so the argument ran, would soon broaden and deepen the role of the Community in the economic and political life of the member states. Thus, the Community would enjoy increasing legitimacy among citizens and their representatives. With the growing rivalry and dominance of national governments in the Community decision-making process during the 1960s, the gloom of the integrationists was only allayed by the thought that public opinion might still be rallied in support of a genuine supranational European government. Thus, the role of public opinion took on special significance.

Implicit in these views of Community development is the notion of a set of institutions created by elites in which the public merely plays a legitimizing role. More precisely, in the earlier scenario, the public is legitimizing the *status quo*; in the later scenario, with the growing rivalry of national governments, the public is seen as the preserver of the European ideal, pushing elites towards full integration. Either way, it is the relationship between elites and public which has an important influence on the development of the Community.

Let us now consider the roles of political elites and the mass public in the development of the Community. Before proceeding, the briefest explanation of terms will be useful. *Political elites* refers to governments, governing political parties, and associated groups and organizations.

The term *rival political elites* is used to denote opposition groups and parties.

• POPULAR INDIFFERENCE TOWARDS EUROPE

To what extent has the public been indifferent towards the European Community? Most of the available data on this question comes from opinion polls. Surveys have been carried out since the 1950s. But many of the early polls were quite limited in scope. Few questions were asked and not all the member states were surveyed. Since 1973, the *Eurobarometre* studies have provided much more detailed coverage. Long time series, however, are relatively rare, with many interesting questions not being asked on a regular basis. Bearing in mind the shortage of data for earlier years, we can, nonetheless, provide a useful picture of public opinion towards Europe.

. . .

Clearly, there is not great public enthusiasm for the Community. But, neither has there been, except in [the] cases of Britain, Denmark, and Greece, any great hostility to Community membership. In all the new member states, save Ireland, it is clear that the Community issue became far more politicized than in the original Six. This fact is also indicated by the relatively high levels of interest in Community affairs in these countries. Interestingly, the initial opposition to Community membership among the new members has not disappeared as might have been expected. Indeed, it has shown a tendency to increase. Mixed with this antagonism, it is fair to say that in both old and new member states, there is a continuing high level of apathy towards the European Community. This apathy shows all the signs of being on the increase. Direct elections to the European Parliament have not appeared to bring Community institutions very much closer to their public. There is little public understanding of or interest in the Community. Clearly, the work of the Community is not something that has captured the imagination or interest of the public. A difficult problem for the Community is that where it has attracted public attention, the publicity is all too often negative. The Community, for instance, frequently finds itself unpopular with farmers over the fixing of agricultural prices and with British tax-payers over the question of budget contributions. Few people are prepared to make personal sacrifices for European integration. The alternative public reactions seem to range between apathy and irritation. A high level of diffuse support for European unification seems to have little relevance for public attitudes towards more concrete aspects of European integration.

The apparent remoteness of the European Community coincided during the 1960s and 1970s with a growing public mood towards popular participation and the decentralization of state power. To the extent that the public has challenged the legitimacy of the nation state, it has been in the direction of regional government and devolution. Throughout Western Europe, there was an upsurge in public support for ethnoregional political movements. France, Britain, Italy, Spain, and Belgium have all made moves towards increasing the power of regional government. There seems little doubt that the drift of popular opinion has been towards a view of the Community and its institutions as increasingly remote.

Clearly, the functionalists' hoped-for shift in public loyalties from national to supranational government has not occurred. The strong but vague reservoir of support for European unity has not been translated into a firm commitment which might allow European institutions to exercise authority over national institutions. Instead, the Community has increasingly become the stage on which national rivalries are fought out. National governments, first, through the Council of Ministers, and, later, through the European Council, have come to dominate the Community decision-making process. As a result of national rivalries, progress towards common policies has been extremely slow and haphazard.

Having looked at public opinion in the European Community, let us now turn to a more detailed examination of the role of political elites and public in the various stages of Community building. I will begin by looking at the early years of the Community.

- ### CREATING THE COMMUNITY:
  ### POPULAR INDIFFERENCE AND THE ROLE OF POLITICAL ELITES

It could be argued that the high level of diffuse support for European unification provided a suitable climate for the creation of the European Communities. Throughout the 1950s, up until the formation of the EEC in 1957, a series of polls revealed a high level of support for unification: an average of 56 percent in France; 59 percent in Italy; 67 percent in the UK; and 76 percent in Germany.

More specific questions on the new European institutions also elicited favorable responses from the general public. In September 1952, 61 percent of Italian respondents, 60 percent of Germans, 50 percent of French, and 43 percent of British favored their country's participation in the European Coal and Steel Community. In May 1957, 65 percent of Italians, 71 percent of Germans, and 60 percent of French approved of EEC membership. Two and a half years earlier in October 1954, a majority of respondents in Britain, France, Germany and Italy wanted their countries to participate in a common European government. The evidence at this time seemed to confirm Hallstein's earlier quoted remark that political elites had lagged behind public opinion on European integration. Most obviously in the case of Britain, public opinion was well out-of-line with the decisions which were eventually taken by the political elite.

What gave the British government, and indeed the other governments involved, virtual autonomy in decision-making was the public's lack of intensity in its attachment to European integration. Though the public may have favored integration, it hardly knew what it was, nor what national leaders were negotiating on its behalf. In September 1952, 11 percent of French respondents, 21 percent of Germans, and 46 percent of Italians had never heard of Schuman's Plan for a European Coal and Steel Community. Surprisingly, even fewer had heard of EURATOM and the EC at an equivalent time. In May 1957, 47 percent of French respondents, 59 percent of Germans, and 44 percent of Italians had never heard of EURATOM. Less than half had been able to correctly identify their country as a participant. Almost as high a proportion had never heard of the EEC—35 percent of French respondents, 38 percent of Germans, and 33 percent of Italians. Further, in France and Germany, only 49 percent of the sample managed to identify correctly their country as a member of the EEC. The percentage in Italy was 63 percent.

Though political elites may have had a relatively free hand and could also rely on high levels of support for European unification, the creation of a political community out of so many diverse cultures was in itself a remarkable achievement. It was made possible because of an unusual coalition between national and pan-European elites. Not even nineteenth-century nationalists had known such consensus among their elites. In Italy, for instance, the Catholic Church had remained estranged from the new political community for several decades. At the end of the Second World War, however, there were few national political leaders who did not positively support a united Europe. The evils of competitive nationalism were all too apparent. There were also a number of pan-European pressure groups calling for European unification. However, judging by the vagueness of many of the speeches at the 1948 Hague Congress, there was little agreement on the form that integration might take.

In the event, it was up to a small group of pan-European idealists, led by Jean Monnet, to give concrete form to the idea of European unity. Realizing that immediate political union was too ambitious a goal, they proposed instead the formation of specialized supranational authorities. The first successful plan, proposed by Schuman, was the European Coal and Steel Community, which came into existence in July 1952. There followed the failure of the European Defence Community in 1954. The setback was temporary. In 1957, the Treaty of Rome was signed creating EURATOM and the European Economic Community.

There is no need to go into further detail about the formation of these communities. But, a number of points can be made about the role of political elites and their relationship with the mass public.

1. First, the pan-European idealists were the main motivating force behind the Communities. Significantly, it was an elite movement that did not involve the wider public. The most influential pan-Europeanists were those led by Jean Monnet. They saw integration as a cumulative process. The ECSC, EURATOM, and the EEC were the bases on which full political union could be built. The path to union could only start through cooperation on relatively uncontroversial problems. The influence of the pan-Europeanists was remarkable. To press their goals, they had formed a number of pressure groups. But these pressure groups were highly elitist organizations that did not rely on popular support. Monnet's technique was not to exert public pressure. Instead, he sought to influence national political leaders through strategically placed individuals with the political establishment. In a sense, by moderating his own goals, he achieved a coalition between the pan-Europeanists and the national political elites.

2. The price of the coalition was that the new communities corresponded to the pragmatic interests of the national political elites. For the French, the ECSC was a partial solution to the "German problem." So, too, was the EDC [European Defence Community]. Though, by the time it came to be ratified by the French National Assembly, the question of German rearmament had largely been resolved. Thus, the bill failed in the Assembly when Mendès-France refused to tie the vote to one of confidence in the government. French interests in the EEC were clearly protected and furthered by the Common Agricultural Policy. In addition, French participation in the European Communities allowed the country to grasp firmly the mantle of political leadership in Europe. For the Germans, membership of the European Communities was a means of regaining national autonomy after defeat in war. Also, the Communities opened European markets to German industry. Similar economic advantages were also apparent to political elites in Italy and the Benelux. In addition, leaders in these nations saw themselves exerting greater international influence as part of a united Europe than as minor European powers. Back at the Hague Congress in 1948, Paul-Henri Spaak had proclaimed:

> A hundred and fifty million Europeans have not the right to feel
> inferior to anyone, do you hear! There is no great country in this
> world that can look down on a hundred and fifty million Europeans
> who close their ranks in order to save themselves.

Spaak's conception of a unified Europe might have been aptly described
as super-nationalist. It was certainly different from the conception of
many of the pan-European idealists.

3. Just as the interests of national political elites in the Six explain
their joining the Communities, so too does national interest explain why
others stayed outside. The British political elite was unable to perceive
that it had any interest in European cooperation of the type proposed.
The U.S. special relationship, the Commonwealth, and Britain's pre-
sumed status as a world power were powerful arguments against
cooperation. Only much later, after Suez, decolonization, and Britain's
poor economic performance compared to members of the European
Community did the British political elite become convinced of the value
of Community membership. President Kennedy's influence was also
important in encouraging the British government to revise its position
on Europe.

The other nations eligible for Community membership—Denmark, Norway, and Ireland—followed Britain's lead. Britain was their
major economic market. They also enjoyed close political links with
Britain. It was unthinkable to abandon these economic and political
interests. In addition, Denmark and Norway, particularly, were reluctant to enter a Community which in its early years showed a conservative, Catholic dominance.

4. This conservative, Catholic dominance of the Community in its
early years highlights the ideological cohesion which contributed to its
formation. All the governments of the Six were Catholic, or had
dominant Catholic elements. Later on, France became the only exception when it was Mollet's decision to take the country into Euratom and
the EEC. There was also a shared anti-Communism. At the height of the
Cold War, European cooperation looked as though it might constitute
a powerful bulwark against Communist expansionism. In the cases of
France and Italy, the threat was internal as well as external. This
cooperation was to some extent seen as a means of consolidating
internal political power.

5. There were no rival political elites powerful enough to offer an
alternative avenue of development. Quite clearly, the form that the
Community took and its membership composition were determined by
the perspectives of the national governing elites. Within the Six, the main
opposition to membership came from the left. Though the left, and
particularly the Communists in France and both the Communists and

Socialists in Italy, constituted a rival political elite, their opposition was relatively ineffectual. They had been discredited by the Cold War, and had been cast in the role of permanent opposition. With the Communities still very much an idea rather than a concrete set of institutions, they were unable to muster very much political support in opposition. Their grounds of opposition—the strengthening of capitalist Europe, loss of control in central planning, and the implicit anti-Sovietism of the Community—was indicative of the weakness and isolation of their position.

6. In terms of the institutional development of the Community, the initial pattern was one of consensus politics with a gradual transition to majority rule. The Commission and the Council were seen as having equal weight in the decision-making process. With close cooperation among national political elites, along with their shared interests and ideologies, there were few fears about this pattern of development. The Community was seen very much as an institution run by and answering to elites. The status of the European Assembly indicated the low level of importance attached to popular participation. Indeed, there was no public pressure for popular participation. If one views political institutions as mechanisms for resolving conflict, then clearly the political elites of the time envisaged no major conflicts emerging in the popular arena. Instead, they envisaged mainly national conflicts, emerging from their own national governments, which could be dealt with in the Council of Ministers. Neither the national governments of the Six nor the pan-Europeanist elite thought to involve the mass public in the decision-making process in any meaningful way.

In conclusion, as a result of widespread public apathy and the failure of rival elites to emerge, national political elites formed, during the early stages of Community building, a comfortable coalition with one another and with the pan-Europeanist political elite. By the 1960s, however, this coalition had begun to show its limitations.

• CHANGING ELITE-MASS RELATIONS WITHIN THE COMMUNITY

From the 1960s onwards, the pattern of elite coalitions and popular indifference had begun to change. Let us examine these developments and their consequences.

The first major development was the break-up of the coalition between national political elites and the pan-Europeanists. The form that this development took also meant the break-up of cooperation among the national elites, and the growth of national rivalries. In the context of the Community's institutional structure, the Commission represented the pan-Europeanists and the Council, the national political elites. The first break occurred with de Gaulle's veto of the British membership application in January 1963. The veto showed clearly the power of national interests in the Community. De Gaulle was concerned that Britain would disrupt the Common Agricultural Policy and was suspicious of Britain's links with the United States over a nuclear deterrent. French interests, rather than Community interests or the interests of the other members, were at stake. The second break in the coalition of political elites was again precipitated by de Gaulle in 1965 with his "empty chair" strategy. The Luxembourg compromise that followed in January 1966 consolidated the authority of national governments within the Council over the Commission.

There is little argument that de Gaulle was the precipitating force in the break-up of the old coalition of political elites. It has been argued that de Gaulle pursued a very personal strategy. A single strategically placed politician, it is claimed, was quite able to pursue his own whim in disregard of French elite opinion. Evidence shows that in 1964, 83 percent of a sample of French elites favored some further limitation on national sovereignty. But views were mixed as to the most desirable form of integration. Respondents were fairly equally divided in their desire to see a confederation; a mixed system with supranational dominance; a mixed system with national dominance; a confederation; and the existing international system. With regard to the question of British membership, only a quarter of the elites interviewed wished the Community to be limited to the Six. The rest wanted various forms of expansion of the Community which would include British membership. Despite the contrariness of a large segment of the elite to de Gaulle's views, it is important to note that most of those who identified with the Gaullist party shared de Gaulle's views. It was to this group initially that de Gaulle looked for his political support. He also looked to the mass public. Certainly, in the case of his rejection of British membership, de Gaulle made a successful appeal to the mass public. In February 1963, only 43 percent of French respondents in a public opinion poll approved of Britain joining the EEC; 21 percent disapproved. A far higher proportion approved of Norwegian membership (62 percent); with only 4 percent disapproving. Despite these differences, it is clear from the high number of uncommitted respondents that British membership was not an issue of very great importance to the majority of the French public. On this kind of issue, de Gaulle certainly had sufficient elite and public support for his actions.

De Gaulle alone cannot be held responsible for the break with Europeanist ideals. In the case of Britain's application, the other member states were not prepared to force France's hand by continuing to negotiate with Britain. Adenauer, in particular, was more interested in pursuing Franco-German friendship despite the fact that a majority of the German public were prepared to loosen ties with France in order to gain Britain's inclusion in the EEC. Again, we see an instance of a national political elite ignoring its mass public with impunity, no doubt because of the low level of intensity of public feeling. The British could also be held responsible for events on the grounds that had they joined the Community at the beginning, some of the problems between France and Britain might have been less intractable.

The rejection of British membership was a blow to the pan-Europeanists as much as it was to the other member states. It meant the predominance of national interests over European interests. This time they did not overlap. The 1965 crisis was a more obvious attack on European interests. The French government, in seeking to protect its freedom for unilateral action, brought to an end any possibility of the development of majority rule in the European context.

The result in institutional terms was the growing dominance of the Council of Ministers over the Commission, and the use of the technical veto in the Council. The consolidation of nationalist power also meant the development of new institutions around the Council—COREPER, and later the European Council. The mass public remained largely peripheral to these developments, and there were no changes in the status of the European Parliament. The biggest losers, however, were the pan-Europeanists. Had there been a mass base to their movement, they could perhaps have successfully defended the pre-existing institutional structure. As it was, the public remained indifferent or even began to see things through an increasingly nationalistic perspective. Nowhere was this truer than in the new member states.

In some ways, the expansion of the Community in the 1970s contributed to the consolidation of national governmental power. The public in the new member states helped to legitimate the dominance of the Council. Whereas in the original Six, the public remained indifferent to the Community, in the newer member states, public interest was much more intense. There are several reasons.

1. The initial rejection of Britain's application in the 1960s had allowed the debate over national interests to develop much more fully than would otherwise have been the case. Clearly, the governments of all the applicants had decided in 1961 that national interests could best be served by membership of the Community. At this time, the public was still largely indifferent. Hilary Allen notes in the case of Norway's application:

> The suddenness with which the question had arisen and the widespread unfamiliarity with it meant that initially, at least, there were not only many voters, but also many politicians and party activists who had no very firm opinion on it.

Had membership been attained at this stage, there would probably have been considerably less controversy. As it was a counter-elite had time to mobilize support against membership.

2. It was the growth of a rival political elite opposed to membership that for the first time brought real public involvement to the issue of EEC membership. This rival elite was particularly active in Britain, Denmark, and Norway. The early decisions taken by the governments of the latter two countries to hold a popular referendum was both a cause and an effect of the wide-ranging public debate about the national implications of Community membership. The level of public debate was in sharp contrast to the manner in which the Six had formed the Communities in the 1950s.

3. The circumstances of membership were very different for the new applicants. Britain, Denmark, Norway, and Ireland were intending to join a community that was already well established. Though some flexibility was possible in negotiating the terms of entry, the new members were nonetheless obliged to accept the Community as a given. The Community was no longer merely an idea in the minds of a small political elite. Its basic structure and identity were set. It was visible to the public. It was not surprising, therefore, that Community membership should have generated such passionate debate.

4. Finally, opposition to EC membership in the applicant-states was based on substantive, and often substantial arguments, on which various interests could take sides. Many people were skeptical of the supposed economic benefits of membership. The CAP [Common Agricultural Policy] came in for particular criticism; in the case of the Norwegians because it threatened the livelihood of the country's small and inefficient farmers, heavily subsidized by the Norwegian state; in the case of the Danes and the British because it threatened their cheap food policies. The other major issue was the loss of sovereignty by national governments to the European Community. Only in Ireland was Community membership largely uncontentious. The small Labour party alone opposed membership, but in a somewhat half-hearted manner.

Voting turn-out was high in the referendums, particularly in Denmark where it reach 90.1 percent. The results showed a positive commitment to the EC by the Irish, Danes, and British; but membership was rejected by the Norwegians. In the case of Norway, it was a severe defeat for the political establishment. But, it had not been achieved by public opposition alone. A rival political elite, largely extra-parliamentary, and organized in the People's Movement had been successful in mobilizing a majority of the public against membership.

As we noted earlier, the result of the politicization of the European issue has meant that public opposition to EC membership has continued in Britain and Denmark. There is also a reasonable expectation that opposition will continue in the case of Greece, a member since 1981. This public opposition has often been interpreted as a threat to the viability of the Community. Two points need to be made. First, the development of rival political elites opposing membership was a far greater challenge to the national political establishment than it ever was to the Community. In both Denmark and Norway, the issue of Community membership precipitated major and long-lasting splits within the party systems. In Britain, too, the EC issue has been a major cause of the realignment in British politics which took place in 1981. Second, the only possible threat to the Community of the arguments over membership was that they were couched in terms of national interests. But, where cooperation is achieved by consensus (as it is in the EC), there is no alternative framework in which members of a particular nation state can decide upon membership. What has happened in the new member states has no doubt consolidated the existing institutional structure, but it has not changed it.

In the cases of the original Six, membership remained largely uncontroversial because no rival political elites were willing or able to mobilize public opinion against membership. As we noted earlier, it is always easier to mobilize public opinion against a concrete set of institutions, than against an idea. By the 1960s with several years of successful economic growth behind them, which had coincided with the formation of the EEC, the publics of the original Six were in no mood to reopen the issue. In 1962, a poll revealed that three-quarters of German, French, and Italian respondents approved their country's membership of the European Community.

• PAST, PRESENT, AND FUTURE

During the past decade, the European Community appears to have become increasingly beleaguered by national differences, and the resulting inability to develop common policies. In fact, the Community has probably been under less stress than national governments. There is surely no more consensus within the various member states on how to deal with the economic, social, and political crises which have emerged during the 1970s and 1980s than there is in the European Community. Thus, the failures of the EC to achieve consensus among its members should be seen in the context of the serious cleavages that exist in national political systems with regard to government policies.

. . .

A change in public attitudes is unlikely given the present institutional structure of the Community. Despite the efforts of members of the European Parliament, there is no indication that they have caught or will succeed in catching the public's interest and support on a really broad scale. The best hope for institutional change still lies with the national governments themselves. Though this might occur as the result of the failures of consociationalism in the European context, it is not clear that majority rule will be an entirely acceptable replacement. National governments have themselves found it increasingly difficult to satisfy a fickle public. In a general desire for decentralized democracy, there is no good reason why the Community should expect to find it any easier.

Organized Interests
and the Europe of 1992

PHILIPPE C. SCHMITTER AND WOLFGANG STREECK

Neofunctionalists, unlike federalists such as Spinelli, did not believe that the mass public would rise up and demand a European constitution. They did argue, however, that groups, representing the specific interests of the people, would recognize the tangible benefits of integration and pressure the national governments and Community institutions to speed the process.

Philippe Schmitter (Stanford University, Stanford, California) and Wolfgang Streeck (University of Wisconsin–Madison) argue that the neofunctionalist system of interest representation and policymaking would look very much like the neocorporatist models adopted by many European governments in the 1960s and 1970s. They contend, however, that at the European level, interest representation best approximates the fragmented pluralistic model found in the United States, despite the efforts of the Commission. They cite two important reasons: the absence of a strong European state, and the dominance of business over labor interests at the European level. Also significant to the fragmentation of interests, however, was the implicit bargain between business elites (who wanted less government regulation) and national governmental elites (who wanted to regain some control of their economies) that opened the way for further integration in the late 1980s. This bargain excluded labor and limited EC intervention in the economy, thus leaving no place for major interests to act in concert.

Underlying Schmitter and Streeck's discussion of interest groups in

Reprinted from *Political Power and Social Change: The United States Faces a United Europe*, eds. Norman J. Ornstein and Mark Perlman (The AEI Press, 1991) with the permission of The American Enterprise Institute for Public Policy Research, Washington, D.C. Notes omitted.

the European Community is an explanation of the "relaunching" of Europe in the late 1980s. They view the integration process as one profoundly influenced by the international political economy. The failure of postwar international institutions to govern the global economy led European governments to try domestic solutions to their problems. When that failed they turned to supranational institutions, and the result was Project 1992. This explanation draws heavily on an article by Wayne Sandholtz and John Zysman (see Chapter 18) that launched a new era of grand integration theory.

I know what the EC *really stands for: Executive Committee—as in the "Executive Committee for managing the common affairs of the bourgeoisie"! These businessmen really do expect to recuperate at the level of Europe as a whole what they have lost at the level of national states— the capacity to govern as they please in the interest of capitalism as a whole.*

—Overheard at a conference for businessmen
on Europe 1992, Berkeley, December 1989.

No one can doubt that business interests have played a prominent role in European integration. Although the Treaty of Rome was drafted exclusively by politicians and higher civil servants, many firms and sectors, well-protected at the national level, resisted the idea of interregional competition at first, and the representatives of business interests soon found their way to Brussels. During the 1960s and 1970s, policymaking in the European Community (EC) settled into a bilateral, sectoral mold with business association executives and Eurocrats negotiating among themselves over a series of detailed (and excruciatingly obscure) issues. Representatives of labor and consumers were by and large absent from the process—whether by design or indifference.

The agreements of 1985 that established the goals of completing Europe's internal market by December 31, 1992, came from a different process and motivation. They did not merely spill over from the previous technical deliberations but imposed a different multilateral, cross-sectoral, political dynamic upon the process of regional integration. In so doing, they radically changed the structure of incentives for the participation of organized interests at the European level.

Moreover, contrary to numerous previous *relancements*, the Single European Act was quickly followed by significant changes in the behavior of business firms, which entered into numerous mergers, acquisitions, plant locations, and marketing arrangements. In addition, national policy makers scrambled to bring their respective policies up to speed, and there were important shifts in the expectations of mass publics who began to imagine moving about unimpeded in an enlarged social space. These factors increased the visibility of and potential stake in the European process for business interests as well as for workers, consumers, environmentalists, and policy takers of all sorts.

Our task here is to assess the impact of the 1992 process upon the structure and behavior of organized interests in Europe, particularly business associations. We describe the system of interest intermediation emerging at the European level and explain how it differs from previous national and regional practices and what this may imply for the future configuration of a united Europe.

• THEORIES OF INTEGRATION AND PRACTICES OF INTEREST GROUPS

Organized socioeconomic groups—interest associations—have been assigned a prominent place in virtually all theories and "pre-theories" of European integration, especially in the neofunctionalist vision of Europe's would-be polity of the 1960s and mid-1970s. Supranational association formation and bargaining were expected to serve, at least temporarily, as a substitute for popular identification with the new polity that was emerging beyond and above the narrow confines of existing nation states. Most observers and participants of the fledgling integration process thought that individuals would continue for the foreseeable future to cling to their respective national passions and identities. If a United Europe had to wait until its citizens identified themselves as "Europeans"—rather than as Frenchmen, Germans, Italians, and so on—then the small Eurocracies that had been created in Luxembourg, Brussels, and Strasbourg in the 1950s with only fragile support from national governments stood no chance of contributing very much to the integration process, certainly not in the lifetimes of their founders.

The professional representatives of specialized interests within national polities were expected to provide the missing link between indifferent publics and innovative Eurocrats. Unlike the voters trapped in traditional partisan identities, they would orient themselves rationally and opportunistically toward the new policy action at the regional level. Moreover, in response to the frustrations that such an imperfect consensus on convergent objectives was likely to produce, these representatives would insist on expanding the scope and authority of the new institutions—thereby contributing to what the neofunctionalists called spillovers.

In attitude and outlook, association officials and European civil servants appeared to be birds of the same feather. Both were appointed rather than elected; both were experts with a technocratic approach to problem solving; both were professionally trained (often in the same institutions) to manage complex interdependencies; and both possessed a cosmopolitan orientation and life-style and were likely to be indifferent to the traditional rituals of nationhood. Just as civil servants such as Jean Monnet had been persuading and cajoling the elected politicians and administrative cadres of national states to accept emergent supranationalism, so the *Geschäftsführer* of business associations and trade unions were expected to enlighten their respective elected leaders and members that the locus of interest satisfaction had migrated to a higher level of authority. Armed with specialized perceptions of opportunity, they would arrive in Brussels long before their fellow politicians and citizens, who were still focusing on national goals and symbols.

With more supranational lobbyists participating in the policy process, the Community would have better payoffs, especially for the Commission. This cooperative arrangement would not only provide Eurocrats with indispensable factual information for their highly complex decisions, but it would also socialize powerful forces within European civil society into a worldview and conception of interest that would continuously spill over into new areas of supranational authority. Having been drawn into the ambit of the Commission, representatives would learn from experience that it was more efficient and effective to manage issues on a European scale than at the national level. Upon returning to their respective capitals, they would serve as a reverse lobby—not for their national interests in front of the Community, but for the Community's interests in front of national governments and publics. By fostering the development of a transnational system of interest representation, the Community and the Commission in particular, would contribute indirectly to its own growth as a policy arena and executive body and thereby overcome the constraints of parochial national calculations and purely intergovernmental negotiation to build a brave (and better) new world of supranational political management.

• INTEREST INTERMEDIATION AT THE NATIONAL LEVEL

In many ways, the status imagined for organized interests in the future European polity bore a strong resemblance to a model of interest politics within national polities that only later came to be labeled "neocorporatist." The emergent Euro-state was expected to be primarily concerned with governing a "mixed economy," according to rational (read, "Keynesian") principles of public intervention and professional expertise whose prudent application would ensure social peace and citizen consent. This involved a shift from the territorial-electoral-parliamentary arena of adversarial liberal politics toward the creation of mechanisms for functional representation by monopolistic, hierarchically structured associations. Through a growing, dense, and institutionalized, web of bi-, tri-, and multilateral relationships, involving both public and private entities, mutual constraints on class, sectoral, and professional behavior could be negotiated—and implemented. These, when supplemented by the shared values of a technocratic intelligentsia, would help to satisfy the strategic imperatives of self-restraint, moderation, and compromise imposed by the sheer complexity and interdependence of a modern society and economy.

Ironically, it was not to the European, but to the national level that the practice of modern corporatism gravitated during the 1960s and 1970s. Almost universally, existing states—inside and outside the European Community—turned to centralized bargaining between firmly institutionalized functional interest associations, admittedly, with varying degrees of success. Governments of the left and right (although predominantly the former) facilitated these developments as an antidote to economic dislocations and crises, especially to the threat of inflation in societies with a strong labor movement. Where they were afraid to renege on the political guarantee of full employment, the cornerstone of the postwar Keynesian welfare state, they turned to "neocorporatist concertation" and "incomes policies." In effect, national governments were practicing what integration theorists had been preaching for the European Community and its Commission: to integrate their political systems by relying more and more on deals with interest groups, as opposed to depending on electoral and parliamentary majorities and alliances, and to generate new, higher-level loyalties and obligations through compromises about specific payoffs rather than by mobilizing mass publics around partisan slogans and national symbols.

The system of interest representation that has emerged in the Community looks more pluralist than corporatist; it is more organizationally fragmented, less hierarchically integrated, and more internally competitive, and less control is vested in peak associations over their affiliates or in sectoral associations over their members. The contrast with what was happening at the national level is especially striking. By the early 1970s, when neofunctional approaches to integration were beginning to be declared obsolescent, it had become clear that Community-level associability was not developing along the lines that had been anticipated or advocated.

Why did the has-been polities of national states—and not the "would-be polity" of the European Community—develop in the anticipated direction? Why did supranational pluralism emerge and persist in the face of growing national corporatism?

One possible explanation may lie in the need—especially in liberal, democratic, voluntaristic settings—for large, encompassing, and potentially monopolistic interest associations to be assisted, encouraged, privileged, even created by state agents. Only where there is active and more or less purposive intervention by external, legitimate, and coercive power in the organizational design of associations will a corporatist outcome emerge and prevail. This is not to say that modern corporatism must be a "plot" of public authorities, since its success depends on the willing acceptance and usually on the initiative of private actors, but that group interests, if left purely to their own devices and calculations, will follow a path of pluralist development. Applied to the weak, fledgling pseudostate that is (or was) the European Community, with its strictly limited resources for direct policy implementation, the implication is clear: it had sufficient material incentives to attract the attention of organized interests, but not sufficient coercive resources to influence their organizational design.

Another possible explanation relates to the balance of class forces, especially during the formative period of corporatist arrangements. Only where labor is well organized and capable of mounting a credible threat to employer prerogatives—for example, through the mobilization of the electorate and a friendly party in government (hence, the importance in most national cases of Social Democracy)—does corporatist concertation emerge as a second-best alternative to outright state allocation or competitive market clearing as a means for resolving class-based interest conflicts. It is the collective strength of organized labor that affects the interventionist policies of the state that, in turn, lead to the state's relatively autonomous role in affecting the design of organized interests.

Again the negative implication for prospective European corporatism is obvious. Labor at the EC level has always been (and remains) highly disorganized as a class. It has been difficult to articulate even on a sectoral basis, especially in comparison with business interests. In the absence of anything resembling a balance of class or sectoral forces, the Community as would-be state has never had the autonomy to act and thereby to institutionalize a system of concertation—despite, as we shall see, several attempts to do so.

- **PATTERNS OF INTEREST INTERMEDIATION**
  DURING THE 1960s AND 1970s

Before the European Economic Community was formed in 1958, class, sectoral, and professional interests in Europe had been involved in collective action across national lines only a few times, and very little of it had been successful. Industry cartels among business firms had emerged around the turn of the century, along with proletarian internationalism between trade unions and some cooperative ventures among professional groups. But World War I put an end to most of this activity. After World War II, the continuing presence of the United States—and especially its insistence, through the Marshall Plan, OEEC [Organization for European Economic Cooperation], and the EPU [European Payments Union] that European countries should act in concert on matters of postwar reconstruction—laid a different foundation. Nonetheless, there is little evidence, until the stimulus of the Treaty of Rome, that national interest associations were prepared to establish permanent European-level organizations.

Immediately after 1958 European peak associations began to form to represent broadly encompassing industrial, commercial, and agricultural employer interests: UNICE for industry (1958); COPA for agriculture (1958); Permanent Conference for Chambers of Commerce (1958); UNACEE for craft industries (1958); COGECA for agricultural cooperatives (1959); BFEC for banking (1960); and GCECEE for savings banks (1963). The interests of workers (ETUC) and consumers (BEUC) took a while longer to find their way to Brussels—both were established in 1973. SEPLIS, which represented the liberal, intellectual, and social professions, was only created in 1975. By then, roughly at the time of the enlargement to include Great Britain, Ireland, and Denmark, virtually all of the main categories of functional interest were covered. These broadly encompassing organizations were composed exclusively of national associations, most of which continued to command far greater resources than their nominally superior *Spitzenverband*, and all of which continued to act autonomously on matters of particular relevance. For example, the national associations of industrialists for each member state opened their own offices in Brussels. None of the European associations of this first wave had individuals or firms as direct members.

Meanwhile, a myriad of more specialized, sectoral associations were also being formed at the European level. Some of these did have individuals or firms as direct members, but few were affiliated (and none subordinated) to the peak associations mentioned above. By 1985, the total of all types and all interest bases had reached 654, according to a census carried out by the Commission. Needless to say, the resources available to these organizations differ considerably, as does the frequency of their access to EC decisionmaking. The associations representing business interests vastly outnumber those representing labor, artisans, and consumers. The situation at the national level was similar, and there are several reasons why capitalists choose to work through a greater variety of specialized intermediaries than workers. The EC imbalance seems disproportionate, however: 583 business associations to 112 associations representing the interests of workers, artisans, professionals, and consumers combined!

• THE FAILED ATTEMPT AT EURO-CORPORATISM

The Commission seems to have deliberately encouraged the formation of these associations and quickly established a procedure for recognizing their special Community status. This implied privileged access to its deliberations, even if recognition was not always limited to one organization per category. Each of its Directorates-General soon surrounded itself with a vast number of standing, advisory, and management committees, most of which were based on functional rather than territorial principles of representation. In the early stages, the Commission apparently attempted to confine lobbying to interactions with certified Community associations, but this practice was subsequently relaxed to permit an increasing volume of direct contacts with representatives of national interests.

This structure of advisory committees and expert groups expanded over the subsequent years. The Commission itself has never employed many officials and has depended heavily on the advice of interest representatives, national government employees, and experts for both drafting its directives and monitoring compliance with them. The number of consultative bodies was close to 700 by the time the Single European Act was signed in 1985, and since then it has almost doubled. Interest representatives are well remunerated for attending these meetings, and these payments could even be interpreted as a conscious subsidy for the development of an appropriately structured system of interest intermediation.

The capstone of this early corporatist design was to have been the Economic and Social Committee (ESC). This body was inserted in the Treaty of Rome and persists to the present day. Its 189 members (as of 1985) represent three "grand categories" of interest: employers, workers and various agricultural, transport, shopkeeper, artisan, consumer, environmental, and other groups, but they do not represent specific interest associations. They are nominated as individuals by member governments and appointed by the Council of Ministers to a term of four years. The ESC likes to think of itself as the "other European Assembly"—a sort of functional shadow to the territorially based European parliament—but it has actually accomplished very little. Even its own propaganda admits that "it was regarded as the most unobtrusive of the Community institutions," protesting, of course, that it is now becoming more significant!

When, in 1970, the Council began taking advantage of the subsequent development (and relative success) of corporatist arrangements at the national level and tried to replicate them at the European level, the ESC was set aside as too cumbersome and insufficiently *paritaire* to bear the burden of leading the Community into the brave new world of social partnership. Instead, the ministers of social affairs and, later, the ministers of economic and financial affairs decided to convoke a series of Tripartite Conferences bringing together the European peak associations and national representatives of capital and labor with national civil servants and Eurocrats. They met six times until 1978—often in highly publicized settings—to discuss a wide range of macroeconomic and social policies. Their concerns paralleled those of the national concertation efforts of the same period: full employment, inflation, wage restraint, fiscal policy, worker training, and productivity measures. The Standing Committee on Employment with tripartite representation was established, and there was even a plan for creating a set of sectoral councils wherein capital, labor, and state officials were expected to hammer out collective agreements for governing the steel, shipbuilding, textile, aerospace, and telecommunications industries.

All this effort came to naught in 1978. Business associations had consistently shown no enthusiasm for concertation practices within the Community. They were already reluctant participants in analogous national arrangements and often led the struggle to get rid of these arrangements during the 1980s. The great proponent of this approach had been the European Trade Union Confederation, aided and abetted by the Commission. When it withdrew its support in 1978 because of the lack of progress (and because of some dissent within its ranks), all that was left of Euro-corporatism in macroeconomic policy was the Standing Committee on Employment and a few specialized working groups that continued to recycle the by-now tattered idea of concertation, until, during the French presidency of the Council in 1984, a new initiative came from its minister of employment, Pierre Bérégovoy. As "an interested private person"(!), he invited high-level representatives of European and national associations to an informal discussion at the Val

Duchesse castle just outside of Brussels. This formula closely approximates the loose organizational structure that characterizes the more successful national experiences with concertation: the Harpsund meetings in Sweden, the Parity Commission in Austria, and the Chancellor's Fireside Talks in the Federal Republic. These secretive encounters continued during the year but were interrupted in 1985 when the initiative shifted to the hands of the new president of the Commission, also a French socialist, Jacques Delors. He came up with an ambitious proposal for a European social policy complete with European-level collective bargaining and the possible harmonization of industrial relations and welfare policy throughout the region. The activity surrounding the signing of the Single European Act and the momentum it imparted to Community decisionmaking seem to have subsequently eclipsed this initiative, but, as we shall see, some of its content (if not its tripartite form) is contained in the discussions about adding a "social dimension" to the 1992 Package.

• THE LINK WITH CONCOMITANT
   EFFORTS AT NATIONAL CORPORATISM

So far, we have made the (comforting) assumption that national corporations and supranational corporatism are not only compatible, but causally implicated with each other. It seemed just a simple matter of replication, of transferring lessons learned from the lower to the higher level of aggregation. A closer look at the critical period of the 1970s suggests a different answer.

This, in retrospect, heyday of national corporatism was rooted in exclusively domestic responses to the deinstitutionalization and ensuing disorder of the capitalist world economy that had begun in the late 1960s. Except in the United States—where a long decline in unionism had set the stage for privatization and deregulation (a strategy that was to have severe consequences for smaller capitalist countries a decade later)—governments almost everywhere in advanced industrial societies tried centrally negotiated social contracts as a sort of home-made replacement for the defunct international arrangements that had been providing some rules and assurance among competing national economies. These agreements served to impose and enforce informal equivalents to the external balance of payments constraint and helped public officials and union leaders to hold down wage demands. To an important degree, they should be understood as a desperate recourse to domestic political and institutional solutions for what were actually international problems. The link between corporatism and economic nationalism holds not only for the 1930s, but also for the 1970s.

Member states of the European Community were among those that resorted to such solutions, although it is significant that the more extreme (and successful) practitioners of the new art of social contracting—Austria, Sweden, Norway and, eventually, Finland—were not EC members. Even the most enthusiastic proponents of regional integration could hardly have avoided noticing how useless the Community was as an instrument for restoring a stable global monetary environment, for working out a common energy policy with the United States and OPEC, or for combating inflation and unemployment. The "dark ages of intergovernmentalism" in the European Community coincided with the period when national elites came to believe that the system of supranational institutions they had set up in the 1950s and 1960s, a time of relatively stable international order, could not be exploited to deal with the rising turbulence in their policy environments.

Moreover, by resorting to domestic concertation on a large scale, these elites made international concertation even more difficult to achieve. This is the underlying factor that brought the formation of a European system of interest politics to a momentary halt. Once the attention of policy makers and association officials had been diverted away from Brussels and back to national capitals, regional cooperation and compromise became more difficult because domestic political constituencies had to be satisfied first. Perhaps even more important, member countries had quite different institutions for adopting such a policy. Corporatism worked well in some places—most of them outside the European Community—and it dismally failed in others. In still others, it worked for a while but accumulated problems that could not be resolved. As a result, the performance of national economies diverged greatly in the 1970s. If anything, the uneven distributions of costs and benefits seemed to make them even more resolute not to give up an iota of sovereignty. The weak countries were no doubt afraid of becoming subservient to the strong ones; and the strong countries saw no advantage to be gained in making concessions to the weak, fearing a dilution of their national success.

- **THE DECLINE OF NATIONAL CORPORATISMS
  AND THE CRISIS OF THE 1980s**

It follows from the above analysis that the demise of national corporatisms in the early 1980s was more than coincidental with the resurgence of interest in regional integration via the Single European Act and the internal market project. Behind the change was the shared experience that all European countries were finding their effective sovereignty declining. It was crucial to believe in this national capacity if they were to sustain the social contracts they had entered into during the crisis of the 1970s. These had been last-ditch attempts to shore up the so-called postwar settlements of the 1950s and 1960s by prolonging their life in an international environment that was quite distinct from the one in which they had originally been embedded.

This turned out to be an impossible task, in large part because of changes in the international role and position of the United States. No longer the benevolent hegemon willing to make sacrifices for a reliable world order and no longer bound to the class compromise forged during the New Deal, American policy makers sought to renew competition through deregulation and deunionization. In the early 1980s, this strategy paid off handsomely by giving the United States flexible markets and encouraging world investors to underwrite an expansionist fiscal and monetary policy that has aptly been characterized as "Keynesianism in one country."

From the perspective of other capitalist countries, this policy was particularly ominous, as the French socialist government after 1981 was soon to find out. The international political economy after the second oil crisis behaved as though it was under the sway of the old Roman imperial maxim, *quod licet Jovi non licet bovi*. Keynesianism had become limited not just to one, but to only one country. Since the United States was so much larger than everybody else and therefore much less internationalized, had broken its unions, was still in control of the *de facto* world currency while no longer being the world banker, and could still attract and maintain the confidence of the financial market (despite gigantic and growing deficits in its budgetary and foreign trade balances), it could effectively prime the pump with fiscal stimuli. The Europeans could not do so without suffering capital flight, as François Mitterrand and the others quickly learned.

The key point is that some sort of Keynesian capacity for expanding effective national demand seems indispensable for the viability of corporatist concertation. If a state cannot apply its most potent collective measures to alleviate unemployment—namely, fiscal and monetary policy—it cannot hope to gain concessions from workers or even to influence settlements between trade unions and employers' associations. To be able to put its domestic sovereignty up for negotiation to class interests, public authorities need to have sufficient sovereignty from foreign entanglements in the first place. As that sovereignty declined, the Keynesian capacity of European states faded, along with corporatism and the associated social-democratic project of politically guaranteeing full employment.

Not everything can be blamed on the deinstitutionalization of the international economy or on the policies of the United States and the deflationary bias they introduced in the world capitalist system of the 1980s. A more general explanation would involve the growing interdependence between market economies. As a result, the typical West European country now finds that it can no longer treat the external trade component in its national accounts as a mere addendum to a primarily domestic economy. As the French learned from their experiment in reflation from 1981 to 1983—and as everybody else learned from the French—it is possible to create jobs by Keynesian stimuli, but unless a country has the size, the currency, and the social and the industrial relations system of the United States, much of this induced employment will emerge outside the territory of the government that has incurred the national debt necessary to create the expanded aggregate demand.

Given the absence of effective international institutions to manage such interdependence, governments in the early 1980s were tempted to withdraw the political guarantee of full employment and rely for the restoration of prosperity upon internationalized markets for goods and services, as well as upon a deregulated national market for labor. The temptation first spread from the United States to Britain, the country with the most open capital markets in Europe, and from there to the Continent. It took the form of a more or less forceful (and successful) attack on the "rigidities" accumulated during three decades of mixed economy. In many cases, this included dismantling, or at least disregarding, the structures of collective bargaining and compromises among domestic interests. Where this proved politically impossible and did not progress very far, the inability of governments to deliver on employment, growth, price stability, or international competitiveness created an atmosphere of "Europessimism" or "Eurosclerosis," which spread throughout Europe during the first half of the 1980s.

- **THE 1992 PROJECT AND ITS IMPACT**
  ON EUROPEAN INTEREST POLITICS

European integration gained new momentum in the mid-1980s as a result of an alliance between two broad interests: (1) those of large European firms struggling to overcome perceived competitive disadvantages in relation to Japanese and U.S. capital; and (2) those of state elites seeking to restore at least part of the national sovereignty they had gradually lost during the growth of international interdependence. The firms seem to have come to the conclusion that using their clout in national political arenas to protect themselves from foreign competition through subsidies, discriminatory technical and health standards, or privileged access to public procurement contracts had become counter-productive, given the increased size of production runs and the volume of investment required to sustain world market competitiveness. Instead of trying to benefit again from the economic nationalism that had ground the integration process to a halt in the 1970s, big business throughout Europe became willing in the 1980s to join forces with political and administrative elites that were under pressure to seek a supranational pooling of eroded national sovereignties in order to recapture autonomy with regard to the United States and organize a competitive response to the Japanese challenge.

In return for business going along with the 1992 project, governments conceded that the future integrated European political economy would be significantly less subject to regulation—national or supranational—than under the corporatist arrangements of the 1960s and 1970s. That meant assuring business interests that supranational sovereignty would be used primarily for external reassertion, not for internal intervention. Instead of relying exclusively, as before, on the cumbersome process of harmonizing norms and conditions throughout the Community, a novel method of defining and governing the internal market known as "mutual recognition" was adopted for cases in which agreement could not be reached. Any product or practice that was legal in one member country would be legal in all member countries. For all practical purposes, this amounts to a subtle form of deregulation and is obviously inimical to any resurgence of Euro-corporatism.

This "negative" mode of resolving the conflicts of regional integration not only undermines what is left of existing national corporatisms at both the macro- and meso-levels, but it would also rule out their eventual replacement by supranational structures of policy concertation. Hence, the *relancement* around the 1992 goals coincides with—and was advanced by—the decline in social contracting at the national level, but the more it progresses, the more it seems destined to push the European system of interest intermediation further in a pluralist direction. Organized capital and labor are less likely to play such a pivotal role in a centralized, tripartite management of the economy as a whole or even in the governance of its sectors. This does not mean that European interest associations will be any less present in the EC policy process of the future, just that their *modus operandi* may resemble that of American interest associations much more than it has in the past.

· · ·

• **CONCLUSION**

Basic uncertainty about the institutional impact of the 1992 process makes it difficult to predict the future course of European interest politics. Let us first return to the two "lessons" we drew from the national studies of corporatist concertation—the role of the state and the significance of class balance—and then examine some other properties of the integration process to see if we can discern what is emerging.

At present, the Community is not a state. Its Commission may have more autonomy than other international organizations, but it lacks the core attributes of a state. It has neither a monopoly over the legitimate exercise of coercion nor a centralized capacity for administering exchanges within a given territory. The 1992 directives and associated spillovers may eventually increase its relative stateness—especially if they promote the harmonization and direct implementation of policies—but it will still lack sufficient resources to intervene successfully in the design of a coherent system of interest intermediation at the European level. For the foreseeable future, this system will be formed by the voluntary choices of firms and individuals as molded and deflected by national political intervention.

The European Community does not reflect a balance of class forces. Business interests have always predominated over those of workers, artisans, professionals, and consumers in the integration process. In fact, large European firms played a direct role in initiating and promoting the 1992 measures. So far, European trade unions have supported the project, but they have had virtually no influence over its content. Because of a number of recent changes in the economy—lower growth rates; persistently high unemployment; labor market segmentation due to smaller, more dispersed work sites; the rise of part-time, temporary, and irregular jobs; flexible specialization in production; the decline in blue-collar occupations and rise in white- and pink-collar ones; extensive restructuring in specific industries; new transnational systems of ownership and sourcing—unions are everywhere on the defensive. Some are losing members or being forced into mergers. Some are losing the effective monopoly of representation and semipublic status they gained during the heyday of national corporatism. Some are being compelled to decentralize their bargaining strategies to the sectoral and even to the plant or firm level. Some are suffering from rising conflict *within* the ranks of the working class: between public and private employees; between older and younger workers; between those in sectors that are sheltered and those in sectors exposed to international competition; between those who are regularly employed and those who are not. The trends are by no means uniform from sector to sector and country to country, and the resultant disparities have undermined the capacity for trade unions to act in solidarity at the national and supranational levels.

Previous efforts at European collective action in the 1970s—to impose a thirty-five-hour workweek or to pass a uniform European company law that would have guaranteed worker representation in management—were easily defeated by the mobilization of business interests. Nevertheless, the prospect of adding a social dimension to the 1992 package might have provided just the sort of class-based threat or opportunity that led to higher levels of national associability in the past. Moreover, it emerged as an issue in the context of the informal Val Duchesse meetings and was initially backed by the dynamic new president of the Commission, Jacques Delors, a Socialist with a background in the French Catholic workers' movement.

The Commission's proposal went through several drafts, some of which contained ambitious measures to advance union rights and worker consultation, as well as to set high standards of social welfare for all member states. By the time it finally was approved at the Strasbourg Summit in 1989, it was watered down beyond recognition. Most of what was left dealt only with health and safety guidelines! As with the previous resistance to the Vredeling proposals on company law, business interests (in this case, strongly assisted by the Thatcher government) easily defeated a policy measure that would have improved the balance of class forces—and, with it, the incentive for a more corporatist and concertive system of intermediation.

Other factors, too, have conspired to promote a more pluralist outcome. By the mid-1980s, conservative governments were well entrenched in several EC member states and the Social Democrats governing in France and Spain had turned to austerity policies that were incompatible with the voluntary practice of concertation and the deliberate promotion of monopolistic self-organization. This might have changed as a result of the German elections in December 1990. They did not produce a Social Democratic majority, however—quite the contrary! The Thatcher government in Britain lagged badly in the polls, but its leader was replaced by her hand-picked successor, John Major, not a rotation of party in power. Only a massive shift toward the left could bring the social dimension back to the EC agenda and, with it, a different approach to organized interests. This now seems highly unlikely within the twelve members. Only the accession of such solidly social democratic countries as Austria, Norway, and Sweden could tip the balance.

The two successive enlargements have certainly contributed to the social and economic heterogeneity of the Community, making it increasingly difficult for class, sectoral, and professional associations at that level to adopt common policies. Labor in the poorer, low-wage countries of southern Europe may not see much advantage in the harmonization of welfare policies; capitalists in the small and medium-size firms that predominate in these regions may not have that much in common with the big-business of northern Europe. Needless to say, if enlargement were to continue and were to include not only the wealthy countries of the European Free Trade Association but also the recently marketized and markedly less efficient economies of Eastern Europe, it is hard to imagine what the basis of effective, systemwide, interest aggregation could be. The likely outcome would be a further decline in the role of encompassing peak associations and a proliferation of specialized and autonomous organizations, crosscut by region, level of development, and size of firm.

Faced with the imperative of restructuring declining industries in the 1970s and early 1980s and, more recently, with the need for programs for improving international competitiveness in advancing industries, the Commission has found it necessary to deal in more direct and differentiated ways with its "policy takers." At first, this brought it into contact with specific sectors—hence, the shift toward more specialized trade associations with direct membership noted during that period. The new programs for promoting cooperative research and development, such as ESPRIT, BRITE, CRAFT, EUREKA, JESSI, and RACE, and the new responsibilities for regulating competition and distributing regional funds now bring the Eurocrats increasingly face to face with individual firms. In this context, interest associations can lose their most precious political commodity—the capacity to monopolize the transaction space between clients and authorities.

One sign that this has already occurred is the virtual invasion of Brussels by representatives from the government relations departments of major European and American corporations, and by European and American law firms. This has created a quite different atmosphere of informal and multilayered exchanges, of "lobbying," to use the American expression, with the more formal and collective representations of interest associations playing a less pivotal role. All that is missing to make this truly resemble the United States is the political action committees (PACs), which have heretofore been absent from European politics. The closest equivalent is the European Round Table of Industrialists, consciously modeled on the Business Round Table of American fame. It is composed of some forty chief executive officers of leading European firms—not all of whom are in the European Community. Already credited with playing a major role in initiating the internal market proposal in 1985, it has since intervened with short position papers and direct personal exchanges with commissioners or ministers on a wide range of issues.

The Community has always had a complex and multilayered decision-making structure. With the Luxembourg compromise of 1966, authority came to be concentrated at the level of the Council of Ministers and this gave privileged access to national interest representatives—especially to those that wished to block new measures. With the Single European Act, this bottleneck has been enlarged (but has not been broken) with qualified majority voting on most issues. Even one of the larger members can no longer hold up approval, unless it can find two or more allies among the smaller countries. The Commission has kept its monopoly on the formal initiation of new measures. In the past, it has been the focal point of associational activity, particularly through the recognized European peak associations. As already mentioned, the Commission now finds itself dealing with a much wider range of actors, including individual firms and subnational governments. Moreover, its most salient structural characteristic is its compartmentalization into twenty-three Directorates-General, each with its own commissioner and cabinet, and each with its own set of advisory and administrative councils.

One of the main themes in the literature on American interest politics is the way in which such a fragmented and layered decisional system provides multiple points of access and encourages a proliferation of strategies of influence. No single form of collective action—least of all one that is unitary, hierarchical, and encompassing, as in the corporatist model—can expect to predominate. Pluralism, in other words, is written into the structure of authority, as well as into the diversity of interests.

The European Community has yet to attain its definitive institutional configuration. The internal market objectives could be met in a variety of ways, including some that would concentrate a good deal of regulatory and even financial power in Brussels. The Commission could take advantage of three key policy areas—competition, the environment, and regional questions—for which it already has authority for direct implementation, and make them into the central core of a *dirigiste* Euro-state. If one relied on Delors's idea that the integration process consists of concentric circles, the new functional tasks—promoting research and development, providing aid for Eastern Europe, and monetary union and the social dimension—could all be manipulated from Brussels by reaching out to incorporate other rings of actors. If so, the outcome would come close to replicating the French or British pattern of building a unitary state around a single core area and might well lead to a revival of Euro-corporatism. If not—if direct implementation is resisted in the name of subsidiarity and the new tasks are assigned to a wide variety of European institutions with differing memberships and dispersed locations—then, the resulting configuration would look more like a Switzerland, a West Germany, or the United States—and the trend we have observed toward Euro-pluralism would be greatly reinforced.

In the words of one well-informed observer, "Brussels is getting closer to Washington than to Bonn, Paris, or London." The implications for the future of European politics could be quite substantial. As early as Andrew Shonfield's *Modern Capitalism*, it was recognized that the institutions of Europe's political economy, although they varied considerably within the region, differed from those of other advanced capitalist countries, especially the United States. The role of formal interest intermediaries in screening and diverting group preferences into broader class and sectoral channels and in subsequently governing the behavior of their members was central to this matrix. These organizations permitted, even encouraged, a distinctive mode of production and distribution of benefits. The more extreme national versions were called "organized capitalism," some form of which was expected to become the hallmark of supranational integration.

Instead, we find growing evidence of "Disorganized Capitalism" at the Community level, without the elements of official recognition, ensured access, hierarchy, and monopoly. In such a disjointed and competitive setting, interest associations are not necessarily privileged interlocutors, and higher-order peak associations may not be preferred over more specialized ones. They must compete for influence with a wide variety of other units: national states, parastatal corporations, subnational governments, large private firms, and even lobbyists and lawyers intervening on behalf of individual clients. The policy outcomes become less predictable, and majorities become more difficult to mobilize. The power of public coercion is blunted, but so is the capacity of the state to overcome private exploitation. Moreover, in the European Community of 1992, this trend toward supranational pluralism in both the structures of authority and the associations of interest can advance unchecked by powerful mechanisms of territorial representation and electoral accountability. Here, at long last, the bourgeoisie may have found the executive committee for managing its common affairs that it lost (or never had) at the level of the national state.

18   1992: Recasting the European Bargain

WAYNE SANDHOLTZ AND JOHN ZYSMAN

The adoption of the White Paper on Completing the Internal Market (1985) and the passage of the Single European Act (1986) revitalized the European Community and marked a new stage in the European integration process. The new enthusiasm in the Community awoke grand integration theory from a long slumber as scholars—some new, some veterans of former debates—attempted once again to explain what was happening in Europe. They initially focused their attention on the decision to create a single market and to revise the Treaty of Rome to expedite the process. Ultimately, they were trying to explain why, after years of stagnation, the integration process was suddenly moving forward again. These scholars drew on neofunctionalism and a number of other approaches derived from international relations and EC decisionmaking to provide answers to their theoretical questions.

Wayne Sandholtz (University of California, Irvine) and John Zysman (University of California–Berkeley) opened the theoretical debate in 1989 with an attempt to explain the "1992 process" by focusing on supranational institutions. They argue first that changes in the international structure—specifically the decline of the United States and the rise of Japan—"triggered the 1992 process." They then couple this idea with neofunctionalist and domestic politics notions to explain the timing and specific nature of the new integration process. From neofunctionalism, they draw the importance of supranational institutions (primarily the Commission) and European interest groups (organized European industrialists); from theories of domestic politics, they emphasize the importance of the domestic political context to the

Reprinted with permission from *World Politics*, 41(1)(1989):95–128. Copyright 1989 by The Johns Hopkins University Press. Notes omitted.

receptiveness of national governmental elites to initiatives from the Commission and European business. Thus in their view, recent integration is best viewed as a bargain between elites in EC institutions, European industry, and member governments, with the Commission supplying most of the policy leadership.

The focus for Sandholtz and Zysman is primarily, although not exclusively, on the actors working in the realm above the member states. For this reason, other scholars have often labeled their view supranationalist.

Under the banner of "1992," the European Communities are putting in place a series of political and business bargains that will recast, if not unify, the European market. This initiative is a disjunction, a dramatic new start, rather than the fulfillment of the original effort to construct Europe. It is not merely the culmination of the integration begun in the 1950s, the "completion" of the internal market. The removal of all barriers to the movement of persons, capital, and goods among the twelve member states (the formal goal of the 1992 process) is expected to increase economies of scale and decrease transaction costs. But these one-time economic benefits do not capture the full range of purposes and consequences of 1992. Dynamic effects will emerge in the form of restructured competition and changed expectations. Nineteen ninety-two is a vision as much as a program—a vision of Europe's place in the world. The vision is already producing a new awareness of European strengths and a seemingly sudden assertion of the will to exploit these strengths in competition with the United States and Japan. It is affecting companies as well as governments. A senior executive of Fiat recently declared, "The final goal of the European 'dream' is to transform Europe into an integrated economic continent with its specific role, weight and ability on the international scenario vis-à-vis the U.S. and Japan."

But why has this process begun, or begun again, now? In this article, we propose that changes in the international structure triggered the 1992 process. More precisely, the trigger has been a real shift in the distribution of economic power resources (crudely put, relative American decline and Japanese ascent). What is just as important is that European elites perceive that the changes in the international setting require that they rethink their roles and interests in the world. The United States is no longer the unique source of forefront technologies; in crucial electronics sectors, for example, Japanese firms lead the world. Moreover, Japanese innovations in organizing production and in manufacturing technologies mean that the United States is no longer the most attractive model of industrial development. In monetary affairs, some Europeans argue that Frankfurt and Tokyo, not Washington, are now in control. In short, shifts in relative technological, industrial, and economic capabilities are forcing Europeans to rethink their economic goals and interests as well as the means appropriate for achieving them. American coattails, they seem to have concluded, are not a safe place when the giant falters and threatens to sit down.

While economic changes have triggered the 1992 process, security issues may shape its outcomes. Europe's economic relationship with the United States has been embedded in a security bargain that is being reevaluated. This is not the first reassessment of the alliance, but it is the first time that it takes place against the backdrop of Soviet internal reform and external overtures to dismantle the symbols of the cold war. The point is that the security ties that underpinned U.S.-European economic relations are being reconsidered in Europe. But we need not look deeply into the security issues to understand the origins of the 1992 movement, though some believe that the nuclear horsetrading at Reykjavik accelerated the 1992 process. Eventually, the economic and security discussions will shape each other.

We hypothesize that structural change was a necessary, though not a sufficient, condition for the renewal of the European project. It was a trigger. Other factors were equally necessary and, in combination, sufficient. First, 1992 emerged because the institutions of the European Communities, especially the Commission, were able to exercise effective policy leadership. International structural shifts and a favorable domestic setting provided a motive and an opportunity for restarting the Communities. The Commission played the role of policy entrepreneur. The renewed drive for market unification can be explained only if theory takes into account the policy leadership of the Commission. To be sure, the Commission did not act alone; a transnational industry coalition also perceived the need for European-level action and supported the Commission's efforts. The Commission, aided by business, was able to mobilize a coalition of governmental elites that favored the overall objective of market unification. Member governments were receptive to the 1992 initiatives because of the domestic political context in the member states, which had altered in ways that made European-level, market-oriented initiatives viable. The most important elements of the domestic political setting were the failure of existing, purely national economic strategies, the decline (or transformation) of the left, and the presence of vigorously market-oriented governments on the right. Without these shifts, an EC-based response to the changing international structure would have been politically impossible.

We therefore propose to analyze 1992 in terms of elite bargains formulated in response to international structural change and the Commission's policy entrepreneurship. In the sections immediately following, we lay out an analytical framework and examine the origins of the 1992 movement and its constituent bargains.

The 1992 process has so far been limited to the Community institutions, the governments, and leaders of major companies. National parliaments, political parties, and trade unions have not yet become centrally involved. That will change. How and when the 1992 process will draw in other political actors (like labor) is one of the many uncertainties.

. . .

• EXPLAINING 1992: ALTERNATIVE APPROACHES

Analysis of the 1992 project in Western Europe could follow any one of three broad approaches, each with a different focus. One approach would look to the internal dynamics of the integration process itself, as in integration theory. A second would concentrate on the domestic politics behind the regional agreements. The third approach, for which we argue, focuses on elite bargains in response to the challenges and opportunities posed by international and domestic changes. The analysis of elite bargains incorporates the strengths of the other two approaches while avoiding their major weaknesses. Although we have no intention of elaborating three different theoretical frameworks, we will briefly describe what appear to be the chief shortcomings of the integration theory and domestic politics approaches.

Consider integration theory. Instead of a single theory, there were numerous permutations, each employing different concepts and definitions. But what distinguished integration theory from other, traditional analyses of international politics was that it assigned causal significance to the process of integration itself. Indeed, a genuine integration theory would have to posit some specific political effects stemming from the internal logic of integration. This was the contribution of neofunctionalist integration theories, which were in turn partly inspired by the functionalist theory of David Mitrany.

Integration begins when governments perceive that certain economic policy problems cannot be solved by national means alone and agree to joint policymaking in supranational institutions. Initially, therefore, experts in the supranational organization apply technical solutions to (primarily) economic problems. Integration proceeds through the "expansive logic" of spillovers. Spillovers occur when experience gained by one integrative step reveals the need for integration in functionally related areas. That is, in order to accomplish the original objectives, participants realize that they must take further integrative steps. Creating a common market, for example, might reveal the need for a regional fund to manage short-term current accounts imbalances among the members. That would constitute a spillover. In the long term, according to the formulations of Ernst Haas, as more technical functions shift to the integrated institutions, the loyalties and expectations of the populations transfer from the historical nation states to the larger supranational entity.

Haas and other scholars later modified these initial neofunctionalist conceptions. Nye noted that integration could progress by means of deliberate linkages that created "package deals." He also argued that functional links among tasks did not always lead to spillovers, but could have a negative impact on integration. Others further refined the kinds of internal dynamics of integration to include "spill-back," "spill-around," and "forward linkage." Haas recognized that spillovers could be limited by the "autonomy of functional contexts" and that integration turned out not to be the steady, incremental process originally envisioned.

For a number of reasons, we do not believe that integration theories are well suited for analyzing the 1992 movement. The major weaknesses were recognized by the integration theorists themselves; two of their criticisms are most relevant to the concerns of this paper. (1) The internal logic of integration cannot account for the stop-go nature of the European project. One possibility is that the Community attained many of its objectives, which led to "the disappearance of many of the original incentives to integrate." The question then becomes, why did the renewed drive for the single internal market emerge in the mid-1980s and why did it rapidly acquire broad support among governments and business elites? (2) Even where the Community did not meet expectations or where integration in one area pointed out problems in functionally related areas, national leaders could frequently opt for national means rather than more integration. That is, even in issue areas where the pressure for spillovers should have been strong, national means appeared sufficient and were preferred. In the 1960s, efforts to establish a common transport policy fell flat because national policies appeared adequate to interested parties. During the 1970s, the Commission's efforts on behalf of broad Community science and technology planning (the Spinelli and Dahrendorf plans) got nowhere because governments perceived science and technology as areas in which national policies could and should be pursued. The national option always stands against the EC option and frequently wins.

An explanation rooted in the domestic politics of the various

European countries is a second possible approach to explaining 1992. Certainly the shift of the socialist governments in France and Spain toward market-oriented economic policies (including privatization and deregulation) was essential for acceptance of the 1992 movement. The Thatcher government in the U.K. could also support measures that dealt primarily with reducing regulations and freeing markets. Thus, the favorable domestic political context was one of the necessary conditions that produced 1992.

But domestic politics cannot carry the full analytical burden, for three main reasons. (1) An argument based on domestic politics cannot answer the question, why now? Such an argument would have to account for the simultaneity of domestic developments that would induce states to act jointly. Attention to changes in the international context solves the problem. International changes posed challenges and choices to all the EC countries at the same time. (2) The political actors that figure in analyses of European domestic politics have not yet been mobilized in the 1992 project, though perhaps that is now beginning. Although the political parties and the trade unions now talk about 1992, they were not involved in the discussions and bargains that started the process. Governments (specifically, the national executives) and business elites initiated and defined 1992 and have moved it along. (3) An argument based on domestic politics cannot explain why domestic political change produced the 1992 movement. The project did not bubble up spontaneously from the various national political contexts. On the contrary: leadership for 1992 came from outside the national settings; it came from the Commission.

The third approach to analyzing 1992 is the one we advance in this paper. It focuses on elite bargains formed in response to changes in the international structure and in the domestic political context. The postwar order of security and economic systems founded upon American leadership is beginning to evolve after a period of relative U.S. decline and Japanese ascent. These developments have led Europeans to reconsider their relations with the United States and within the European Communities. The international and domestic situations provided a setting in which the Commission could exercise policy entrepreneurship, mobilizing a transnational coalition in favor of the unified internal market.

The 1992 movement (as well as the integration of the 1950s) can be fruitfully analyzed as a hierarchy of bargains. Political elites reach agreement on fundamental bargains embodying basic objectives; subsidiary bargains are required to implement these objectives. The fundamental bargains agreed upon for 1992 are embodied in the Single European Act and in the Commission's White Paper which outlined specific steps toward the unified internal market. The Single European Act extended majority voting in the Council and cleared the way politically for progress toward unifying the internal market. Endorsement of the Commission's proposals in the White Paper represents agreement on the fundamental objective of eliminating barriers to the movement of persons, goods, and capital. The specific measures proposed by the Commission (some 300 of them) can be thought of as implementing bargains.

. . .

The original European movement can be seen in terms of this framework. The integration movement was triggered by the wrenching structural changes brought about by World War II; after the war, Europe was no longer the center of the international system, but rather a frontier and cushion between the two new superpowers. Political entrepreneurship came initially from the group surrounding Robert Schuman and Jean Monnet. The early advocates of integration succeeded in mobilizing a transnational coalition supportive of integration; the core of that coalition eventually included the Christian Democratic parties of the original Six, plus many of the Socialist parties.

The fundamental objectives of the bargains underlying the European Coal and Steel Community (ECSC) and the expanded European Communities were primarily two: (1) the binding of German industry to the rest of Europe so as to make another war impossible, and (2) the restarting of economic growth in the region. These objectives may have been largely implicit, but they were carried out by means of a number of implementing bargains that were agreed upon over the years. The chief implementing bargains after the ECSC included the Common Market, the Common Agricultural Program, the regional development funds, and, most recently, the European Monetary System (EMS).

The fundamental external bargain made in establishing the Community was with the United States; it called for (certainly as remembered now in the U.S.) national treatment for the subsidiaries of foreign firms in the Common Market. That is, foreign (principally American) firms that set up in the Community could operate as if they were European. American policy makers saw themselves as willing to tolerate the discrimination and potential trade diversion of a united Europe because the internal bargain of the EEC would contribute to foreign policy objectives. Not only was part of Germany tied to the West, but sustained economic growth promised political stability. All of this was framed by the security ties seen as necessary on both sides of the Atlantic to counter the Soviet Union.

The European bargains—internal and external—were made at the moment of American political and economic domination. A bipolar security world and an American-directed Western economy set the context in which the European bargain appeared necessary. Many expected the original Community to generate ever more extensive integration. But the pressures for spillover were not that great. Economics could not drive political integration. The building of nation states remains a matter of political projects. Padoa-Schioppa has put it simply and well: "The cement of a political community is provided by indivisible public goods such as 'defence and security'. The cement of an economic community inevitably lies in the economic benefits it confers upon its members." The basic political objectives sought by the original internal bargain had been achieved: the threat of Germany was diminished and growth had been ignited. When problems arose from the initial integrative steps, the instruments of national policy sufficed to deal with them. Indeed, the Community could accommodate quite distinct national social, regulatory, and tax policies. National strategies for growth, development, and employment sufficed.

Several fundamental attributes of the economic community that emerged merit emphasis, as they prove important in the reignition of the European project in the mid-1980s. First, the initial effort was the product of governmental action, of intergovernmental bargains. Second, there was the partial creation of an internal market; that is a reduction, but not an elimination, of the barriers to internal exchange. The success of this initiative was suggested by the substantial increase in intra-European trade. Third, and equally important, there was toleration of national intervention; in fact, in the case of France such intervention was an element of the construction. There was an acceptance of national strategies for development and political management. Fourth, the European projects were in fact quite limited, restricted for the most part to managing retrenchment in declining industries and easing dislocations in the rural sector (and consequently managing the politics of agriculture) through the Common Agricultural Policy. There were several significant exceptions, including the European Monetary System that emerged as a Franco-German deal to cope with exchange-rate fluctuations that might threaten trade relations; however, the basic principle of national initiative persisted. Fifth, trade remained the crucial link between countries. Joint ventures and other forms of foreign direct investment to penetrate markets continued to be limited. Sixth, American multinationals were accepted, if not welcomed, in each country.

When the global context changed, the European bargains had to be adjusted for new realities. Wallace and Wessels have argued that "even if neither the EC or EFTA had been invented long before, by the mid-eighties some form of intra-European management would have had to be found to oversee the necessary economic and industrial adjustments."

- ## THE POLITICAL MEANING OF
  CHANGING ECONOMIC STRUCTURES

Changing international economic structures altered the choices and constraints facing European elites. Europe's options shifted with the changes in relative economic power resources. The relative position of the United States declined, prior to 1970, as its trade partners reconstructed themselves and developed. Gaps closed in technology, wealth, and productivity. The U.S. now has difficulty controlling its own economic environment, let alone structuring the system for others. The changed international setting is equally a story of the emergence of Japan, which has grown into the second-largest economy of the world, overtaking all of the individual European nations and even the Soviet Union. The significance of Japan's rise is frequently hidden rather than revealed by data about its growing share of world gross domestic product and its booming exports. The substantial consequences of the international changes are qualitative as well as quantitative. They alter the political as well as the economic choices for Europe. It is not a matter of trade quantities or economic well-being, though it may eventually be viewed in that way. For now, the problem is one of control and influence.

. . .

The choices for European elites in technology, money, and trade have changed. Previously, the options had centered on the United States. If Europe could not lead in technology, at least it could acquire it relatively easily from the U.S. If Europe could not structure financial rules to its liking, at least it could accommodate to American positions. If Europe was not first, it was second, and a series of individual bargains by governments and companies could suffice. However, it would be quite another matter to be third. To be dependent on Japan in monetary and technology matters, without the integrated defense and trade ties that link the Atlantic partners, was a different problem. The new international structure required new bargains.

The structural changes we have been depicting do not "cause" responses. Structural changes pose challenges and opportunities. They present choices to decision makers. Three broad options, individually or in combination, were open to the countries of the EC. First, each nation could seek its own accommodation through purely national strategies; but, for reasons we explore below, going it alone appeared increasingly unpalatable. Second, Europe could adjust to Japanese power and shift ties from the U.S. to Japan. But the Japanese option had significant counts against it: (1) there were no common security interests with Japan to undergird the sorts of relations Europe has had with the United States; and (2) Japan has so far been unwilling to exercise a vigorous leadership role in the international system. The third option was that Europe could attempt to restructure its own position to act more coherently in a changing world. The international changes did not produce 1992; they provoked a rethinking. The 1992 Project emerged because the domestic context was propitious and policy entrepreneurs fashioned an elite coalition in favor of it.

- **POLITICAL ENTREPRENEURSHIP:**
  UNDERSTANDING THE CHANGING BARGAINS

The surprisingly sudden movement by governments and companies toward a joint response does not have a clear and simple explanation. Uncertainty abounds. In a situation so open, so undefined, political science must rediscover the art of politics. The 1992 movement cannot be understood as the logical response to the situation in which actors and groups found themselves, and cannot therefore be understood through such formal tools as theories of games or collective action. Neither the payoff from nor preferences for any strategy were or are yet clear. European choices have been contingent on leadership, perception, and timing; they ought to be examined as an instance of elites constructing coalitions and institutions in support of new objectives.

This is not a story of mass movements, of pressure groups, or of legislatures. In the 1950s, the European project became a matter of party and group politics. In the 1980s, the EC institutions were not the object of debate; they were a political actor. Indeed, the Commission exercised leadership in proposing technical measures for the internal market that grabbed the attention of business and government elites, but were (in the initial stages at least) of little interest to the organs of mass politics. The governments and business elites had already been challenged by the international changes in ways that the parties and unions had not been. Some business and government leaders involved in 1992 are, in fact, trying to sidestep normal coalition politics in order to bring about domestic changes.

Consequently, any explanation of the choice of Europe and its evolution must focus on the actors—the leadership in the institutions of the European Community, in segments of the executive branch of the national governments, and in the business community (principally the heads of the largest companies)—and what they have achieved. These are the people who confronted the changes in the international environment and initiated the 1992 process. Each of these actors was indispensable, and each was involved with the actions of the others. The Community remains a bargain among governments. National governments—particularly the French—have begun to approach old problems in new ways and to make choices that are often unexpected. The Commission itself is an entrenched, self-interested advocate of further integration, so its position is no surprise. The multinationals are faced with sharply changed market conditions, and their concerns and reactions are not unexpected. The initiatives came from the EC, but they caught hold because the nature of the domestic political context had shifted. The interconnections and interactions among them will almost certainly defy an effort to assign primacy, weight, or relative influence.

In this section, we first address the domestic political context that prepared the ground for the Commission's plans. We then look at the Commission's initiatives, and finally at the role of the business elite in supporting the 1992 project.

The question is why national government policies and perspectives have altered. Why, in the decade between the mid-1970s and the mid-1980s, did European governments become open to European-level, market-oriented solutions? The answer has two parts: the failure of national strategies for economic growth and the transformation of the left in European politics. First, the traditional models of growth and economic management broke down. The old political strategies for the economy seemed to have run out. After the growth of the 1960s, the world economy entered a period of stagflation in the 1970s. As extensive industrialization reached its limits, the existing formulas for national economic development and the political bargains underpinning them had to be revised. Social critics and analysts in fact defined the crisis as the failure of established formulas to provide even plausible guides for action. It was not simply that the price of commodities rose, but that the dynamics of growth and trade changed.

Growth had been based on the shift of resources out of agriculture into industry; industrial development had been based on borrowing from abroad the most advanced technologies that could be obtained and absorbed. Suddenly, many old industrial sectors had to be closed, as in the case of shipbuilding. Others had to be transformed and reorganized, factories continuously upgraded, new machines designed and introduced, and work reorganized. The arguments that eventually emerged held that the old corporate strategies based on mass production were being forced to give way to strategies of flexibility and adaptability. Despite rising unemployment, the steady pace of improvement in productivity, coupled with the maintenance and sometimes reestablishment of a strong position in production equipment in vital sectors, suggested that Europe's often distinctive and innovative approaches to production were working. However, that was only to come toward the end of the decade. In short, during the 1970s, national executive and administrative elites found themselves facing new economic problems without adequate models for addressing them.

The 1970s were therefore the era of Europessimism. Europe seemed unable to adjust to the changed circumstances of international growth and competition after the oil shock. At first, the advanced countries stumbled, but then the United States and Japan seemed to pick themselves back up and to proceed. Japan's growth, which had originally been sustained by expansion within domestic markets, was bolstered by the competitive export orientation of major firms in consumer durables. New approaches to manufacturing created substantial advantages. In the United States, flexibility of the labor market—meaning the ability to fire workers and reduce real wages—seemed to assure jobs, albeit in services and often at lower wages, despite a deteriorating industrial position in global markets. Japan experienced productivity growth; the United States created jobs. Europe seemed to be doing neither and feared being left behind by the U.S.-Japanese competition in high technology.

For Europe, the critical domestic political issue was jobs, and the problem was said to be labor market rigidity. In some sense that was true, but the rigidities did not lie exclusively or even primarily with the workers' attitudes. They were embedded in government policy and industrial practice. In most of Western Europe, the basic postwar political bargain involved governmental responsibility for full employment and a welfare net. Consequently, many European companies had neither the flexibility of their American counterparts to fire workers or reduce wages, nor, broadly across Europe, the flexibility Japan displayed in redeploying its labor force. As unemployment rose, the old growth model built on a political settlement in each country was challenged—initially from the left by strategies of nationalization with state investment, and then from the right by strategies of deregulation with privatization. The political basis, in attitude and party coalition, for a more market-oriented approach was being put in place.

For a decade beginning with the oil shocks, the external environment for Europe was unstable, or turbulent, but its basic structure remained unchanged. While the United States was unwilling or unable to assure a system of fixed exchange rates, it remained the center of the financial system even as it changed the rules. The European Monetary System was an effort to create a zone of currency stability so that the expansion of trade inside Europe could continue. In the 1960s and 1970s, a long debate on technology gaps and the radical extension of American multinational power had not provoked joint European responses. During the 1970s, the mandate for the European Community was not altered; it was stretched to preserve its original objectives in the original context. The international economic turbulence and fears of a relative decline in competitive position did not provoke a full-blown European response. The extent of the shifts in relative economic power was not yet apparent. National strategies in many arenas had not yet failed, or at least were not yet perceived as having failed. In other arenas, the challenges could be dealt with by accommodations within the realm of domestic politics.

The question remains: Why did national policy change, why did the perceptions of choice evolve, the range of options shift? Policy failure must be interpreted; it can be assigned many meanings. National perceptions of position are filtered through parties and bureaucracies, shaped and flavored by factions, interests, and lobbies. In 1983, the French Socialist party was divided between those led by Laurent Fabius, who concluded that pressure on the franc was a reason to reverse policy direction and to stay within the European Community, and those like Chevènement, who felt the proper choice was to withdraw from the EMS, even if that resulted in an effective weakening of the Community. The choice, to stay in the EMS, was by no means a foregone matter. The French response to the currency crisis was a political choice made in the end by the president.

Thus, the second aspect of the changed domestic political context was the shift in government coalitions in a number of EC member states. Certainly the weakening of the left in some countries and a shift from the communist to the market-socialist left in others helped to make possible a debate about market solutions (including unified European markets) to Europe's dilemma. In Latin Europe, the communist parties weakened as the era of Eurocommunism waned. Spain saw the triumph of Gonzalez's socialists, and their unexpected emergence as advocates of market-led development and entry into the Common Market. Italy experienced a weakening of the position of the communists in the complex mosaic of party positioning. In France, Mitterrand's victory displaced the communists from their primacy on the left. The first two years of the French socialist government proved crucial in turning France away from the quest for economic autonomy. After 1983, Mitterrand embraced a more market-oriented approach and became a vigorous advocate of increased European cooperation. This had the unexpected consequence of engendering independence for the state-named managers of nationalized companies. When the conservative government of Jacques Chirac adopted deregulation as a central policy approach, a second blow was dealt to the authority of the French state in industry. In Britain and Germany, the Labour and Social Democratic parties lost power as well as influence on the national debate.

Throughout Europe the corporatist temptation waned; that is, management of the macroeconomy by direct negotiations among social groups and the government no longer seemed to work. In many union and left circles an understanding grew that adaptation to market processes would be required. (As the 1992 movement progressed, unions in most countries became wary that the European "competitive imperative" might be used to justify policies that would restrict their influence and unwind their positions and gains. As a counterpoint on the right, Thatcher began to fear a bureaucratized and socialized Europe.)

In an era when deregulation—the freeing of the market—became the fad, it made intuitive sense to extend the European internal market as a response to all ailments. Moreover, some governments, or some elites within nations, can achieve purely domestic goals by using European agreements to limit or constrain national policy choices. The EMS is not only a means of stabilizing exchange rates to facilitate trade, but also a constraint on domestic politics that pushes toward more restrictive macroeconomic policies than would otherwise have been adopted. There is little doubt that the course of the social experiment in 1981 would have been different if France had not been a member of the EMS, which required formal withdrawal from commitments if a country wanted to pursue independent expansionary policies. In a different vein, some Italians use the threat of competitive pressures as a reason to reform the administration. As one Italian commentator put it, "Europe for us will be providential. . . . The French and Germans love 1992 because each thinks it can be the key country in Europe. The most we can hope for is that 1992 straightens us out."

In any case, in Europe we are watching the creation of like-minded elites and alliances that at first blush appear improbable—such as Mitterrand and Thatcher committed to some sort of European strategy. These elites are similar in political function (though not in political basis) to the cross-national Christian Democratic alliance that emerged in support of the original Community after World War II in Germany, France, and elsewhere. European-level, market-oriented solutions have become acceptable.

This was the domestic political soil into which the Commission's initiatives fell. Traditional models of economic growth appeared to have played themselves out, and the left had been transformed in such a way that socialist parties began to seek market-oriented solutions to economic ills. In this setting, the European Community provided more than the mechanisms of intergovernmental negotiation. The Eurocracy was a standing constituency and a permanent advocate of European solutions and greater unity. Proposals from the European Commission transformed this new orientation into policy, and, more importantly, into a policy perspective and direction. The Commission perceived the international structural changes and the failure of existing national strategies, and seized the initiative.

To understand how the Commission's initiatives led governments to step beyond failed national policy, let us examine the case of telematics, the economically crucial sector combining microelectronics, computers, and telecommunications. By 1980, European policy makers were beginning to realize that the national champion strategies of the past decade or so had failed to reverse the steady international decline of European telematics industries. Throughout the 1970s, each national government in Europe had sought to build up domestic firms capable of competing with the American giants. The state encouraged or engineered mergers and provided research-and-development subsidies; state procurement heavily favored the domestic firms. By 1980, none of these approaches had paid off. Europe's champions were losing market shares both in Europe and worldwide, and most of them were operating in the red. Even Europe's traditional electronics stronghold, telecommunications equipment, was showing signs of weakness: the telecommunications trade surplus was declining annually while U.S. and Japanese imports were accounting for ever larger shares of the most technologically advanced market segments.

In telematics, European collaboration emerged when the Commission, under the leadership of Etienne Davignon, struck an alliance with the twelve major electronics companies in the EC. Because of the mounting costs and complexity of R&D, rapid technological and market changes, and the convergence of hitherto separate technologies (e.g., computing and telecommunications), these twelve companies were motivated to seek interfirm partnerships. Although such partnerships were common with American firms, the possibilities within Europe had not been explored. The twelve firms designed the European Strategic Programme for Research and Development in Information Technology (ESPRIT) and then sold it to their governments. The RACE program (Research in Advanced Communications for Europe) emerged via a similar process. In short, the Community's high-technology programs of the early 1980s took shape in a setting in which previous national policies had been discredited, the Commission advanced concrete proposals, and industry lent essential support. In a sense, the telematics cases prefigure the 1992 movement and display the same configuration of political actors: the Commission, certain political leaders and specific agencies within the national governments, and senior business leaders.

The Commission again took the initiative with the publication of its "White Paper" in June 1985. The initiative should be seen as a response to the stagnation of the Community enterprise as a result of, among other things, the budget stalemates. When Jacques Delors took office as president of the European Commission in 1985, he consciously sought an undertaking, a vision, that would reignite the European idea. The notion of a single market by 1992 caught the imagination because the need for a broader Europe was perceived outside the Commission. Helen Wallace and Wolfgang Wessels suggest that if the EEC and the European Free Trade Association (EFTA) had not existed by the late 1980s, they would have had to be invented. Or, as was the case, reinvented.

The White Paper set out a program and a timetable for the completion of the fully unified internal market. The now famous set of three hundred legislative proposals to eliminate obstacles to the free functioning of the market, as well as the analyses that led up to and followed it, expressed a clear perception of Europe's position. European decline or the necessities of international competitiveness (choose your own phrasing) require—in this view—the creation of a continental market.

The White Paper's program had the political advantage of setting forth concrete steps and a deadline. The difficult political questions could be obscured by focusing on the mission and by reducing the issues to a series of apparently technical steps. Advocates of market unification could emphasize highly specific, concrete, seemingly innocuous, and long overdue objectives rather than their consequences. In a sense, the tactic is to move above and below the level of controversy. The broad mission is agreed to; the technical steps are unobjectionable. Of course, there is a middle ground where the questions of the precise form of Europe, the allocation of gain and pain in the process, become evident. A small change in, say, health and safety rules may appear unimportant, but may prove to be the shelter behind which a national firm is hiding from European and global competitors. Here we find the disputes about outcomes, both in terms of market results and of social values. Obscuring the issues and interests was crucial in developing Europe the first time, one might note, and has been instrumental once again.

Implementation of the White Paper required a separate initiative: the limitation, expressed in the Single European Act, of national vetoes over Community decisions. At its core, the Community has always been a mechanism for governments to bargain. It has certainly not been a nation state, and only a peculiar kind of federalism. Real decisions have been made in the Council by representatives of national governments. The Commissioners, the department heads, are drawn from a pool nominated by the governments. Broader representative institutions have played only a fictive (or, more generously, a secondary) role. Moreover, decisions taken by the Council on major issues had to be unanimous, providing each government with a veto. For this reason, it has been painfully difficult to extend the Community's authority, to change the rules of finance, or to proceed with the creation of a unified market and change the rules of business in Europe. The most reluctant state prevailed. Furthermore, domestic groups could block Community action by persuading their government to exercise their veto.

Many see the Single European Act as the most important amendment to the Treaty of Rome since the latter was adopted in 1957. This act has replaced the Luxembourg compromise (which required decisions to be taken by unanimity) with a qualified majority requirement in the case of certain measures that have as their object the establishment and functioning of the internal market. The national veto still exists in other domains, but most of the three hundred directives for 1992 can be adopted by qualified majority. As a result, disgruntled domestic interest groups have lost a source of leverage on their governments; the national veto no longer carries the clout it once did. Perhaps equally important, the Single European Act embodies a new strategy toward national standards that were an obstacle to trade within the Community. Previously, the EEC pinned its hopes on "harmonization," a process by which national governments would adopt "Euronorms" prepared by the Commission. The Single European Act instead adopts the principle affirmed in the famous Cassis de Dijon case. That principle holds that standards (for foodstuffs, safety, health, and so on) that prevail in one country must be recognized by the others as sufficient.

The third actor in the story, besides the governments and the Commission, is the leadership of the European multinational corporations. In a number of ways, they have experienced most directly some of the consequences of the international economic changes. They have acted both politically and in the market. The White Paper and the Single European Act gave the appearance that changes in the EC market were irreversible and politically unstoppable. Businesses have been acting on that belief. Politically, they have taken up the banner of 1992, collaborating with the Commission and exerting substantial influence on their governments. The significance of the role of business, and of its collaboration with the Commission, must not be underestimated. European business and the Commission may be said to have together bypassed national governmental processes and shaped an agenda that compelled attention and action.

Substantial support for the Commission's initiatives has come from the Roundtable of European Industrialists, an association of some of Europe's largest and most influential corporations, including Philips, Siemens, Olivetti, GEC, Daimler Benz, Volvo, Fiat, Bosch, ASEA and Ciba-Geigy. Indeed, when Jacques Delors, prior to assuming the presidency of the Commission in 1985, began campaigning for the unified internal market, European industrialists were ahead of him. Wisse Dekker of Philips and Jacques Solvay of Belgium's Solvay chemical company in particular were vigorously arguing for unification of the EC's fragmented markets. In the early 1980s, a booklet published by Philips proposed urgent action on the internal market. "There is really no choice," it argued, "and the only option left for the Community is to achieve the goals laid down in the Treaty of Rome. Only in this way can industry compete globally, by exploiting economies of scale, for what will then be the biggest home market in the world today: *the European Community home market.*"

It is hard, though, to judge whether the business community influenced Europe to pursue an internal market strategy or was itself constituted as a political interest group by Community action. Business began to organize in 1983, when the Roundtable of European Industrialists was formed under the chairmanship of Pehr Gyllenhammer, of Volvo. Many of the original business discussions included senior Community bureaucrats; in fact, Etienne Davignon reportedly recruited most of the members of the original group. The executives constituting the Roundtable (numbering 29 by mid-1987) were among the most powerful industrialists in Europe, including the non-EEC countries. The group initially published three reports: one on the need for development of a Europe-wide traffic infrastructure, one containing proposals for Europe's unemployment crisis, and one, *Changing Scales,* describing the economies of scale that would benefit European businesses in a truly unified market.

The European Roundtable became a powerful lobby vis-à-vis the national governments. One member of the Delors cabinet in Brussels has declared, "These men are very powerful and dynamic... when necessary they can ring up their own prime ministers and make their case." Delors himself has said, "We count on business leaders for support." Local and regional chambers of commerce have helped to establish about fifty European Information Centers to handle queries and publicize 1992. In short, the 1992 process is repeating the pattern established by ESPRIT: major businesses have allied with the Commission to persuade governments, which were already seeking to adapt to the changed international structure.

At the same time that the business community has supported the political initiatives behind the 1992 movement, it has been acting in the market place. A series of business deals, ventures, and mergers form a critical part of the 1992 movement. Even if nothing more happens in the 1992 process, the face of business competition in Europe is being changed. The structure of competition is being altered.

There has been a huge surge in joint ventures, share-swapping, and mergers in Europe. Many are justified on the grounds of preparing for a unified market, some for reasons of production and marketing strategies, and some as a means of defense against takeovers. But much of the movement is a response to business problems that would exist in any case. Still, the process has taken on a life of its own. The mergers provoke responses in the form of other business alliances; the responding alliances appear more urgent because of the political rhetoric. As the Europeans join together, American and Japanese firms scurry to put their own alliances in place and to rearrange their activities.

The meaning of the process is far from evident. Are we watching the creation of European competition, or the cartelization of industry at a European level? In some sectors, such as textiles and apparel, there already is an effective European market. In others, such as telecommunications, the terms of competition—whatever the corporate reshufflings—will turn on government regulation and choice. Since U.S. firms are already entrenched, the real newcomers are the Japanese. A surge of Japanese investment is taking place in Europe.

. . .

• CONCLUSION

Europe is throwing the dice. It is confronted with a change in the structure of the international economy, with emerging Japanese and dwindling American power and position. It feels the shift in Asian competitive pressure in industry and finance. The problems are no longer those of American production in Europe, but of Japanese imports and production displacing European production. More importantly perhaps, Europe also feels the shift in rising Japanese influence in the monetary and technology domains. The industrial and governmental presumptions and deals with which Europe has operated are changing or will change. Indeed, Europeans may have to construct a coherent political presence on the global stage in order to achieve the most attractive accommodation to the new order.

We hypothesize that change in the international economic structure was necessary for the revival of the European project. A full-fledged test of this proposition will require detailed analysis of the perceptions and beliefs of those who participated in launching the 1992 movement. We have mentioned other analytical approaches—based on integration theory and domestic politics—that appear logically unsuited to explaining 1992. Of course, these approaches are not really alternatives. There are functional links among some of the bargains being struck, and domestic factors clearly shaped governmental responses to the international changes. But tests of alternative explanations often create a false sense of scientism by setting individually weak explanations against each other and finding "confirmation" by denying the worst of them. Competing explanations often represent different types of explanation, different levels of analysis. In the end, it is not a matter of which one is better, but of whether the right questions are being asked. This article is an effort to frame the proper questions and propose analytical links among them.

We argue that structural situations create the context of choice and cast up problems to be resolved, but they do not dictate the decisions and strategies. In other words, the global setting can be understood in neorealist terms, but the political processes triggered by changes in the system must be analyzed in other than structural terms. The choices result from political processes and have political explanations. In this case, the process is one of bargains among nations and elites within the region. The political process for implementing these bargains is labeled "Europe 1992," a complex web of intergovernmental bargains and accommodations among the various national business elites.

In this essay, we showed why 1992 has so far been a project of elites. The commitment of the governments to the process, the fundamental bargain, is expressed by the end of the single-nation veto system, which changed the logic of Community decisionmaking. Europe's states have thrown themselves into the drive for a unified market, unleashing business processes that in themselves are recasting the terms of competition within Europe. The terms of the final bargains are open.

The effort to reshape the European Communities has so far been guided by three groups: Community institutions, industrial elites, and governments. The Commission proposes and persuades. Important business coalitions exercise indispensable influence on governments. Governments are receptive because of changes in the world economy and shifts in the domestic political context. The domestic context has changed in two key ways: (1) with the failure of traditional models of growth and purely national strategies for economic management; and (2) with the defeat of the left in some countries, and with its transformation because of the weakening of communist parties in others. These changes opened the way for an unlikely set of elite alliances. In this context, EC initiatives began to demonstrate that there were joint

European alternatives to failed national strategies. The telematics programs were one precursor. Delors built on the budding sense of optimism and gave energy and leadership to the notion of a genuine single market. Whether a broader range of political groups will become involved is an open issue, one that may determine both whether the process continues and what form it takes.

The outcomes are quite unknowable, dependent on the timing and dynamics of a long series of contingent decisions. But the story, and consequently the analysis, concerns political leadership in creating a common European interest and then constructing a set of bargains that embody that understanding. Many of the choices are simply calculated risks, or perhaps explorations that will be entrenched if they work and refashioned if they don't. Even if we could predict the outcomes of any single choice with a high degree of confidence, the sequencing of diverse decisions and their cumulative effects would be impossible to foresee. It would be ironic if 1992 succeeded formally but economic rejuvenation did not follow. In any case, Europe's choices—particularly the possibility of a coherent Western Europe emerging as an actor on the global stage—will powerfully influence the world economic system, and perhaps the security system as well.

19 Negotiating the Single European Act: National Interests and Conventional Statecraft in the European Community

Andrew Moravcsik

Sandholtz and Zysman (Chapter 18) argued that supranational actors played a major role in relaunching Europe. Neofunctionalism was suddenly back in style among many students of the European Community, who now saw spillover everywhere. Realists, who assume that nation states operating in an anarchic (or near-anarchic) world are still the most important international actors, eventually reacted to the emphasis on supranational institutions and processes with their own explanation of recent events in Europe.

Andrew Moravcsik (Harvard University, Cambridge, Massachusetts), in a widely read article, offers a realist challenge to Sandholtz and Zysman's explanation of the 1992 process. He argues that the "supranational institutionalism" of Sandholtz and Zysman cannot, in fact, account for the "negotiating history" of the Single European Act (SEA). EC institutions, transnational business groups, and international political leaders simply were not as important to the passage of the SEA as the supranationalists claimed. Moravcsik argues instead that the SEA was the result of bargaining among the heads of government of the three most powerful EC countries: Britain, France,

Reprinted from *International Organization* 45(1)(1991):651–688 by permission of The MIT Press. Copyright 1991 by the World Peace Foundation and the Massachusetts Institute of Technology. Notes omitted.

and Germany; that these bargains represented the lowest common denominator; and that each leader jealously protected national sovereignty. Understanding the positions taken by the important states in the negotiations, according to Moravcsik, requires an investigation of the domestic sources of EC policy (see Chapter 15). In this article, he outlines several possible avenues of investigation, but he does not come to a definitive conclusion as to which explanation of domestic policies works best.

The European Community (EC) is experiencing its most important period of reform since the completion of the Common Market in 1968. This new impulse toward European integration — the "relaunching" of Europe, the French call it — was unexpected. The late 1970s and early 1980s were periods of "Europessimism" and "Eurosclerosis," when politicians and academics alike lost faith in European institutions. The current period is one of optimism and institutional momentum. The source of this transformation was the Single European Act (SEA), a document approved by European heads of government in 1986.

The SEA links liberalization of the European market with procedural reform. The first half of this reform package, incorporating 279 proposals contained in the 1985 EC Commission White Paper, aims to create "an area without internal frontiers in which the free movement of goods, persons, services, and capital is ensured." To realize this goal, European leaders committed themselves to addressing issues never successfully tackled in a multinational forum, such as the comprehensive liberalization of trade in services and the removal of domestic regulations that act as nontariff barriers. Previous attempts to set detailed and uniform European standards for domestic regulations ("harmonization") had proven time-consuming and fruitless. With this in mind, the White Paper called for a "new approach" based on "mutual recognition"—a less invasive form of liberalization whereby only minimal standards would be harmonized.

The second half of the SEA reform package consists of procedural reforms designed to streamline decisionmaking in the governing body of the EC, the Council of Ministers. Since January 1966, qualified majority voting had been limited in practice by the "Luxembourg compromise," in which France unilaterally asserted the right to veto a proposal in the Council of Ministers by declaring that a "vital" or "very important" interest was at stake. The SEA expands the use of qualified majority voting in the Council of Ministers, although only on matters pertaining to the internal market.

What accounts for the timing and the content of the reform

package that relaunched Europe? Why did this reform succeed when so many previous efforts had failed?

The findings [of this paper] challenge the prominent view that institutional reform resulted from an elite alliance between EC officials and pan-European business interest groups. The negotiating history is more consistent with the alternative explanation that EC reform rested on interstate bargains between Britain, France, and Germany. An essential precondition for reform was the convergence of the economic policy prescriptions of ruling party coalitions in these countries following the election of the British Conservative party in 1979 and the reversal of French Socialist party policy in 1983. Also essential was the negotiating leverage that France and Germany gained by exploiting the threat of creating a "two-track" Europe and excluding Britain from it. This "intergovernmental institutionalist" explanation is more consistent with what Robert Keohane calls the "modified structural realist" view of regime change, a view that stresses traditional conceptions of national interests and power, than it is with supranational variants of neofunctionalist integration theory. For the source of state interests, however, scholars must turn away from structural theories and toward domestic politics, where the existence of several competing explanations invite further research.

• EXPLANATIONS FOR THE SUCCESS OF THE SEA

Journalistic reportage, academic analysis, and interviews with European officials reveal a bewilderingly wide range of explanations, some contradictory, for the timing, content, and process of adopting the White Paper and the SEA. One French official I interviewed in Brussels quipped, "When the little boy turns out well, everyone claims paternity!" The various accounts cluster around two stylized explanations, the first stressing the independent activism of international or transnational actors and the second emphasizing bargaining between leaders of the most powerful states of Europe.

○ Supranational Institutionalism

Three supranational factors consistently recur in accounts of EC reform: pressure from EC institutions, particularly the Parliament and Court; lobbying by transnational business interest groups; and the political entrepreneurship of the Commission, led by President Jacques Delors and Internal Market Commissioner Lord Arthur Cockfield. Together these supranational factors offer an account of reform guided by actors and institutions acting "above" the nation state.

European institutions. Between 1980 and 1985, pressure for reform grew within the EC institutions. In the European Parliament, resolutions and reports supported the programs of two groups, one "maximalist" and the other "minimalist" in approach. The first group, which included many Italians and quite a number of Germans, advocated European federalism and a broad expansion in the scope of EC activities, backed by procedural reforms focusing particularly on increasing the power of the Parliament. Following the Europarliamentary penchant for animal names, these activists called themselves the "Crocodile Group," after the Strasbourg restaurant where they first met. Led by the venerable Altiero Spinelli, a founding father of the EC, their efforts culminated in the European Parliament resolution of February 1984 proposing a "Draft Treaty Establishing the European Union"—a new, more ambitious document to replace the Treaty of Rome.

The second group, founded in 1981 and consisting of Parliament members who were skeptical of federalism and parliamentary reform, focused on working with national leaders to liberalize the internal market. These activists called themselves the "Kangaroo Group," based on the Australian marsupial's ability to "hop over borders." Their efforts were funded by sympathetic business interests (primarily British and Dutch), and they counted Basil de Ferranti, a leading British industrialist and Tory parliamentarian, among their leaders. The Kangaroos encouraged parliamentary studies on economic topics and in 1983 launched a public campaign in favor of a detailed EC timetable for abolishing administrative, technical, and fiscal barriers, a reference to which was included in the draft treaty.

Transnational business interest groups. According to Wisse Dekker, chief executive officer of Philips, European integration in the 1950s was initiated by politicians, while in its current "industrial" phase it is initiated by business leaders. The evidence presented to date by partisans of this view stresses the actions of pan-European business interest groups. The Commission has long sought to encourage the development of a sort of pan-European corporatist network by granting these groups privileged access to the policy process, though this effort has met with little success.

In the mid-1980s, business interest groups, at times working together with EC officials, hoped to bolster the competitiveness of European firms by calling for a more liberal EC market. Viscount Etienne Davignon, the internal market commissioner from 1976 through 1984, brought together a group of large European information technology firms in 1981 to form the Thorn-Davignon Commission, which developed proposals for technology programs and European technical norms and reportedly also discussed market liberalization. In 1983, Pehr Gyllenhammer, the chief executive officer of Volvo, and Wisse Dekker helped found the Roundtable of European Industrialists, made up of the heads of a number of Europe's largest multinational corporations, some of whom were selected on Davignon's suggestion. Once the SEA was adopted, the Roundtable formed a "watchdog" committee to press for its implementation. In February 1984, the Union des Confederations de l'Industrie et des Employeurs d'Europe (UNICE), the leading EC industrial interest group, called for majority voting, and it has been active since then in promoting market liberalization.

In a series of speeches delivered in the autumn of 1984 and early 1985, Dekker proposed what became the best-known business plan for market liberalization, the "Europa 1990" plan. Its focus on internal market liberalization, its division of the task into categories (reform of fiscal, commercial, technical, and government procurement policies), its ideology of economies of scale, its recognition of the link between commercial liberalization and tax harmonization, its identification of the ultimate goal with a certain date, and many of its other details were echoed in Delors' proposal to the European Parliament a few months later and in the White Paper of June 1985. Transnational business pressure, some have argued, was "indispensable" to the passage of the SEA.

International political leaders. The Commission has traditionally been viewed as the agenda-setting arm of the EC. When Delors was nominated for the presidency of the Commission, he immediately sought a major initiative to rejuvenate the EC. When he assumed the office in January 1985, he visited government, business, and labor leaders in each of the European capitals to discuss possible reforms. According to his account, he considered reform in three areas—the EC decisionmaking institutions, European monetary policy, and political and defense collaboration—before deciding to "return to the origins" of the EC, the construction of a single internal market. Like Jean Monnet two decades before, Delors identified the goal with a date. He aimed to render the achievement of the program irreversible by 1988 and to complete it by 1992, coeval with the duration of two four-year terms of commissioners. It is commonly argued that Delors used the institutional power of the presidency as a platform from which to forge the link between the procedural improvements proposed by Parliament and the internal market liberalization advocated by Brussels-based business groups. According to this view, he encouraged Cockfield to elaborate the internal market agenda in the White Paper and then exaggerated the sense of economic decline to secure the approval of European heads of government.

○   *Supranational Institutionalism and Neofunctionalism*

An elite alliance between transnationally organized big business groups and EC officials, led by Delors, constitutes the core of the supranational institutionalist explanation for the 1992 initiative. The explanation is theoretically coherent in that each of its elements emphasizes the autonomy and influence enjoyed by international institutions and transnational groups acting "above the state." Two leading scholars [Sandholtz and Zysman, see Chapter 18] have recently argued that the key role played by supranational actors decisively distinguishes the politics of the SEA from those of the Treaty of Rome three decades earlier: "Leadership for 1992 came from outside the national settings. . . . It came from the Commission."

This explanation is consistent with a certain variant of neofunctionalist theory. In *The Uniting of Europe*, Ernst Haas distinguishes between processes of integration that take place at what he called the "supranational" and "national" levels. Three key elements of the supranational process are the ability of a central institution (the EC) "to assert itself in such a way as to cause strong positive or negative expectations," the tendency of "business and labor . . . to unite beyond their former national confines in an effort to make common policy," and the "demonstration by a resourceful supranational executive that ends already agreed to cannot be attained without further united steps." An examination of the role of supranational actors in initiating the SEA tests this particular variant of neofunctionalism, though not, of course, the entire model.

○   *Intergovernmental Institutionalism*

An alternative approach to explaining the success of the 1992 initiative focuses on interstate bargains between heads of government in the three largest member states of the EC. This approach, which can be called "intergovernmental institutionalism," stresses the central importance of power and interests, with the latter not simply dictated by position in the international system. Intergovernmental institutionalism is based on three principles: intergovernmentalism, lowest-common-denominator bargaining, and strict limits on future transfers of sovereignty.

Intergovernmentalism. From its inception, the EC has been based on interstate bargains between its leading member states. Heads of government, backed by a small group of ministers and advisers, initiate and negotiate major initiatives in the Council of Ministers or the European Council. Each government views the EC through the lens of its own policy preferences; EC politics is the continuation of domestic policies by other means. Even when societal interests are transnational, the principal form of their political expression remains national.

Lowest-common-denominator bargaining. Without a "European hegemon" capable of providing universal incentives or threats to promote regime formation and without the widespread use of linkages and logrolling, the bargains struck in the EC reflect the relative power positions of the member states. Small states can be bought off with side-payments, but larger states exercise a *de facto* veto over fundamental changes in the scope or rules of the core element of the EC, which remains economic liberalization. Thus, bargaining tends to converge toward the lowest common denominator of large state interests. The bargains initially consisted of bilateral agreements between France and Germany; now they consist of trilateral agreements including Britain.

The only tool that can impel a state to accept an outcome on a major issue that it does not prefer to the status quo is the threat of exclusion. Once an international institution has been created, exclusion can be expensive both because the nonmember forfeits input into further decisionmaking and because it forgoes whatever benefits result. If two major states can isolate the third and credibly threaten it with exclusion and if such exclusion undermines the substantive interests of the excluded state, the coercive threat may bring about an agreement at a level of integration above the lowest common denominator.

Protection of sovereignty. The decision to join a regime involves some sacrifice of national sovereignty in exchange for certain advantages. Policymakers safeguard their countries against the future erosion of sovereignty by demanding the unanimous consent of regime members to sovereignty-related reforms. They also avoid granting open-ended authority to central institutions that might infringe on their sovereignty, preferring instead to work through intergovernmental institutions such as the Council of Ministers, rather than through supranational bodies such as the Commission and Parliament.

o   *Intergovernmental Institutionalism
      and Modified Structural Realism*

Convergent national interests, interstate bargains, and constraints on further reform constitute the intergovernmental institutionalist explanation for the SEA. This explanation is theoretically coherent in that it stresses the autonomy and influence of national leaders vis-à-vis international institutions as well as the importance of power resources in determining the outcomes of intergovernmental bargains.

Intergovernmental institutionalism affirms the realist foundations of what Keohane calls the "modified structural realist" explanation of regime formation and maintenance. States are the principal actors in the international system. Interstate bargains reflect national interests and relative power. International regimes shape interstate politics by providing a common framework that reduces the uncertainty and transaction costs of interstate interactions. In the postwar system, Keohane argues, regimes have preserved established patterns of cooperation after the relative decline of the United States. Similarly, the EC regime, though neither created nor maintained by a hegemon, fixes interstate bargains until the major European powers choose to negotiate changes.

The emphasis of intergovernmental institutionalism differs decisively from that of modified structural realism, however, in that it locates the sources of regime reform not only in the changing power distribution but also in the changing interests of states. States are not "black boxes"; they are entities entrusted to governments, which themselves are responsible to domestic constituencies. State interests change over time, often in ways which are decisive for the integration process but which cannot be traced to shifts in the relative power of states.

• NATIONAL INTERESTS AND 1992

The intergovernmental approach suggests that an analysis of the 1992 initiative must begin by examining the underlying preferences of Germany, France, and Britain. As indicated above, Delors identified four issue-areas that might have served as the vehicle for major EC reform: monetary coordination, political and defense cooperation, institutional reform, and internal market liberalization. A glance at the national preferences for monetary coordination and for political and defense cooperation suggests that there was little possibility of a formal agreement, since in both cases France was opposed by Britain and Germany. Procedural reform in the EC decisionmaking institutions and liberalization of the internal market offered more promise and later became the two components of the 1992 initiative.

○ Germany: Consistent Support

Among the three largest member states of the EC, Germany has enjoyed since the late 1950s the least partisan opposition to further European integration. As Europe's leading exporter, dependent on the EC for nearly half its exports, Germany profits directly from economic integration. German Foreign Minister Hans-Dietrich Genscher, leader of the Free Democrats, has also been a strong supporter of European political cooperation, which he views as a vital complement to *Ostpolitik*. Moreover, a greater role for the European Parliament is widely viewed as a desirable step toward political union. On the other hand, in the mid-1980s, Germany was suspicious of proposals for a European defense organization, was ambivalent about altering the agricultural policy so it would pay more or receive less, and was opposed to further monetary integration, at least until capital flows were liberalized.

○ *France: The Road to Damascus*

Although traditionally pro-European, the French Socialist party all but ignored the EC during the first few years of the Mitterrand presidency. France did call for more qualified majority voting and, to the surprise of many, supported a majority vote to override the threatened British veto of the cereal price package in May 1982. But substantive disagreements undermined Franco-German cooperation for EC reform. The most important French initiatives of this period, one in October 1981 on *un espace social européen* and another in the autumn of 1983 on *un espace industriel européen*, did not amount to much. The first initiative, which was an antiunemployment program of fiscal stimulation billed as the initial step toward a "socialist Europe," found few friends in either Bonn or London and was never discussed at the Council. The second offered support for technology policies already in the process of adoption by the EC.

France's role as a European outsider during this period reflected its unorthodox domestic economic policies, which ran counter to the more conservative policies of Germany and Britain. Until 1983, French economic policy was conceived by the more radical wing of the Socialist party, led by politicians such as Jean-Pierre Chevènement and Pierre Bérégovoy. Nationalization, direct intervention to increase employment, and increases in social welfare spending undermined international business and financial confidence in the French economy. By March 1983, the French government had already negotiated two devaluations of the franc within the European Monetary System (EMS) and was rapidly heading for a third. The governments of other European states, particularly Germany, made it clear that a continuation of expansive policies was incompatible with continued membership in the EMS.

Many Socialists urged Mitterrand to move toward autarky—import protection, capital controls, and repudiation of the EMS—to protect expansionist domestic policies. Others in the moderate wing of the Socialist party, represented by politicians Michel Rocard and Jacques Delors and backed nearly unanimously by the French economic technocracy, advocated continued EMS membership, external free trade, and an austerity policy consisting of wage restraint and cuts in public expenditures. Some moderates also realized that the economic fundamentals underlying traditional French support for the Common Agricultural Policy (CAP) were shifting. Although domestic politics dictated that the government not move too quickly against agricultural interests, France was no longer a large net beneficiary from the EC budget, and its prospects after the entry of Spain and Portugal were even bleaker.

Mitterrand's decision to remain in the EMS, announced on 21 March 1983, marked a turning point not only in French domestic politics but also in French policy toward the EC. While the EMS decision may have been influenced in part by an independent desire to remain "European," other factors included the failure of the autarkic policies, which would ultimately have compelled the French government to impose as much austerity as the policy they chose, and the decline of the Communist party, which allowed Mitterrand to align himself with moderate Socialists. French economic decisionmaking was thus vested in the hands of Rocard, Delors, and other politicians convinced of the virtues of conservative economic policies and firm in their belief that France must work within Europe to achieve its economic goals.

With the advent in January 1984 of the French presidency in the Council of Ministers and with elections to the European Parliament just two months away, Mitterrand—true to the European idealism he had espoused since the 1940s but undoubtedly also conscious of the political advantage to be gained by making a virtue out of necessity—announced a major diplomatic initiative for a relaunching of Europe. From that point on, Mitterrand played a decisive role in settling European disputes. French leadership and concessions helped resolve British agricultural and budget complaints. French negotiators began to support internal market liberalization and collaborative research and development. Mitterrand began to adopt the rhetoric of European federalism. He spoke of reconsidering the Luxembourg compromise and supporting procedural reform, as long as it was limited to the Council and the Commission and did not imply a radical democratization of EC politics. Although committed to using the EC to combat economic decline, the French government remained uncertain whether monetary policy, internal market liberalization, or cooperative research and development should be the heart of the new initiative. Thus, Mitterrand, without being entirely sure where the initiative was leading, became the primary spokesman for relaunching Europe. One senior French diplomat observed dryly, "Monsieur Mitterrand's term as president of the European Council has become his road to Damascus."

○   *Britain: The Road to Milan*

With France converted to the European cause, Britain remained the major obstacle to an initiative linking internal market liberalization and procedural reform. Britain's entry into the EC in 1973 had expanded the Community without strengthening it. Insofar as Thatcher was pro-European, it was largely because she saw the EC almost exclusively as an organization for promoting economic liberalism in the industrial and service sectors. By British standards, however, this represented a considerable commitment, since the opposition Labour party was against market liberalization and against European integration. Having abolished exchange controls in 1979, having begun liberalization of telecommunications services in 1981, having publicly promised to lower European air fares, and, last but not least, being fully aware that the city of London contained highly competitive banking and insurance sectors, Thatcher began to call for pan-European deregulation of services. The British government also favored strengthening European political cooperation, although without creating an independent bureaucracy.

In the early 1980s, the most important British objection to EC policy stemmed from the heavy British deficit under the CAP. With its small, efficient agricultural sector concentrated in areas not generously subsidized by the CAP (for example, in sheep husbandry), Britain gained little from the agricultural programs that comprise 70 percent of the EC budget. At the same time, Britain was by far the largest per capita net contributor to the budget. Thatcher campaigned to get "her money back" from the EC, and her frugality bolstered British opposition to the budgetary policy. When she was elected to office, she insisted that two-thirds of the British deficit over the past few years be rebated and that permanent adjustments be made to limit agricultural spending and to prevent future budgetary disequilibria.

More was at stake in the British objections than temporary budgetary imbalances. In 1973, Britain had been forced to accept the agricultural and budgetary policies as part of the *acquis communautaire*, the corpus of existing EC institutions. For those who had worked for decades in the Community and who saw the CAP as part of the initial Franco-German bargain at the heart of the EC, the British demand called into question the very foundation of European cooperation. French Foreign Minister Claude Cheysson declared in 1982 that "the United

Kingdom [seeks] *juste retour,* which is not a Community idea. We and the British are not speaking of the same community."

The Thatcher government, even more than previous British governments, was wary of attempts to strengthen the Commission and Parliament and to expand EC competence into areas not directly connected with trade, such as indirect taxation and social legislation. Thatcher also firmly opposed format changes in Council procedures, in part because of a suspicion of written constitutions, a suspicion shared by most British conservatives. Although she was opposed to any treaty changes that undermined the sovereign prerogatives recognized by the Luxembourg compromise, she recognized the need for some movement away from unanimous decisionmaking and thus favored informal means of encouraging majority voting.

. . .

- **INTERPRETING THE NEGOTIATIONS**

○ *Assessing Supranational Institutionalism*

The historical record does not confirm the importance of international and transnational factors. Let us consider each element in turn.

European institutions. The supranational model stresses the role of EC institutions, particularly the Parliament. Yet after Fontainebleau, government representatives, abetted by the Commission, deliberately excluded representatives of the Parliament from decisive forums. One of the Dooge Committee's first actions was to reject the Parliament's "Draft Treaty Establishing European Union" and begin negotiations with a French government draft instead. From that moment on, key decision makers ignored the maximalist agenda. National governments viewed the Parliament's proposals as too open-ended ("real reform . . . requires a treaty encompassing all Community policies and the institutions needed to implement them"), too democratic (the powers of the Parliament should be "extended to new spheres of activity"), and too automatic (the draft treaty would have gone into effect without unanimous Council approval). The Parliament members' continuous protests against the emasculation of the draft treaty and their exclusion from the "real participation" in the discussions were ignored. The fact that the member states parried parliamentary pressure with ease certainly casts doubt on the argument that the SEA was necessary to co-opt rising demands for even more thoroughgoing institutional reform. In the end, the Parliament overwhelmingly passed a resolution protesting that the

SEA "in no way represent[s] the real reform of the Community that our peoples need," but it had little alternative but to accept the *fait accompli.*

Transnational business interest groups. The internal market program, like the EC itself thirty years before, appears to have been launched independently of pressure from transnationally organized business interest groups. The Kangaroo Group in Parliament, which had close contacts with business interests, remained relatively small until after the 1992 initiative was launched and established no formal links with the Council until 1986. The activities of the Roundtable of European Industrialists focused primarily on the concerns of its non-EC European membership. Before 1985, its chief involvement was in European infrastructure projects such as the Channel tunnel. The Roundtable was based in Geneva and did not move to Brussels until 1988, when Dekker assumed its presidency.

Most transnational business lobbies got involved late. By the time Dekker delivered his oft-quoted speeches, nearly a year had passed since the beginning of the path-breaking French presidency and the discussions of the Dooge Committee were well under way. But a few business groups, such as UNICE, had been pushing vainly for liberalization for a long time. Given their persistence, what needs to be explained is why governments finally listened.

International political leaders. Cockfield's boldness and Delors' extraordinary political skill are not in question. Cockfield and Delors acted on the margins to broaden the White Paper and the SEA, and they may have contributed to the remarkable speed of decisionmaking at the intergovernmental conference. Nevertheless, the broader outlines of both documents were proposed, negotiated, and approved, often in advance of Commission initiatives, by the heads of government themselves. Indeed, the breakthrough in the relaunching of the EC had already occurred before Delors became president of the Commission. The causality of the supranational explanation is thus reversed: the selection of a prestigious politician for the presidency was merely a symptom of mounting trilateral pressure for reform. In this regard, ironically enough, Delors' actions as Finance Minister of France may have contributed more to the SEA than those as president of the Commission.

It is worth dwelling for a moment longer on the intergovernmental conference, for this is the point at which the supranational institutionalist hypotheses about Commission influence might appear most plausible. Four specific arguments can be advanced, but none suggests that supranational actors influenced the substance of the SEA. First, the remarkable speed of the conference might be attributed, at least in part, to the role of Delors and the Commission in proposing and revising the specific wording of treaty amendments. While logistical support from the Commission may indeed have hastened a final agreement, there is little evidence that it altered its substance. Second, the Commission might be credited with having quietly slipped some new EC functions, such as environmental and research and development programs, into the revised treaty. But these were functions that the EC had been handling under indirect authorization for a number of years, and there was little opposition from member states to extending a concrete mandate to cover them. Third, in late September and early October 1985, Delors dropped strong advocacy of monetary and social reform and chose to stress instead the links between internal market reform, majority voting, and the increases in structural funds needed to gain support from Ireland and the Southern countries. Delors' conciliatory move, particularly the proposal for structural funding, may have facilitated a political compromise, but his position on these issues was nonetheless closely circumscribed by the views of the major states. This is particularly true in regard to monetary policy, where Delors' elimination of monetary reform from the package resulted from the direct pressure of domestic officials. Fourth and finally, Cockfield's White Paper might be seen as a key act of agenda setting. But the White Paper was a response to a mandate from the member states expressed both in the Council, which commissioned the paper, and in the interim report of the Dooge Committee. In previous years, the Commission had proposed many of the nearly three hundred items as part of various reform proposals, but governments had simply rejected them.

Delors' most important contributions to the process resulted not from his role as an initiator of unforeseen policies but instead from his keen awareness of the extreme constraints under which he was acting. A reexamination of his memoirs reveals that his arguments (as distinct from his tone) stress intergovernmental constraints rather than personal influence. Procedural reform without a substantive program, he reasoned, would get bogged down in ideological battles over sovereignty; a plan for European monetary union would encounter the opposition of the governors of the central banks, who, led by the Germans, had just rejected an expansion of the EMS; and European defense cooperation was neither within the current competence of the EC nor widely supported among member states. The sole remaining option was internal market reform. In this regard, Delors' most statesmanlike judgments concerned the proper moment to compromise—as he did in September and October 1985.

○   *Supranational Institutionalism and Neofunctionalism*

None of the three supranational variables—European institutional momentum, transnational business interest group activity, and international political leadership—seems to account for the timing, content, and process of negotiating the SEA. Moreover, governments did not bargain by "upgrading" the common interest or by linking issues but, rather, by accepting the lowest common denominator, backed by the threat of exclusion. The resulting bargain places major obstacles in the path of attempts to extend the reform to new issues, such as monetary policy.

In this regard, one striking aspect of the negotiations for the SEA is their parallel to the negotiations for the ECSC and EC in the 1950s. Even regional integration theorists are inclined to accept that the founding of the ECSC was an extraordinary act of political statecraft, but they contend that once it occurred it sparked a qualitatively different and potentially self-sustaining process of spillover. The negotiating history of the SEA, however, suggests that three decades later the factors encouraging a greater commitment to European unity are essentially the same: the convergence of national interests, the pro-European idealism of heads of government, and the decisive role of the large member states.

The importance of interstate bargains in the SEA negotiations is consistent with the broader experience of the EC since the mid-1960s. European integration did not proceed steadily and incrementally; it proceeded in fits and starts. Moreover, since the Luxembourg compromise in 1966, the EC has moved toward intergovernmental ("state-to-state") decisionmaking centered in the Council and summit meetings, rather than toward increasing authority for international bodies such as the Commission and Parliament. One detailed study concluded that the systems change in the EC has in fact proved to be more political and less technical than Haas predicted. While spillover and forward linkages may in some cases suffice to prompt the intensification of international decisionmaking under a specific mandate within a given sector, they play a minimal role in the processes of opening new issues, reforming decisionmaking procedures, and ratifying the accession of new members. Movement in these areas requires active intervention by heads of state and a considerable amount of nontechnocratic interstate bargaining.

The SEA negotiations suggest, furthermore, that in the 1980s, just as in the 1950s, pan-European business groups were relatively ineffective at influencing policy. Business, at least on the supranational level, was mobilized by the emerging interstate consensus for reform, rather than the reverse. This casts doubt on at least one mechanism underlying the long-term historical prediction of neofunctionalism—namely, that over time, growth in the autonomy and responsibility of supranational actors and organizations will facilitate further integration.

○   *Assessing Intergovernmental Institutionalism*

The historical record confirms the importance of the three elements of intergovernmental institutionalism. Again, these elements can be considered in turn.

Intergovernmentalism. Heads of government and their direct representatives carried out the negotiations. The result represents the convergence of domestic policy preferences in the largest member states. The dominance of the three largest states is revealed most clearly by the lack of cases (with the possible exception of the Danish stand on workers' rights) in which a smaller nation either initiated or vetoed a central initiative. The Southern nations and Ireland were appeased *en masse* with the promise of a sidepayment in the form of increased structural funds; the Benelux countries had been prepared in any case to go further than the others. The election of a Conservative government in Britain and, more important, the shift in French economic policy preferences in 1983 were the key turning points on the road to 1992.

Lowest-common-denominator bargaining. The only major exception to lowest-common-denominator bargaining concerned whether to amend the Treaty of Rome to promote majority voting on internal market matters. On this point, the British yielded to Franco-German pressure to convene an intergovernmental conference, at least in part because the Franco-German position was backed by the threat of exclusion. As Paul Taylor has observed, "British diplomacy . . . had to balance two objectives: that of satisfying specific interests, and that of staying in the game. A measure of compromise in the former [became] necessary to achieve the latter." Nonetheless, given the lowest-common-denominator bargaining characteristic of systems change in the EC, it is not surprising that the British were most satisfied with the final outcome. Thatcher's success in negotiating a fundamental revision of the rules for calculating the net obligations to the EC budget can be viewed as the end of extended negotiations over the terms of British accession. While the agricultural *acquis communautaire* represented a Franco-German deal, the new agreement reflected more closely the new trilateral balance of power within the EC. The British also succeeded in limiting institutional reform to internal market issues.

Protection of sovereignty. The steady narrowing of the institutional reform to a "minimalist" position in which majority voting is restricted to internal market policy, the power of the Parliament is limited, and the future spillover to areas such as monetary policy is blocked confirms the enduring preoccupation of all three major states with maintaining sovereignty and control over future changes in the scope of EC activities.

○   *International Institutionalism and Domestic Politics*

While the intergovernmental approach, based on the relative power of member states and the convergence of their national policy preferences, offers a satisfactory account of the SEA negotiations, it raises a second, equally important question: Why did underlying national policy preferences converge at this point in time? As indicated earlier, part of the answer can be found in the domestic politics of France, Germany, and Britain. Four paradigmatic explanations can also be identified: autonomous action by political leaders, pressure from state bureaucracies, support from centrist coalitions, and pressure to replace failed economic policies. Each offers a promising starting point for analyzing the domestic roots of European integration, but none is entirely satisfactory.

Statism: The autonomy of political leaders. The convergence of policy preferences in the mid-1980s may have reflected the views, either pro-European or neoliberal, of the three major European leaders of the time — Mitterrand, Kohl, and Thatcher — and their close associates. The history of the SEA suggests that heads of government in the three largest member states possessed considerable autonomy from domestic bureaucracies, political parties, and interest groups, at least in the short run.

In 1984, Mitterrand's personal advocacy, against the opposition of the Quai d'Orsay and the left wing of his own party, gave a decisive impetus to reform efforts. Delors himself stressed the importance of Mitterrand's shuttle diplomacy, recalling that Mitterrand met six times each with Kohl and Thatcher during his 1984 Council presidency alone. The key decisions in France were made in meetings *à quatre* with Mitterrand, Dumas, Delors, and the French Minister of European Affairs.

Like Adenauer and de Gaulle before them, Kohl and Mitterrand viewed economic integration as part of a geopolitical grand strategy. In this sense, French support for the EC could not be separated from French initiatives in areas such as armaments coproduction, coordinated conventional defense, and nuclear strategy. Similarly, Kohl followed Genscher in viewing German support for the EC as an indispensable precondition for German unification within a pan-European framework.

Thatcher's role in the reform effort was as important as Mitterrand's role, though somewhat more ambivalent. Obstacles to reform stemmed from Thatcher's personal crusade to constrain European bureaucracy, particularly in the social and monetary areas, despite the more pro-European sentiments of her closest civil service advisers and a majority of her own party. On the other hand, her extreme neoliberalism lent the SEA much of its substance.

In the case of Mitterrand and Thatcher, current views toward European unification reflect positions held for decades. In the case of Cockfield, Rocard, Delors, and others, support may also reflect positive experiences working with and within EC institutions.

Bureaucratic politics: The role of technocracy. The importance of bureaucracies is suggested by the long-term evolution of European policymaking. Since 1966, when the Luxembourg compromise was accepted, the EC has institutionalized an intergovernmental style of internal decisionmaking, centered in the Council. Committees consisting of national bureaucrats, members of permanent delegations (COREPER), or ministers (the Council of Ministers) have met regularly in Brussels and interacted through an increasingly cooperative and specialized mode of decisionmaking. By the early 1980s, a clear trend had emerged away from the traditional practice of consulting foreign ministries in each European state and toward specialization of functions in the Council. While the foreign ministries tended to be suspicious of transferring or pooling sovereignty through mechanisms such as majority voting, the bureaucratic specialists have often been strong supporters of European economic integration. Thus, increased specialization may have encouraged a steady increase in majority voting, with ten decisions based on qualified majority voting between 1966 and 1974, thirty-five between 1974 and 1979, and more than ninety between 1979 and 1984. In this sense, as Helen Wallace points out, the SEA represents "a return on investments made over many previous years" in developing a set of common norms for Council negotiating.

According to the bureaucratic politics view, this evolution in EC negotiating may also have had an effect at home. That is, as technocrats have internalized norms of cooperation, the national leaders have increasingly supported European integration. At a number of points in the negotiating history of the SEA, for example, domestic bureaucracies appear to have intervened to change the views of heads of government, most notably when British officials helped convince Thatcher to join the intergovernmental conference.

Like the statist explanation, the bureaucratic politics explanation has several weaknesses. First, both overlook the evidence that changes in domestic political support facilitated or frustrated the efforts of national leaders to implement policies favoring further European integration. Neither national leaders nor bureaucracies enjoy complete autonomy. Second, both of the explanations fail to offer a plausible account of the stop-and-go process of European integration over the past twenty years. Technocratic explanations overlook evidence of the splits between bureaucracies and the strong opposition among top officials to the dilution of national sovereignty through majority voting. But despite the weaknesses of these explanations, autonomous decisionmaking by heads of state or bureaucrats should be retained as a null hypothesis in future research on the domestic roots of policy initiation in the EC.

Partisan support: The role of centrist coalitions. A more promising explanation for the convergence of national policies stresses the role of political parties. While heads of government have some autonomy in European affairs, they are constrained, in this view, by the party coalitions that support their rule. Since Europe is a low-priority issue for the voters of the three largest member states, it is implausible to posit a mechanism by which politicians launch policy initiatives to seek direct electoral advantage, except perhaps immediately before European elections. European integration thus remains an elite affair. Nonetheless, the evolution of conceptions of national interest over time and the key role of partisan splits over European policy, as demonstrated by the decisive French turnaround in 1983 and the importance of British Tory support for neoliberal policies, suggest that the autonomy of heads of government in pursuing a European policy may be constrained by elites within their domestic partisan base.

Over the years, centrist parties, particularly those of the center-right, have tended to support EC reforms, while the strongest opposition to further integration has been located on the extremes of the ideological spectrum. At the founding of the EC, Christian Democratic parties provided the core of partisan support for European integration. Over the years, Germany's center-weighted party system, which pivots on alliances with the pro-European Free Democrats, generated constant support for European integration. Since the completion of the Common Market in 1968 and Britain's accession in 1973, however, a reform package of internal market liberalization and majority voting was blocked by the presence of an anti-EC party in at least one ruling coalition. In the 1970s and early 1980s, the far left (the British Labour party, the West German Greens, the French Communist party, and the more radical French Socialists) remained suspicious of economic liberalization, while the far right (the Thatcherite wing of the British Conservative party, the Gaullists and the party of Jean-Marie Le Pen in France, and the German Republicans) opposed the dilution of national sovereignty. The SEA thus had to navigate a narrow passage between the Scylla of far left opposition to economic liberalization and the Charybdis of conservative opposition to institutional reform.

In the mid-1980s, the dominance of centrists in ruling coalitions created a rare opening for reform. The election of Thatcher and the shift to the moderate wing of the French Socialist party in early 1983 dramatically altered the political landscape. For the first time in over a decade, ruling coalitions in each of the three major states of Europe were ideologically committed to relatively liberal domestic economic policies and were also committed, in varying degrees and for diverse reasons, to liberalization of the European market. If the Labour party had held power in Britain or if either the Gaullists or the Communists had held power in France, reform would have encountered bitter opposition. The SEA still had to satisfy British complaints about agricultural policy and surmount Thatcherite opposition to institutional reform. The first obstacle was overcome by the carrot of budget reform and the second by the stick of threatened exclusion. The partisan support explanation thus accounts for the high level of international conflict over budget and institutional reform, as compared with the low level of conflict over the central substantive agenda of market liberalization. Yet this explanation nonetheless shares several weaknesses with the following explanation, as discussed below.

Economic functionalism: The role of policy failure. The convergence of policy preferences in the major European states may also have resulted from the failure of purely national strategies of economic policy, which created or legitimated pressure for coordinated liberalization at the European level. According to the statements of European leaders, the plan for market liberalization by 1992 was in part a response to the declining industrial competitiveness of Europe. In the late 1970s and early 1980s, "Eurosclerosis"—the combination of persistent high unemployment, low growth rates relative to those of other countries in the Organization for Economic Cooperation and Development (OECD), and long-term decline in international competitiveness vis-à-vis the United States and Japan in high-technology industries such as electronics and telecommunications—was widely interpreted as an indication of policy failure.

In the 1970s and early 1980s, the economic difficulties of Britain, France, and Germany could ostensibly be attributed to problems common to all OECD countries, such as disruption from the two oil shocks and the need for tight monetary policies to combat inflation. By 1982, however, French and German economic performance lagged significantly behind that of the United States and Japan. This relative failure in economic performance undermined the last excuse for slow growth. After the British experience in the mid-1970s, the German experience with internationally coordinated reflation in 1977, and the French experience with "Keynesianism in one country," reflation was no longer credible. The business-labor bargains on which corporatism and incomes policy are based were disintegrating.

Poor economic performance may have been translated into pressure for internal market liberalization through at least three distinct, though not mutually exclusive, mechanisms. The first mechanism is electoral. Although European integration itself is rarely an issue of electoral importance, leading politicians in advanced industrial democracies face a structural imperative to provide steady economic growth, on which electoral success often depends. Growth requires constant investment, which in turn is stimulated by business confidence. Internal market reform can thus be seen as a way to generate business confidence and stimulate investment by removing market barriers.

The second mechanism is ideological. With other economic policies discredited, European governments turned to new ideas, particularly the American and Japanese models of development. The idea of creating an internal market the size of the United States was one of the few untried policies. It seemed particularly attractive when tied to firm-led high-technology cooperation programs patterned on the Japanese model, such as ESPIRIT, the European Programme for High Technology Research and Development (EUREKA), and Research in Advanced Communications for Europe (RACE). Moreover, the idea of economic renewal through economies of scale and industrial flexibility underlies the 1992 initiative and reflects the new supply-side and privatization orthodoxy that was sweeping Europe during this period.

The third mechanism involves sectoral or firm-level business pressure at the domestic level. In general, as trade and investment interdependence increase, these interests grow stronger. Specifically, the more competitive a given firm or sector and hence the greater the level of net exports or foreign investment, particularly within the EC, the greater is the likelihood that the firm or sector will support internal market liberalization. Moreover, as sectors become globalized and sensitive to competition from outside the EC, particularly from the United States and Japan, liberalization may appear necessary to create the economies of scale required to compete effectively. The greater the potential for common gains vis-à-vis non-EC countries, the greater is the incentive to bear the costs of adjustments to liberalization within Europe.

This sort of sectoral logic might also be used to explain the initial bargain upon which the EC was founded. In the early years of the EC, Germany agreed to finance a disproportionate share of the budget, much of which went to France in the form of subsidies to its relatively efficient agricultural sector, in exchange for market liberalization for industrial goods, in which Germany enjoyed a comparative advantage. Today, British support would be expected from the financial and business service sectors, while German support would draw on industrial and capital-goods exporters.

The economic functionalist explanation and the partisan support explanation are both more plausible than the first two explanations set forth above. Yet anomalies plague these accounts as well. Neither a functionalist nor a partisan sectoral approach seems to explain French support for internal market liberalization. France appears to lack a natural constituency analogous to German industry or British financial services. And if the 1992 initiative was a capitalist conspiracy, Mitterrand was a most unlikely instrument. The economic functionalist approach also faces difficulties in explaining the pressure in some member states for institutional change in areas other than internal market policy. Despite these anomalies, however, the activities of interest groups and political parties should serve as a springboard for further inquiry.

Domestic analysis is a precondition for systemic analysis, not a supplement to it. The existence of significant cross-national variance in state policy preferences and diplomatic strategies invites further research into the domestic roots of European integration. Yet most theories of international cooperation, including regime theory, have neglected the problem of domestic interest formation, often electing instead to specify interests by assumption. None of this is meant to exclude theories of state interests based on international processes, such as economic and social interdependence. But at the very least, domestic politics offers a mechanism—a "transmission belt"—by which international impulses are translated into policy. Testing domestic theories of integration invariably raises many questions traditionally treated by students of comparative politics: Which domestic actors take the lead in promoting and opposing economic liberalization? Are they state or societal actors? How do they perceive their interests? How do they influence one another? What is their relation to the world economy? Future research on these questions will necessarily connect the literatures on international cooperation and state-society relations in an interdependent world economy.

- ## CONCLUSION: THE SEA IN PERSPECTIVE

Neofunctionalism remains the sole attempt to fashion a coherent and comprehensive theory of European integration. The standing of neofunctionalist theory among political scientists is a lagged function of the standing of the EC in the eyes of Europeans. When the EC stagnates, as in the 1970s, scholars speak of the obsolescence of regional integration theory; when it rebounds, as in 1985, they speak of the obsolescence of the nation state. Regional integration theory, we read today, has been "unjustly consigned to the dustbin."

This article challenges the notion, implicit in these statements, that progress in the EC necessarily supports all the claims of neofunctionalists. It does so by testing and rejecting a particular variant of neofunctionalism, supranational institutionalism, which rests on the argument that international institutions and transnational interest groups play a vital and increasing role as integration progresses. The approach proposed here, intergovernmental institutionalism, accords an important role to supranational institutions in cementing existing interstate bargains as the foundation for renewed integration. But it also affirms that the primary source of integration lies in the interests of the states themselves and the relative power each brings to Brussels. Perhaps most important, the intergovernmental approach demonstrates that even this explanation is incomplete, thus clearing the ground for further research into the international implications of European domestic politics.

PART ④

Integrating the Theories

20 Institutional Change in Europe in the 1980s

ROBERT O. KEOHANE AND STANLEY HOFFMANN

The debate between "supranationalists" (Chapter 18) and "intergovern-mentalists" (Chapter 19) over why the European Community revived in the 1980s was more apparent than real. Although both positions were rooted in different approaches to international relations, they were not at all irreconcilable. If viewed not as competing models, but as different levels of analysis, supranationalist and intergovernmentalist perspectives could be combined to offer a more complete picture of the dynamics of European integration. The syntheses that are now emerging in the 1990s may not be as elegant as more abstract theories, such as neofunctionalism, but they are less likely to become disconnected from reality, for, in fact, they are theories that have emerged from the practice of EC decisionmaking.

Robert Keohane and Stanley Hoffmann (both of Harvard University, Cambridge, Massachusetts), writing as negotiations leading to the signing of the Maastricht treaty commenced, look back on the surprising relaunch of Europe in the 1980s. To explain the surprise, they begin by asserting that the EC is both supranational and intergovernmental by nature. It is a complex network of relationships and overlapping authorities that operates supranationally; that is, its participants "seek to attain agreement by means of compromises upgrading common interests." It is also intergovernmental in the sense that all the "negotiation and coalition-building takes place within the context of agreements between governments." With the EC so described, Keohane and Hoffman then go on to examine three possible sources of institutional change: spillover

Reproduced from William Wallace, ed., *The Dynamics of European Integration*, 1990 by permission of Pinter Publishers Ltd., London. All rights reserved. Notes omitted.

(drawn from neofunctionalism), the international political economy (a reflection of Sandholtz and Zysman, Chapter 18), and preference-convergence (a reflection of Moravcsik, Chapter 19). They conclude that all of these explanations must be combined to understand the development of the EC in the 1980s.

Since the revolutions in Eastern Europe in 1989, the position of Europe in world politics has been transformed. No longer do Soviet troops occupy the eastern portion of a divided Germany. The limitations on German sovereignty resulting from the rights in Germany of the four occupying powers, which persisted for forty-five years, came to a formal end in September 1990. The European Community (EC) is coordinating Western aid to the incipient democracies of Czechoslovakia, Hungary, and Poland and, more cautiously to Bulgaria, Romania, and Yugoslavia. No longer is it meaningful to speak of "Western Europe" and "Eastern Europe" as distinct entities; for the first time since World War Two, "Europe" is a political as well as geographical reality.

This Europe, however, is very different from the Europe of 1938. The most important institutional difference is that in the 1990s, much European policy is made not in national capitals but in Brussels, capital of the European Community. As of 1990, the EC comprised twelve countries with a joint population of about 340 million people and a gross domestic product of over $5,000 billion. The progressive elimination of trade barriers within the Community had created the world's largest market. It also meant that between 1970 and 1989, while EC countries' exports to the rest of the world grew ten times (in nominal terms), their exports to each other grew fifteen times, so that by 1989, 60 percent of these countries' exports went to each other.

Not only have European Community rules prevailed in internal trade, its members have given up national trade policies to the Community, which has negotiated international trade rules with the United States, Japan, and other external trade partners. Furthermore, between 1984 and early 1987, EC members agreed on the Single European Act (SEA), which reformed Community decisionmaking and mandated the creation of an internal market, without internal barriers or discrimination, by the end of 1992. By fall 1990, the successful implementation of these plans for an internal market seemed all but assured, and EC members were planning to extend the Community's powers in two respects: toward economic and monetary union (EMU) and by making far-reaching constitutional changes. It was expected that these constitutional reforms, discussed at the Intergovernmental Conference (IGC) beginning in December 1990, would help to define European citizenship, strengthen security cooperation, and, in particular, expedite European decisionmaking and make it more democratically accountable.

The success of the SEA was indeed a surprise. In the years immediately before the signing of the SEA in February 1986, few observers foresaw more than halting progress, and many expected stagnation or even decay of European movement toward regional centralization of decisionmaking. In his skeptical analysis of European decisionmaking during the 1970s, published in 1983, Paul Taylor stressed the limits imposed by states on European integration, arguing that "the challenges to sovereignty were successfully resisted and the central institutions failed to obtain the qualities of supranationalism." His academic analysis echoed the cover of *The Economist* on March 20, 1982, showing a tombstone with the words, "EEC born March 25th, 1957, moribund March 25th, 1982, *capax imperii nisi imperasset*" (it seemed capable of power until it tried to wield it). Even after agreement on the Single European Act, as Albert Bressand points out, the significance of the Act was underestimated both by skeptics and by federalists. Margaret Thatcher referred to it as a "modest decision," and Altiero Spinelli predicted that it "will almost certainly have proven its ineffectiveness within two years." The *Economist* commented that "Europe has labored long to produce a mouse."

The unexpected success of European institutional change in the mid-1980s makes a more general theoretical point, which could be reinforced by the collapse of the Soviet empire in Eastern Europe in 1989. Because informed observers failed to anticipate such a centralization of Community policymaking any more than they later forecast the unification of Germany and democratization in Eastern Europe, our efforts to explain Europe's institutional dynamism should be viewed with skepticism. What was unpredicted by analysts working with established theories cannot, in general, be adequately explained *post hoc* through the use of such theories.

. . .

The central puzzle addressed in this chapter is how to account for the pooling of sovereignty and the unexpected set of institutional changes that have accompanied this process. Political scientists interested in theory development thrive on such puzzles—contradictions between what we should expect based on the conventional wisdom, or what passes for theory, and what we actually observe. During the past two decades, such contradictions have appeared between the realist state-centric view of world politics and the spread of transnational relations; and between the view that hegemony is essential to cooperation and the reality of extensive cooperation after the waning of U.S. dominance. The sudden and unexpected success of the Single European Act similarly confronts us with an analytical challenge.

. . .

• THREE PROPOSITIONS ABOUT EUROPEAN INSTITUTIONS

We begin with three propositions about the nature of the institutions of the European Community, which will form the basis for our subsequent exploration of institutional change. These propositions are largely static, although the third edges into description of processes of change. They can be summarized as follows:

1. The EC is best characterized as neither an international regime nor an emerging state but as a network involving the pooling of sovereignty.
2. The political process of the EC is well described by the term "supranationality" as used by Ernst Haas in the 1960s (although not as often used subsequently).
3. However, the EC has always rested on a set of *intergovernmental bargains*, and the Single European Act is no exception to this generalization.

○ The European Community as a Network

Like international regimes, such as the trade regime under the auspices of the General Agreement on Tariffs and Trade (GATT), the European Community establishes common expectations, provides information, and facilitates arm's-length intergovernmental negotiations. It is designed to protect its members against the consequences of uncertainty, as the formation of the European Monetary System (EMS) during a period of dollar volatility and weakness indicates. Yet the flexible and dynamic Community is much more centralized and institutionalized than an international regime and receives a much higher level of commitment from its members. It has gone well beyond any known "international organization."

The originality of the Community is also evident in foreign affairs. Traditionally, confederations, federations, and unitary states confer to their central institutions what Locke had called the "federative power"— the power to act for the state in international affairs, or, to use the correct legal term, external sovereignty. This is not the case in the EC, whose central institutions have full jurisdiction over only external trade, no more than a power of coordination over the rest of foreign policy, and no power yet over defense. In international meetings other than those of the GATT, the Community is not yet a distinctive actor. At best it is represented along with its members (as at the Group of Seven, or G7, meetings); usually the member states are the actors in world monetary, diplomatic, and military affairs. The "principle of subsidiarity," which prescribes that, in the creation of the single market, the Community take over only those functions the states cannot adequately perform, has not really been applied in foreign affairs and defense, for if it had been, the role of the EC as an actor would be far more important than it is—indeed it would perhaps even be the exclusive actor in matters of security.

As students of world politics and political economy, we are struck by the distinctiveness of the Community among contemporary international organizations. Most evident, perhaps, is the Commission, a coherent executive body composed of over 10,000 professionals that is able to take initiatives and whose President plays a role at summit meetings of heads of government of industrialized countries. When Jacques Delors became its head in early 1985, he decided that the best realm of a *relance* (or "relaunch") of the Community would be the internal market rather than either monetary union or diplomacy and defense, areas in which there was no good prospect of inter-state bargains and convergence of interests. And when the Council met in Milan in June 1985, it found on its table the commission's famous White Paper on the creation of a single market. It is hard to imagine the European Community without the initiatives undertaken by the Commission.

Another distinction of the European Community is its legal status: no other international organization enjoys such reliably effective supremacy of its law over the laws of member governments, with a recognized Court of Justice to adjudicate disputes. The Community legal process has a dynamic of its own. Despite a number of cases of nonimplementation of Community law, by the standards of international organizations implementation has been extraordinary. A recent study concludes that national administrations implement Community law about as effectively as they apply national law, and in its own analysis of such issues, the Commission has concluded that most national courts "are collaborating effectively in the implementation of Community law." Indeed, of all Community institutions, the Court has gone farthest in limiting national autonomy, by asserting the principles of superiority of Community law and of the obligation of member states to implement binding national acts consistent with Community directives.

In addition to its executive capacity and legal powers, the Community has financial resources at its disposal. Furthermore, unlike any other organization in the world political economy, it makes trade policies for twelve states, constituting the largest market in the world. From an institutional standpoint, the transformation of Europe during the last two or three decades has been dissimilar to the evolution of institutions elsewhere in the area of the Organization for Economic Cooperation and Development (OECD).

Boundaries are difficult to draw in a world of complex interdependence: because relationships cross boundaries and coalitional patterns vary from issue to issue, it is never possible to classify all actors neatly into mutually exclusive categories. Europe is no exception. But institutional boundaries are clearer than those of trade or loyalty. The twelve EC states make decisions jointly, whereas EFTA [European Free Trade Association] members, no matter how important they are to the European economy, do not participate in that decision-making process. Europe has an institutional core, which is the European Community.

The kind of entity that is emerging does not, however, much resemble the sort of entity that the most enthusiastic functionalists and federalists had in mind. For they envisaged a transfer of powers to institutions whose authority would not derive from the governments of the member states, and a transfer of political loyalty to the center. According to the most optimistic scenarios, a "United States of Europe" would have come into being—a state with the key attributes of internal and external sovereignty: "supremacy over all other authorities within that territory and population" and "independence of outside authorities."

Portrayals of the state are often bedeviled by the image of an ideal-typical "state" whose authority is unquestioned and whose institutions work smoothly. No such state has ever existed: viewed close up, all modern states appear riddled with inefficiencies and contradictions. Nevertheless, the European Community by no means approximates a realistic image of a modern state, much less an idealized one. If in comparison with the authority of contemporary international organizations the Community looks strong, in comparison with highly institutionalized modern states it appears quite weak indeed. This weakness is reflected in that individual economic agents do not have direct access to the European Court of Justice for redress of grievances. But it is also political: the Community depends inordinately on one state—Germany. The European Community political system rests on national political systems, especially that of the Federal Republic.

The European Community looks anomalous from the standpoint of traditional state-centric theory because it is essentially organized as a network that involves the pooling and sharing of sovereignty rather than the transfer of sovereignty to a higher level. Unlike international organizations, the European Community as a whole has gained some share of states' sovereignty: the member states no longer have supremacy over all other authorities within their traditional territory, nor are they independent of outside authorities. Its institutions have some of the authority that we associate with institutions of sovereign governments: on certain issues individual states can no longer veto proposals before the Council; members of the Commission are independent figures rather than instructed agents. Especially with a leader of vision and method, such as Delors, the Commission is an indispensable fount of proposals and prodding; under the complex provisions of the Single European Act, furthermore, the Council can amend Commission recommendations only with great difficulty.

Yet national governments continue to play a dominant role in the decision-making process. Policy is fragmented by sector, although within sectors a great deal of informal coordination, among national bureaucrats and interest groups, takes place. There are innumerable committees of national experts and bureaucrats preparing the Commission's proposals and the Council's decisions. The execution of the Council's directives by the Commission is closely supervised by committees of national bureaucrats, some of which can overrule the Commission's moves. The Community has a highly complex policy-making process in which formal and informal institutions at different levels in the formal structure, if in the formal structure at all, are linked by a variety of networks.

The European Community operates neither as a political "market"—characterized by arm's-length transactions among independent entities—nor as a "hierarchy," in which the dominant mode of regulation is authoritative rule. Rather, the EC exemplifies what sociologists refer to as a "network form of organization," in which individual units are defined not by themselves but in relation to other units. Actors in a network have a preference for interaction with one another rather than with outsiders, in part because intense interactions create incentives for self-interested cooperation and for the maintenance of reputations for reliability. In the Community, authority remains dispersed, but joint benefits can be gained by the exchange of reliable information—which long-term partners have more incentives to provide than do rivals. The complex system of committees, working groups, and expert groups creates networks of European bureaucrats and of national administrators who play a dual role as representatives of their states and as European agents. Transnational networks associated with each council of ministers link Europe-wide interest groups, national and Commission administrations, and committees of the European Parliament. The EC is not run by a few European specialists but is serious business "for the ministers and high civil servants alike."

The notion of a network is more a metaphor than a theory. It helps to emphasize the horizontal ties among actors and the complexity of their relationships, but it does not elaborate clear hypotheses about behavior. In 1975 Ernst Haas sought to take related notions a step farther by characterizing the European Community as a "semi-lattice" form of organization, somewhat between a hierarchy and a simple matrix: "There is a clear center of authority for some activities and decisions, but not for all. Lines of authority duplicate and overlap; tasks are performed in fragments by many subsystems; sometimes authority flows sideways and upwards, at other times the flow is downward."

Haas went on to predict that in a semi-lattice form of organization, actors would first react to increased complexity and interdependence by incremental, piecemeal approaches—seeking to "decompose" issues. In the longer run, he speculated, these actors might realize that they were sacrificing potential benefits with such a response and might devise new policies. As Haas recognized, the networks of the European Community constitute neither a hierarchy nor a *gemeinschaft*, despite the community rhetoric. With respect to the latter, it is enough to recall the quarrels during the early 1980s over Britain's payments to the Community budget. Britain argued on the basis of equity, whereas its Continental opponents lamented what they saw as reinstitution of the principle of *juste retour*, characterized by Foreign Minister Claude Cheysson of France as "not a community idea." Reciprocity in Europe is often quite specific—demanding tit-for-tat exchanges of equivalent value. Yet as in the Community's North-South bargain, actors in the EC sometimes practice "diffuse reciprocity," transferring resources to others in the expectation that doing so will increase the legitimacy of the Community and its long-term stability, as well as providing the donors with political influence in the interim.

The inappropriateness of statist, strictly intergovernmental, or even confederal models of how European politics operates stems from the inconsistency of these images with the network metaphor or the semi-lattice model, which serve as the best approximation to the evolving reality. "Supranationality," despite the unfortunate connotations of federalism encrusted onto the term, is compatible with these notions. The Community political system can best be visualized as an elaborate set of networks, closely linked in some ways, particularly decomposed in others, whose results depend on the political style in ascendance at the moment. When conditions are propitious and leadership strategies appropriate, as they have been since 1985, the political style of supra-nationality enables connections to be made among points in the network, and from an expanded conception of tasks. When conditions are less benign or strategies inappropriate, the results are policy stagnation and separation of policy spheres.

○   *Supranationality in the European Community*

Perhaps surprisingly, the most appropriate label for the political process of the European Community is Haas's notion of "supranationality." The conception of supranationality, rarely referred to in the recent literature on Europe except with disdain, has suffered grievous misinterpretation and stereotyping over the years. For Haas, supranationality did not mean that Community institutions exercise authority over national governments: "General de Gaulle equates supranationality with a federalism which he detests; Jean Monnet identifies it with a federalism of which he is a leading partisan. Both gentlemen mistake the essence of the phenomenon." Haas also denied a necessary association between supranationality and a "Community viewpoint." That is, supranationality is not at the end of a continuum, whose other end is occupied by strict intergovernmentalism. Instead, supranationality refers to a process or style of decisionmaking, "a cumulative pattern of accommodation in which the participants refrain from unconditionally vetoing proposals and instead seek to attain agreement by means of compromises upgrading common interests." Haas saw this process as implying, structurally, "the existence of governmental authorities closer to the archetype of federation than any past international organization, but not yet identical with it."

Haas viewed supranationality as a style of political behavior through which political interests would be realized, not as a depoliticized form of technical decisionmaking. What Haas called the "three core assumptions" on which theories of regional integration were based can be seen more accurately as the institutional results of the supranational decision-making style: "1) that a definable institutional pattern must mark the outcome of the process of integration 2) that conflicts of interests involving trade-offs between ties with regional partners and ties with nonmembers should be resolved in favor of regional partners, and 3) that decisions be made on the basis of disjointed incrementalism." Haas emphasized that "learning is based on the perceptions of self-interest displayed by the actors," and that lessons will only be generalized "if the actors, on the basis of their interest-inspired perceptions desire to adapt integrative lessons learned in one context to a new situation." And he emphasized connections between politics and economics: "The supranational style stresses the indirect penetration of the political by way of the economic because the 'purely' economic decisions always acquire political significance in the minds of the participants. In short, the kind of economic and social questions here dealt with are those at the very core of the modern welfare state."

The Single European Act reinvigorated Community institutions, particularly by providing for qualified majority voting on issues related to the internal market. It can be argued that what this accomplished, in institutional terms, was the dramatic revival of a largely supranational decision-making style that was lost after 1966, frequently lamented in the years thereafter, and only partially restored with the reforms after the Paris Summit of 1974. Yet this style is supranationality without supranational institutions: the Council is a body of state representatives; the Commission is not a supranational entity in the sense of being an authoritative decision maker above the nation state, nor has loyalty been transferred from the nation state to the Commission. "Progressive regional centralization of decisionmaking," as Haas calls it, has taken place. But we do not observe political integration in the more demanding sense of Haas's formulation in *The Uniting of Europe*: "The process whereby political actors in several distinct national settings are persuaded to shift their loyalties, expectations and political activities toward a new center, whose institutions possess or demand jurisdiction over the pre-existing national states."

The current ascendancy of a qualified supranational style of decisionmaking is shown by the way in which, thanks to the Single Act, the Council now functions. There are no permanent coalitions in it, no country can either dominate or paralyze it, and the major players have repeatedly modified their initial positions in order to reach compromises. But the success of this style does not assure its continuation: the intergovernmental decisions on which the current situation rests (analyzed in the next section) could collapse or entropy could set in as present goals are accomplished without new ones being agreed upon. Least of all does our use of the language of supranationality imply that Europe possesses sovereignty in any simple, unitary way. Quite to the contrary as emphasized in the previous section, the European Community is an exercise in the pooling and sharing of sovereignty.

○ *Intergovernmental Bargains and the European Community*

Although the *process* of European Community policymaking is supranational, all this negotiation and coalition-building takes place within the context of agreements between governments. Without the original Franco-German accord, neither the European Coal and Steel Community nor the Common Market would have ever existed. Likewise, as Moravcsik argues [see Chapter 19], any attempt to understand the Single European Act must begin with a recognition that *governments* took the final crucial steps leading to its negotiation and ratification. Franco-German relations based on a series of mutually beneficial bargains, have always been at the core of the politics of the European Community. The revival of a supranational style of decisionmaking and the strengthening of European institutions in the Single Act resulted most immediately from decisions by governments to press, in their own interests, for a removal of internal economic barriers and for institutional changes that would permit such a policy to be carried out.

Our argument is that successful spillover requires prior programmatic agreement among governments, expressed in an intergovernmental bargain. Such a bargain is clearly important in accounting for the Single European Act. Without the turnaround of French economic policy in 1983 and the decision by the British government to accept Treaty amendment in order to institutionalize deregulation, no consensus could have been reached on a program to dismantle barriers within Europe. The British government was very clear that it was entering into a bargain and not acting on the basis of an ideology of unity or solidarity with Europe. When Margaret Thatcher was asked in May 1989 why she had agreed to ratify the Single European Act, she replied simply that "we wished to have many of the directives under majority voting because things which we wanted were being stopped by others using a single vote. For instance, we have not yet got insurance freely in Germany as we wished."

To say this is not to declare that a state-centric perspective will provide a satisfactory explanation of the Single European Act, only that such an explanation must begin with governmental actions, for these actions are what we observe as leading directly to the Act. The analyst must eventually go beyond these interstate bargains to the domestic political processes of the member states, on the one hand, and to the constraints of international institutions, on the other. Yet these interstate bargains remain the necessary conditions for European integration and must be recognized as such.

- **THREE COMPETING HYPOTHESES**
  ABOUT EC INSTITUTIONAL CHANGE

Even a reader who accepts our argument so far might entertain three quite different hypotheses about the sources of European institutional change in the 1980s. One hypothesis locates the sources of change within Europe, in the political institutions and processes of the Community. Haas made such an argument when he discussed what he called "spillover" from one sector to another.

A second view, the "political economy hypothesis," argues quite straightforwardly that institutional change in the European Community should be seen principally as a form of adaptation to pressures from the world political economy. This hypothesis is, broadly speaking, functional: the form of the European Community follows the functions it must perform to keep its firms, and economies, competitive in a rapidly changing world economy.

The third hypothesis is less often discussed but is consistent with our view that large-scale social change is typically the result of conjunctions of events that are not tightly related to one another. This "preference-convergence hypothesis" holds that a necessary condition for new EC-wide policies, or more centralized decision-making procedures, is convergence of governments' preferences about economic policy, for reasons that do not result principally from prior EC policies or from the pressures of the world political economy.

○   *"Spillover"*

Writing in the late 1950s, Haas characterized the process of spillover not as a manifestation of enthusiasm for the ideology of Europe but as a more prosaic result of "swapping concessions from a variety of sectors":

> Lack of agreement among governments can give rise to increased delegated powers on the part of these [supranational] institutions. Dissatisfaction with the results of partial economic steps may lead labor and industry to demand new central action. Supranational institutions and national groups may create situations which can be dealt with only through central action unless the nations are willing to suffer deprivations in welfare. . . . No statesman, even if he deeply dislikes the process, can permanently isolate his nation from a commitment to unity which is only partially implemented, unless he is willing to pay the price in diminished welfare.

Haas was sophisticated about the politics of spillover—in contrast to the distortions of his views common in the contemporary literature. "The spillover process," as he said, "is far from automatic." It depends on the continued division of Germany and "the tacit recognition of that status in the minds of West German leaders." Furthermore, spillover does not presume continued enthusiasm on the part of elites; indeed, its significance is most evident in the continuation of regional integration even as élan declines.

"Spillover" is, as we have said, an ambiguous term. It can be used simply descriptively, to refer to the enlargement of "an authoritative and legitimate international task." But its theoretical interest derives fr causal conceptualization. Joseph S. Nye, for instance, defines spill as referring to a situation in which "imbalances created by the functional interdependence or inherent linkages of tasks can press political actors to redefine their common tasks." This latter definition can be used either to characterize changing incentives facing states or to a more complex pattern of transnational activity in which national actors "appear as *differentiated* actors, a plurality of negotiating units (classes, status groups, subregions, *clienteles*, bureaucratic agencies, ideological clusters, etc.)."

Neofunctionalists disagreed whether the changing incentives posited by the causal conception of spillover provided an explanation for task expansion. Nye argued that "the functional linkage of tasks has been a less powerful mechanism than was originally believed to be the case" and sought to construct a "revised neofunctionalist process model" in which deliberate linkages, actions of external actors, elite socialization, and other factors played comparable roles. Leon N. Lindberg and Stuart A. Scheingold even sought to refute Haas's conception that spillover led to the Common Market: "The successful transformation that gave birth to the Common Market was not a result of functional spillover."

As argued above, we believe that spillover does not adequately account for major decisions such as those of the Milan summit in 1985 and subsequently those that led to the Single Act. If spillover and pressure from the European institutions had been sufficient to create such a step-level change, it would have occurred much earlier. After all, the members had repeatedly committed themselves to full economic union, but such a union had not been consummated. It is plausible to conjecture that spillover leads to task expansion in the wake of a major intergovernmental bargain, but it would be more difficult to argue that such bargains are themselves explained by endogenous changes in incentives, as a result of past policy change. The 1992 program was much more strongly affected by events in the world political economy outside of Europe—especially by concern about international competitiveness—than it was driven by the internal logic of spillover.

Spillover is an important concept, but it can only be usefully employed within a carefully delimited sphere. Before it is used effectively in research, different meanings will need to be distinguished, as above, and the *conditions* under which spillover can be expected to operate must be kept in mind. The "theory of spillover" has therefore not been discredited: in the wake of an intergovernmental bargain based on subjective similarity and a common policy orientation, actors can have incentives to promote task expansion into new sectors in order to protect gains already achieved. But it remains to be seen, from empirical research, how much this theory will explain of the institutional changes now being observed in the European Community.

Bargains that cover only certain sectors, omitting to provide for sectors linked to these, can stimulate a spillover process either on an interstate basis (as incentives facing states change) or on a transnational one. This core idea of the neofunctionalists is consistent with much of what we know about how changes in the international political economy affect incentives for states. It leaves open for investigation, however, the question of how fast and how far spillover from an initial bargain will extend.

Any explanation of the institutional changes in the Single European Act must take into account that for a decade before the mid-1980s, the Community was preoccupied by its expansion to include twelve governments rather than the original six or the nine of the 1970s. A number of quiet institutional accomplishments occurred during those years: The creation of the European Council in 1974, the decision to have the European Parliament elected directly by the people, the establishment of the European Monetary System, and the enlargement negotiations that added six new members to the original six, all prepared the way for the dramatic events between 1985 and 1990. During these years much concern was expressed about the negative consequences enlargement was expected to have on decisionmaking. For the better part of a decade, the Commission declared that "with twelve members, the institutions and decision-making procedures will be under considerable strain and the Community will be exposed to possible stalemate and dilution unless its practical *modus operandi* is improved."

. . .

Despite prevailing doubts, enlargement did contribute to strengthening Community institutions, not because of idealism or governments' senses of obligations but because governments sought to use Europe to promote deregulation and because decisionmaking was becoming virtually impossible under the practice of unanimity. By the mid-1980s, even the British government believed that it could not attain the predicted large benefits from deregulation without some way to ensure that its partners would open up their markets, and the most credible guarantee that this would occur was treaty amendment, institutionalizing the deregulatory process and instituting qualified majority rule over it. With twelve members, the unit-veto system of the European Council would, in the absence of complex package deals, lead to stalemate on increasing numbers of issues. For a major advance in policy integration to take place, these package deals would have had to be so complex that the costs of negotiating them would have become prohibitive.

The contrast with the French position between 1965 and 1966 is quite instructive. The Common Agricultural Policy (CAP) had been agreed upon, as had the customs union. Both could and did continue without implementation of the EC Treaty provisions for qualified majority voting. De Gaulle could therefore block qualified majority voting, as well as increases in the power of the Commission, without jeopardizing France's economic policy goals. Britain, in 1985, could not do this: changes in the voting procedures, and indeed treaty amendments, were the price to be paid for the 1992 program to complete the internal market, because to achieve this objective, recalcitrant governments had to be outvoted.

Ultimate British willingness to accept majority voting reflected its acceptance of the argument that enlargement made effective use of unanimity impossible. In June 1985 the Minister of State at the Foreign and Commonwealth Office, Malcolm Rifkind, declared: "We believe that enlargement of the Community to 12 will make the existing procedures more unlikely to be capable of reaching early agreement on matters of importance." Similarly, in the French Senate debates on ratification of the Single Act, the French Minister of Foreign Affairs, Jean-Bernard Raimond, stated that "the Europe of twelve could not be administered as was the Community of six and must adapt its decision-making mechanisms to this new enlargement."

Part of the story of the Single European Act, therefore, is that governments decided to strike a bargain on deregulation which seemed to them to require, were it to be effective, reform of the decision-making system. Indeed, the Single European Act can even be seen as partly a way of completing arrangements for the enlargement of the Community to twelve members. A new form of spillover not from one economic sector to another but from one institutional dimension to another, took place. Under conditions of unanimous decisionmaking, expansion of the Community led to anticipation of institutional stalemate, and (because the key actors sought policy changes) created incentives for formal institutional change.

Thus in a dialectical manner, the enlargement from the six to twelve, first appearing as an antithesis to effective decisionmaking, became a decisive element in decision-making reform. Spillover took place not as a functional expansion of tasks but rather in the form of the creation, as a result of enlargement, of incentives for institutional change. Of course, as Haas recognized, spillover was not automatic. Policy change and institutional change also required a convergence of interests between states.

○   *The Political Economy Hypothesis*

As we emphasized at the outset of this chapter, decisions on European integration during the 1980s were made in the context of a political economy of the 1980s that was greatly changed from that of the previous decade. U.S. policy had facilitated European integration in the 1950s and early 1960s, but the economic turbulence of the 1970s had created incentives for competitive extra-European affiliations (especially with oil-producing states). In the 1980s, oligopolistic competition intensified, but for European industry, it appeared increasingly necessary to merge or collaborate to attain sufficient economies of scale and the technological capability to cope with U.S. and Japanese competitors. The "conversion" of the French government in 1983 and the enthusiasm of Britain for deregulation opened the way for elites from big business and the Commission, concerned about the "waning competitiveness" of the EC vis-à-vis the United States and Japan and the perception that "international business seemed to turn its back on the EC." The "national champion" strategy of the 1970s, which had increased the perceived diversity of national situations and competition among European states, was now seen as a failure; European firms could only compete on an international scale if their home market became united rather than fragmented. Thus events in the world political economy were important influences on the governmental decisions associated with the Community's revival.

Yet the political economy hypothesis, however important as part of the puzzle, is not sufficient to explain the sudden strengthening of European institutions during the 1980s. After all, Europe faced serious economic challenges in the late 1960s—when Jean-Jacques Servan-Schreiber coined the phrase, "the American challenge"—and in the 1970s when a combination of U.S. political and economic policies and events in the Middle East produced turbulence in the markets for money and for oil. Had Europe unified itself more strongly in the 1970s, one could have "explained" those actions in functionalist terms as a reaction to instability, and indeed the formation of the European Monetary System in 1978 is often attributed to European concern about errant U.S. policy. Furthermore, from a rational-adaptive perspective the Europeans should have anticipated the effects of technological change on economies of scale and prospects for corporate competitiveness, and altered their institutions in the 1970s in preparation for the competitive struggles of the 1980s. Instead, decisive moves toward the Single European Act were delayed until the perception of crisis was widespread. The political economy hypothesis indeed would have predicted the strengthening of European institutions, but that revival could have occurred at any time after 1973. To understand the timing of the Single

European Act, one also has to look at events within the domestic politics of European countries.

○ The Preference-Convergence Hypothesis

We have argued that although both the spillover and the political economy hypotheses contain some elements of truth, neither alone explains institutional change in Europe. Nor, in our view, are they sufficient for explanation together. A third hypothesis, which focuses on the convergence of preferences of major European governments, is necessary. In formulating this hypothesis, we should keep in mind Haas's own warning that incrementalist strategies, which are necessary for spillover, depend on shared objectives, based on a common understanding of causality as well as ultimate goals. In the 1950s and early 1960s, Europe thrived on what Haas called "a pragmatic synthesis of capitalism and socialism in the form of democratic planning." With such shared objectives, tactics and means can vary as interests and alignments change; furthermore, the specific objectives of the participants can be quite diverse as long as they are complementary with respect to proposed Europe-wide policies. Haas explained the ratification of the European Coal and Steel Community Treaty in the early 1950s as "the convergence, not of six separate national interests, but of a sufficiently large number of separate national party positions to push the Treaty over the top. . . . The very ambiguity of the Treaty, of course, made this pattern of convergence possible. Something seemed to be 'in it' for everybody and a large enough body of otherwise quarreling politicians was persuaded to launch the first experiment in deliberate integration."

There is much in this description that could be applied to the Single European Act. Like the Treaty of Rome, its ratification resulted less from a coherent burst of idealism than from a convergence of national interests around a new pattern of economic policymaking: not the Keynesian synthesis of the 1950s and 1960s but the neoliberal, deregulatory program of the 1980s. Reliance on "mutual recognition" rather than harmonization reflected the decision to focus Community attention on removal of barriers rather than on means of economic intervention. This particular bargain illustrates the general point that the members of a regional organization must regard themselves as having a great deal in common, distinguishing themselves from outsiders. It is, as one of us wrote during the earlier debates, "not that the units be in 'objectively' similar situations but that there be 'subjective' similarity—a conviction on the part of the policy makers that the similarity exists." It was only after the shift in French economic policy in 1983 and the general turn toward deregulatory preferences that such subjective similarity reappeared in Europe.

Focusing on an intergovernmental bargain leaves out one actor: the Commission. When Delors became its head in early 1985, he decided that the best realm in which to relaunch the Community would be the internal market rather than either monetary union or diplomacy and defense, areas in which there was no good prospect of interstate bargains and convergence of interests. When the Council met in Milan in June 1985, it found on its table the famous White Paper prepared by the Commission about the creation of a single market. The Milan summit endorsed that program and also decided on the institutional reform that led to the Single Act. Still it can be argued that Delors's major contribution was to focus states' attention on the one issue—the single market—that was acceptable to the three major actors, Britain, West Germany, and France.

If policy convergence among major governments was so important, we are left with the task of trying to explain why the interests of the major actors became convergent after having failed to be "subjectively similar" for so long, despite many earlier attempts at creating a single market. In the case of Britain, the decisive factor was external: a change in Britain's relation to the EC, whose Council finally made large concessions to Thatcher's demands aimed at reducing Britain's budgetary contribution. This made it possible for her to move on to the task she deemed important, deregulation, and to overcome her own objections to the abandonment of the rule of unanimity, as a qualified majority rule was necessary to the adoption of the single-market program.

The decisive concession to Thatcher had been made possible by a change in French policy. In order to account for the new definition of France's interest, we have to examine both international and domestic factors. The fiasco of the Socialist policy of 1981–1983 did not require a turn to the EC. Many Socialist leaders and business people, as well as the Communists, advocated autarky and the removal of the franc from the EMS. But such a choice would have (1) put François Mitterrand at the mercy of his Communist allies and of the left of his party, (2) cut France off from West Germany and the United States, to which Mitterrand, at that time, wanted France to cling, and (3) most probably undercut even further France's competitiveness.

Thus we end with a tentative conclusion congruent with regime theory: The existence of a "regime"—in this case, the EC—though it did not provoke the new definition of British and French interests, affected these states' calculations of incentives and made it possible for them to see a policy of relaunching Europe as advantageous. And while this relaunch is not a simple case of spillover, the four major actions taken during the period 1973–1984 and other moves such as creating new programs of cooperation in technology and in higher education, made such a relaunch more attractive by making it appear more capable of succeeding. Nevertheless, in contrast to that period when any institutional change required protracted and painful negotiation, there is little doubt that European decisionmaking has since 1985 been more expeditious and effective; we attribute a decisive role in that change not only to incentives for the world political economy and spillover but also to intergovernmental bargains made possible by convergence of preferences of major European states.

. . .

Choosing Union: Monetary Politics and Maastricht

WAYNE SANDHOLTZ

The advances in integration theory in the 1980s came primarily as scholars investigated the causes of the European Community's commitment to create a single market and reform its institutions to accomplish the task. In the early 1990s, scholars had a new chance to test their theories with the signing and ratification of the Maastricht treaty (Chapter 9). Little has so far been written in professional publications about the Maastricht negotiations and ratification process, but what has emerged seems to conform to the eclectic trend begun in the late 1980s.

In this article, Wayne Sandholtz (University of California, Irvine) seeks to explain why the twelve EC countries chose monetary union (a central provision of the Maastricht treaty) over the many other possible methods of governing monetary policy. He argues first that the commitment of all of the member states to macroeconomic discipline in the 1980s was a necessary precondition to considering monetary union an option. To explain the actual decision, however, Sandholtz combines five propositions: spillovers from the process of creating the Single Market, domestic politics, interstate politics in the EMS, foreign policy beliefs and German unification, and concerns about credibility and binding commitments. In doing so, Sandholtz concedes the importance of intergovernmentalism to the integration process, but he steers clear of realist notions that national interests are derived from international power relationships. To find out what leads nations to take the positions they do, according to Sandholtz, we must "look to national decision makers and the sources of their motives and preferences."

Reprinted from *International Organization* 47(1)(1993):1–39 by permission of The MIT Press. Copyright 1993 by the World Peace Foundation and the Massachusetts Institute of Technology. Notes omitted.

*Sandholtz starts us toward an explanation of the Maastricht
negotiations, but he leaves us wondering if we are looking for a unique
explanation for a unique occurrence.*

When heads of state of the European Community (EC) initialed the
Treaty on European Union at Maastricht in December 1991, the road
to monetary union in Europe seemed to have leaped its highest hurdle.
The treaty laid out a plan—complete with deadlines and institutional
blueprints—for a common central bank and a single currency, the
European currency unit (ECU). All twelve member governments committed themselves to ratifying the "Maastricht treaty" by the end of 1992.
Even in the two most skeptical states, Denmark and the United
Kingdom, the major opposition parties endorsed the accord. Since
then, what seemed likely to be an uneventful process of ratification
has become anything but boring. Indeed, the treaty ignited the most
passionate and far-reaching public debate ever concerning the future of
the EC.

Danish voters rejected the Maastricht treaty, including its economic and monetary union (EMU) provisions, by the narrowest of
margins in a June 1992 referendum. Following the Danish "no," public
support for a single currency plunged in Germany to about 25 percent.
In the United Kingdom, a schism opened within Prime Minister John
Major's Conservative party, with the anti-Maastricht Tories emboldened
by the Danish vote. In September, a currency crisis in Europe led to
realignments within the European Monetary System (EMS), but both pro-
and anti-Maastricht forces viewed the turmoil as supporting their
position. On the heels of the EMS crisis, the French electorate endorsed
Maastricht by a margin slim enough to resolve none of the questions.
Yet, after the French referendum President François Mitterrand and
German Chancellor Helmut Kohl declared that it was more important
than ever to ratify the treaty. The plan for monetary union was still alive,
though barely.

The Maastricht saga offers a number of puzzles for students of
international political economy. The fact is that the governments of
twelve independent states, including several of the world's largest
economies, did agree on a far-reaching sacrifice of sovereignty. Participating states not only would give up a major symbol of sovereignty (a
national currency) but also would renounce autonomous monetary
policymaking. Why did national leaders desire to commit their countries
to such a course? The ratification ordeal makes the question even more
pressing, since several governments pushed for Maastricht even in the
face of substantial public reticence. Why?

My objective in this article is to explain why national leaders in the
EC chose to set out on a path toward monetary union! My intent is to
assess neither the bargaining process nor the institutional details of the
treaty. Rather, my purpose is to explain why there was bargaining at all.
In other words, this article is about the definition and evolution of
national preferences. It starts with the premise that national preferences
are endogenous (i.e., not to be taken as given); they themselves can
require explanation.

The first section of the article addresses broad theoretical issues.
The second section argues that a drastic shift in the macroeconomic
policies of several national governments was a necessary precondition
for serious consideration of monetary union. If governments had not
abandoned national economic strategies that required differential rates
of inflation and periodic devaluations, discussion of monetary union
would have been out of the question. The third section shows that there
were several options for a European monetary regime, monetary union
being just one. The fourth section briefly traces the chain of decisions
leading to the conference on monetary union. The fifth section seeks to
explain why EC governments chose to discuss monetary integration
rather than the other options; it examines five propositions. The
conclusion argues that EC governments favored monetary union for
different reasons, at different times. A key implication of this study is
that efforts to formulate a single unified theory of state preferences—
which must precede analytically any theory of bargaining—face formidable obstacles.

• THEORETICAL ISSUES

Theoretical debates concerning the EC often frame the central issue as a
contest between "intergovernmental" and "institutionalist" (or
"neorealist" and "neofunctionalist") perspectives. Intergovernmentalists
hold that nation states dominate EC politics and that outcomes directly
reflect the interests and relative powers of the member states. Institu-
tionalists argue that the supranational institutions of the EC can exercise
an independent effect on EC politics and help shape outcomes. The
intergovernmentalist-institutionalist dichotomy, however, neglects important aspects of community politics that fit neither category. This
stark dichotomy is misleading in two ways. First, the EC is both
intergovernmental and supranational. At the most obvious level, EC
decisionmaking involves intergovernmental institutions (the Council of
Ministers, the Committee of Permanent Representatives) and supranational ones (the Commission of the European Communities, the

European Court of Justice). National governments influence EC policies but are themselves influenced by EC institutions and law. Second, emphasizing the analytical gap between national interests and EC institutions mistakenly suggests that the two are unconnected. The intergovernmentalist argument implies that states form their preferences via some hermetic national process, then bring those interests to Brussels. The implication is that EC institutions have no impact on the formation of state interests. I contend that there is a link between international institutions and state interest formation in the EC. Community decisions are bargains that reflect state interests, but those interests are shaped in part by membership in the EC.

Each member state tries to ensure that EC outcomes are as close as possible to its national interests, but the crucial point is that those national interests are defined in the context of the EC. Membership in the EC has become part of the interest calculation for governments and societal groups. In other words, the national interests of EC states do not have independent existence; they are not formed in a vacuum and then brought to Brussels. Those interests are defined and redefined in an international and institutional context that includes the EC. States define their interests in a different way as members of the EC than they would without it.

With regard to the Maastricht treaty on monetary union, the implication of this logic is that EC institutions and policies influenced the definition, and redefinition, of national interests. In this article my principal goal is to explain why diverse governments came to define their national interests in ways that included monetary integration. Of the five propositions that I examine, three suggest a direct influence of EC institutions and policies on national interest formation. First, the single-market, or 1992, project affected national interest formation by triggering a broad wave of pro-EC enthusiasm. The internal market program therefore enhanced the perceived value of community-level approaches to other issues. Second, the functioning of the EMS influenced national motives and preferences. France and other countries were dissatisfied with what they saw as asymmetries in the EMS. However, they did not want to abandon an EMS that seemed to be working well. The preferred course was therefore to move ahead to monetary union. Third, some member countries were using EC institutions and rules to obtain policy results that they could not achieve through domestic politics. For example, the fragmented Italian political system made it virtually impossible for governments to pursue macroeconomic discipline. The Italian government sought monetary integration as a necessary complement to other EC commitments (in particular, capital liberalization) that would impose macroeconomic discipline from without. In other words,

EC institutions and policies directly affected national interest calculations.

This study carries broader implications as well. Theories of bargaining and strategic interaction take state preferences as exogenously given. In much international relations theory, the exogenous source of preferences is the international system. In its most recent manifestation, the systemic argument holds that anarchy compels states to be concerned for gains or losses of power relative to other states. However, the concern for relative gains is crucial only in a narrow range of settings, namely, settings in which there exist first-mover advantages and the cost of using force is low, and those with two actors. An alternative position, one adopted in this study, is that preferences are endogenous, dependent on actors' perceptions and objectives and on domestic politics.

Having rejected systemic approaches, this study focuses on the national governments in the EC and the diverse motives and interests that led them to favor monetary union. It treats political leaders (presidents, prime ministers, foreign ministers) as the central actors. After briefly describing the shift by European governments toward monetary discipline, I will outline the regime types that would have been compatible with their commitments to low inflation. This frames the issue as one of genuine choice. We must explain not only why EC governments agreed on monetary integration but also why they preferred monetary integration to the alternatives. If the notion of choice is to be meaningful, we cannot imply that the choices made were somehow inevitable. We must place choices in the context in which actors experienced them, that is, as decisions among real options.

• THE CONVERSION TO MACROECONOMIC DISCIPLINE

Shifts in the domestic political economies of several EC states established the necessary foundation upon which discussions of monetary union could build. These conversions to macroeconomic discipline were necessary in the sense that without them, it would have been impossible for key states even to consider monetary integration. The German mark plays the central role in any European-level monetary policy, both because it is the "largest" currency in the EC (with a weight in the ECU basket of over 30 percent) and because of the solid anti-inflation record of the Bundesbank. Since price stability is the first commandment in German monetary policy (and perhaps the second and third commandments as well), no German government could agree to monetary integration with countries wedded to inflationary policies, as many of its EC partners were in the 1970s and early 1980s. By the same token, monetary union would eliminate currency devaluation as a policy option. This would have been unthinkable for France (among other countries) as long as it pursued an economic strategy based on cycles of inflation and devaluation.

Consequently, the shift in domestic political economies toward macroeconomic discipline is a critical factor in explaining the drive for monetary union. Governments did not simply alter their policy tactics within a given economic strategy; they changed strategies. Or, put differently, the policy shifts were not cyclical variations; they represented entirely new attitudes toward inflation and growth. Though a complete explanation of the broad shift to disinflation would require a separate article, I can signal two interconnected processes that worked to bring about this change.

First, technological changes and regulatory liberalization were creating a world in which capital could flow across borders more easily and quickly than ever before. This produced a significant external constraint on national monetary policies, as high inflation in one country would lead to outward capital flows and downward pressure on the currency. Second, governments abandoned the (loosely) Keynesian notion that they could trade employment and growth against inflation and adopted a pragmatic monetarism in which low inflation was a precondition for competitiveness and growth. In other words, governments were abandoning the idea that inflation could be used as a means to achieve domestic economic goals like growth and employment.

The general outlines of the transition to anti-inflationary policies are similar for all of the countries examined. The economic policies of the 1970s had failed dramatically. The combination of full employment, the welfare state, and demand management had been workable as long as economies were growing in the first postwar decades. The coexistence of inflation and stagnation in the 1970s, however, rocked the postwar political consensus. Reflationary strategies seemed unable to produce jobs and growth; rather they accelerated the upward spiral of prices and costs. The recession of the late 1970s and early 1980s finally discredited existing political-economic bargains. Inflation came to be seen by large segments of society and by political leaders as the chief economic evil. New coalitions (sometimes "tacit") supported restrictive fiscal and monetary policies. Policies changed, either when the party in power adapted to the new conditions or when it was replaced. I briefly summarize below the policy transitions in most of the EC states. German motives differed from those of its neighbors; they will be addressed in a later section.

○ *France*

The French case is particularly significant, since the franc is the second largest currency in the ECU basket and French support is essential for any major step in European integration. The French conversion to discipline is also important because it came from the opposite extreme of policy. In the postwar period, the priority had been growth and modernization. French governments employed expansive credit policies to finance growth. The authorities not only tolerated inflation but also used it to squeeze inefficient industries and enterprises. Periodic devaluations counteracted the effects of inflation on the price competitiveness of French firms. Inflation and devaluation were staples of French economic policy—staples that the French gave up in favor of a diet of macroeconomic discipline.

The shift toward restrictive economic policies began in 1976 when the Barre government was installed with the explicit mandate for economic austerity. The Barre government announced monetary targets in 1977, though these had little effect on employers and unions. Furthermore, fiscal austerity was inconsistently pursued, in part because French President Valéry Giscard d'Estaing feared the electoral consequences at a time when the rightist coalition was breaking apart. Ironically, it was a socialist government that finally implemented rigorous macroeconomic policies.

The Mitterrand government, elected in 1981, hoped to reflate its way out of the recession. A pumped-up French economy could then ride the wave of demand that would be generated by worldwide recovery. As it turned out, the expansion drove up prices and imports. Inflation undercut French exporters, so the trade deficit ballooned. The capital that could leave the country did, investment lagged, and there was mounting pressure on the franc. The policy options were stark, each represented by a faction within the Socialist party. On the one hand, France could abandon the EMS, throw up protectionist barriers, and continue to reflate on its own. The alternative was to disinflate, bringing French interest and inflation rates in line with those of its major economic partners. Mitterrand in 1983 chose the deflationary path. Interestingly, Jacques Delors, who would later become President of the Commission of the EC and spearhead the push for monetary union, was one of the most vigorous advocates within the Socialist government of the disinflationary turn.

The socialist government thus committed itself to fiscal austerity and to reducing inflation. After three devaluations in 1983–84, France was prepared to maintain the value of the franc within the exchange-rate mechanism (ERM) of the EMS. However, the policy turnaround carried political costs. The government cut transfer payments, imposed limits on wage increases, and increased taxes on the middle class. As support for the Socialist party fell, reaching a low point in the European elections of 1984, Mitterrand sought to restructure the party's coalitional basis. The Socialists gave up the effort to cooperate with the unions and found support in the growing French managerial and professional class. The technocratic wing of the Socialist party (Michel Rocard, Laurent Fabius, Lionel Jospin) could lead the appeal to that middle-class constituency. In short, the Socialists consummated the conversion from inflation and devaluation to monetary discipline.

o   *Italy*

The slow-moving mechanisms of coalition governments and party-based patronage have prevented Italy from making a decisive break like that which occurred in France. Nevertheless, a pro-reform camp, centered around the Bank of Italy, has succeeded in taking Italy through its first steps toward macroeconomic discipline. The Bank of Italy historically has been subordinated to the Treasury, in the sense that the bank has been required to finance government deficits through Treasury overdrafts or the purchase of Treasury securities. Thus, increasing (and highly indexed) social transfer payments could be financed by monetizing government deficits. Italian inflation ran high. Twice in the 1970s the Bank of Italy pursued restrictive policies—benefitting both times from external support in the form of International Monetary Fund austerity requirements. The effects of inflation on competitiveness could be offset with periodic devaluations.

Officials at the Bank of Italy, opposed to persistently high inflation in the 1970s, began to seek greater independence from the government. A first step, in 1975, allowed the bank to offer Treasury bills at auction (allowing the creation of a private market for Treasury debt). The bank called in 1980 for a separation between the power to expand the money supply and the power to determine state expenditures. The "divorce" between the Treasury and the Bank of Italy in 1981 partially achieved that goal. The divorce eliminated the Bank of Italy's obligation to purchase unsold Treasury securities. In principle, then, the bank could refuse to finance public-sector deficits when doing so would lead to overshooting money-supply targets. There was little public debate over the divorce and little opposition from the government itself, with the Treasury Minister supporting the move.

In practice, as the EMU negotiations began, the Bank of Italy still had not achieved full independence. The Treasury still had the final say on interest rate decisions as well as overdraft privileges at the Bank of

Italy for up to 14 percent of the government budget. Still, Italy has taken additional steps that increase the external pressures for macroeconomic discipline. In July 1989 Italy voted to remove barriers to capital flows in the EC; capital liberalization took effect in July 1990. Also in 1990, Italy moved from the 6 percent to the 2.25 percent band in the ERM. In principle, Italy has reduced the effectiveness of tools it used in the past to sustain inflation rates higher than those prevailing in the EC as a whole: capital controls and currency depreciation. Lamberto Dini, director general of the Bank of Italy, has recognized the constraints: "We are aware of limits to the effectiveness of monetary policy in fixed-rate regimes and in those of full capital mobility." Finally, during the EMU negotiations in 1991, Italy began taking steps to grant the central bank genuine independence in the setting of interest rates.

The pro-discipline camp in Italy has scored some important successes, but the credibility of the Italian commitment to discipline remains shaky, as witnessed by inflation and interest rates persistently higher than those elsewhere in the community. Italy's commitment to low inflation will remain suspect as long as political leaders cannot produce the institutional reforms that would separate government spending from the money supply.

o   *United Kingdom*

The British were among the first to support a political shift toward austerity and disinflation. Margaret Thatcher's election in 1979 put an end to the broad postwar Labour-Tory consensus on economic policy that blended Keynesianism, the welfare state, and full employment. Thatcher received electoral support from British finance and multinational firms. Controlling inflation had become the economic priority for the middle class and for segments of the working class. Thatcher was committed to fiscal and monetary discipline as the means to achieve price stability. Though the government made progress against inflation in the first one-half of the 1980s, after 1986 it crept back up, reaching 10 percent in 1990. The British decision to enter the ERM, though long advocated by business groups and even some Tory political figures, seemed to be for the Thatcher government a last resort for controlling inflation.

The analytically distinctive feature of the British case is this: alone among the EC countries that converted (at least in principle) to disinflation in the 1980s, Britain opposed monetary union. The British advanced as an alternative to monetary union the "hard ECU," which would be a parallel thirteenth currency that would compete with the others for user confidence. One crucial point from the British case is that monetary union was by no means the only policy option for countries committed to monetary discipline.

○   *Other EC Countries*

Greece and Portugal remain problematic, in the sense that inflation rates remain high (about 12 to 14 percent in 1989) and restrictive economic policies could impose high social and political costs. Still, Portugal signaled its intention to make the transition to macroeconomic discipline by placing the escudo in the ERM in early 1992. Greek entry into the ERM and any monetary union will be accomplished after some sort of transition phase. Spain has brought its inflation rate down from over 15 percent in 1979 to 6.7 percent in 1990, though at an exchange rate that was probably overvalued. (Indeed, the EMS crisis of September 1992 included a devaluation of the peseta.) The peseta entered the ERM in June 1989 with a fluctuation margin of 6 percent; Spain has announced a prompt transition to the narrower band.

The remaining countries—Belgium-Luxembourg, Denmark, Ireland, and the Netherlands—have, to varying degrees, made the transition to macroeconomic discipline. The Dutch have committed decisively to low inflation; their inflation rate has been close to and often below the German rate since 1979. The Dutch economy's extreme trade dependence on Germany means that higher inflation reduces exports and, hence, growth. Dutch governments therefore have made a fixed exchange rate vis-à-vis the deutsche mark the first imperative of economic policy. Dutch monetary authorities follow closely changes in the German discount rate and, according to Axel Weber, have thereby achieved an extremely high degree of credibility.

Belgium and Denmark embarked on disinflationary courses in the mid-1980s. Their records in bringing down inflation were similar to that of France through 1987. At that point, Belgium (like France) began to track changes in the German discount rate. As a result, Belgian inflation since 1987 has converged to German levels. Denmark, in contrast, has been slower to embrace the "hard currency option," and its inflation rates have been higher than those in Belgium, France, and Germany. Ireland also followed the French course of gradual disinflation until 1986. At that point, the Irish switched to the hard currency option, joined in the coordinated discount-rate changes, and reduced inflation to German and Dutch levels by late 1989.

This section has underscored two premises upon which the rest of the analysis builds: (1) during the 1980s, a core group of EC states made anti-inflationary discipline its overriding microeconomic objective; and (2) the drive for monetary union can be explained only in the context of this conversion to discipline. Without the new disinflationary zeal, none of the EC states could have entertained the notion of monetary integration. Germany would have been unwilling to tie itself to inflationary partners, and the partners would have been unwilling to sacrifice national economic strategies based on inflation and devaluation. The shift to disinflation was thus a necessary precondition for talks on monetary union. However, it did not make those discussions inevitable.

• **POLICY OPTIONS**

Monetary union is not the only means to sustain low inflation; there are in principle numerous regime options. Indeed, monetary union would seem to be an unlikely choice. Monetary union requires a far-reaching surrender of sovereignty; monetary policy would be set by a supranational central bank and national currencies could eventually disappear. National leaders could therefore be expected to dismiss the idea out of hand. The political logic of monetary union, in short, is not obvious. Furthermore, monetary integration is not an economic necessity for a single-market area like the EC. In fact, there is a striking lack of consensus among economists as to whether monetary union for the EC is a good idea at all. This section lays out the major policy options upon which governments seeking monetary and price stability could draw.

My intent is to describe three broad regime options: unilateral, multilateral, and integrative. In this section I lay out the economic case for each option, in order to show how each might appeal to a political leader pursuing low inflation. Of course, leaders do not choose solely on the basis of economic rationale; a later section turns to political explanations of the choices actually made.

○ *A Unilateral Approach*

At one extreme, governments could commit themselves to macroeconomic discipline without belonging to any sort of fixed exchange-rate regime or currency union. Under a floating exchange-rate regime, the trick is to make the commitment believable without the help of external institutional constraints such that private actors will make economic choices on the expectation that inflation will be low and steady. In theory, such expectations will lead to realistic price decisions including wage agreements, and the belief in future price stability will be self-fulfilling. There are several potential means of achieving such monetary credibility.

One means is via institutional structures. A growing body of research shows that central banks that are independent of political authorities are more successful in maintaining low inflation. The logic is straightforward: a central bank that can resist or ignore the demands of political authorities regarding credit or money policies will be better able to adhere to monetary and inflation targets. More specifically, an independent central bank can refuse political demands to monetize the government's budget deficit or reflate the economy for electoral reasons. The outstanding example is Germany, where the Bundesbank is institutionally independent of the government. The federal government appoints fewer than one-half of the members of the Bundesbank's central board, and the directors' appointments last for eight years. As a result, the Bundesbank's commitment to low inflation is relatively safe from political interference. In other countries (like France) the central bank historically has been subordinate to the treasury and simply has carried out the government's credit and monetary policies.

A second means of providing for a credible commitment to low inflation is to obligate the central bank by law to pursue such a goal. Again, the Bundesbank is a noted example. By law, the primary task of the central bank is to "safeguard the currency" (prevent inflation); other objectives, like supporting the government's economic policies, are subordinate to price stability. A striking and more recent instance of this approach is occurring in New Zealand, where the new central bank law mandates 0 to 2 percent inflation by 1993. If the ceiling is breached, the central bank president stands to lose his or her job (with allowances for certain contingencies outside of central bank control). The rule seems to be producing the desired result, reducing inflation and inflationary expectations (though at the cost of prolonged slow growth).

A third means of unilaterally pursuing a credible commitment to price stability is for a country to peg its currency to a strong foreign currency with a solid low-inflation record (the hard-currency option). This policy is unilateral in that there is no multilateral institution involved; the hard-currency policy continues only at the discretion of authorities in the pegging country. It may take time for the policy to acquire credibility, as private actors may have to be convinced that the national monetary authorities will actually stick to the announced parity and not succumb to the temptation to devalue. The pegging country can increase the credibility of its commitment by announcing a visible intermediate policy target, such as closely following changes in the discount rate of the lead-currency country. A country can unilaterally peg its currency to a low-inflation leader. Austria, not a member of the EMS, has followed this course by consistently tying the schilling to the deutsche mark, and, more recently, Sweden has been tying the krona to the ECU.

○ *A Multilateral Approach*

A second major alternative for EC governments would be to continue with the EMS, perhaps somewhat strengthened. (Following common usage, I will continue to refer to the EMS even though in fact the relevant apparatus is the ERM of the EMS). The EMS is a system of fixed but adjustable exchange rates. Central banks pledge to keep their national currencies within fluctuation bands, both with respect to the central ECU rate and with respect to the bilateral parity for each other participating currency.

The benefits of an EMS-like system vis-à-vis freely floating exchange rates are mainly two. First, as the post–Bretton Woods years showed, exchange-rate fluctuations under a regime of floating rates frequently result from speculative movements and are unrelated to any changes in economic fundamentals. International financial flows now far outweigh trade flows, and exchange rates can fluctuate quite independently of economic fundamentals. Rather than operating to stimulate real adjustments, exchange rates can sometimes disrupt adjustment by sending bogus signals.

Second, for an area with high levels of intraregional trade (like the EC), fluctuating exchange rates do impose higher costs than they would between countries with limited trade ties. Put differently, the costs associated with protecting against exchange-rate shifts are greater, in absolute terms, the greater the volume of trade. For the EC, where the share of intraregional trade in total trade approaches 60 percent, the potential savings from exchange-rate stability must be commensurately large. Indeed, creating a zone of exchange-rate stability was one of the primary motives behind the creation of the EMS.

A system of fixed but adjustable exchange rates like the EMS can also be seen as superior to monetary integration. This line of argument builds on theories of optimal currency areas. In a unified market like that in the United States, the overall economy adjusts to region-specific shocks and regional disparities in productivity and growth through factor movements and fiscal transfers (that is, increased federal expenditures in affected regions). In the EC, because of vast differences in levels of economic development (as between Germany and Portugal), significant differences in productivity and growth will persist. Structural differences between national economies mean that country-specific shocks are likely to occur. Since factor mobility across countries (especially for labor) and EC fiscal transfers (namely, the regional funds) remain limited, that avenue to adjustment is blocked. Exchange-rate shifts remain a viable means of adjusting to cross-national differences without imposing unacceptable costs on any one economy. The EMS can provide for overall exchange-rate and price stability while at the same time permitting adjustment to real economic differences.

○ *An Integrative Approach*

The case for the third major option, monetary integration, also suggests substantial benefits. Naturally, much depends on the nature of the monetary union one envisions. The following assessment is based on the version of monetary union actually being discussed in the EC. It takes into account the general outlines of the ultimate goal, as these have been agreed upon by a solid majority of member states. The sticky questions about how to accomplish the transition can, for the moment, be left aside.

The end point about which there exists broad consensus (the British being the only vigorous dissenters) is a monetary union consisting of permanently fixed exchange rates, giving way eventually to a single currency. Monetary policy for the participating countries would be designed and carried out by a European System of Central Banks (ESCB), which would be legally committed to price stability and independent of national and EC authorities. The Community would be barred from "bailing out" member countries whose government deficits might lead them to default.

The case for this kind of monetary union is as follows. For each member government, a single currency would constitute the most credible possible commitment to low inflation. No longer could a government use devaluation to accommodate higher domestic inflation or declining competitiveness. Indeed, the independent ESCB would provide a low and stable inflation rate for the entire EC. Price stability would lead to increased investment and would provide the basis for higher growth and employment. A single currency would eliminate exchange-rate risk and the transaction costs of exchanging currencies within the EC market. According to the EC Commission, the savings would amount to about 0.5 percent of gross domestic product (GDP) per year for the larger states and up to 1.0 percent of GDP annually for the smaller states—a total savings of some thirteen to nineteen billion ECU ($16.9 to $24.7 billion at December 1991 exchange rates). The ECU would become a major international currency for trade, international bond issues, and reserves. The savings in exchange reserves for the EC could amount to $200 billion. The monetary union could handle shocks that affected some parts of the EC but not others in a variety of ways, including wage and price flexibility, increased factor mobility, and investment (public and private).

- **POLICY CHOICES**

EC political leaders could pursue the goal of monetary discipline through any of several monetary regimes. This section will briefly describe the choices actually made. In the next section I seek to explain why the sum of national and collective (international) choices marked a path toward monetary integration.

At the Hanover summit in June 1988, EC heads of state, over British objections, called for a committee of experts to draw up a plan for monetary union. The committee was composed largely of central bank governors and was chaired by EC Commission President Jacques Delors, whose name became attached to both the committee and its report. The Delors Report (officially, the *Report on Economic and Monetary Union in the European Community*) submitted in April 1989, outlined a three-stage process for creating EMU. The EC heads of state, meeting in Madrid in June 1989, endorsed the suggestion of the Delors Report that stage 1 begin in July 1990, when capital liberalization was scheduled to take place. The summit also unanimously called for an intergovernmental conference to define the subsequent stages in achieving EMU. Whereas a number of EC states held that agreeing to stage 1 implied a commitment to stages 2 and 3 of the Delors Report, Prime Minister Margaret Thatcher vehemently opposed that view. In fact, the British government alone expressed antipathy toward a single European currency and a European central bank.

At the Strasbourg summit in December 1989, as German unification appeared increasingly inevitable, the heads of state voted to convene an intergovernmental conference before the end of 1990. Only Thatcher was opposed. Italian Prime Minister Giulio Andreotti managed the Rome summit in October 1990 so as to outmaneuver Thatcher and win approval for an EMU agenda that included starting stage 3 (fixed exchange rates and a European central bank) in January 1994. The transition would occur, provided relatively undemanding conditions had been met.

By this time there was broad consensus (again, excluding Thatcher) on the outlines of EMU. The emerging design for monetary union largely followed an EC Commission report of August 1990. These were its key points: (1) The overriding policy objective of EMU would be price stability, and a commitment to this goal would be written into the legislation creating its institutions. (2) The ESCB would be independent vis-à-vis national governments and EC authorities. (3) The ESCB would have a federal structure, with the twelve governors of national central banks sitting on the ESCB council. The national central banks, as agents of the ESCB, would be responsible for carrying out its policies. (4) There would be rules prohibiting (a) monetary financing of public deficits and (b) "bailing out" of member states with severe fiscal imbalances. By November, the Committee of Governors of the Central Banks essentially had completed a draft statute for the ESCB, embodying the foregoing principles.

The Intergovernmental Conference on monetary union opened as scheduled in December 1990. In succeeding months the broad consensus on fundamental goals and structures remained unchanged. There was no shortage of disagreement, however, on other points. The starting date for the final stage was pushed from January 1994 to January 1997, a move that some saw as breaking with the agreement reached at the Rome summit in October 1990. Details on how to manage the transition to a European central bank provoked intense wrangling. Two hotly debated topics included (1) the degree of convergence in economic criteria (inflation, interest rates, public budgets) that should be required before moving to EMU and (2) the possibility of delayed entrance for some members. Germany, the Netherlands, and the United Kingdom favored strong conditions—that there would be no move to EMU until a sufficient number of states have met strict and explicit economic conditions. France, Greece, Italy, and Spain favored looser criteria, arguing that EMU would produce full convergence.

A similar split emerged over the question of delayed participation for some countries. Germany and the Netherlands supported a plan whereby a core of strong-currency countries (perhaps as few as six) would move first to monetary union, and the others would join when they qualified. This notion of a "two-speed" EMU was opposed by most of the other states, and especially by Greece, Ireland, and Italy. A potential compromise emerged in the autumn of 1991: all states would participate in planning and decisionmaking for EMU, but some would be granted temporary "derogations" until they met the economic criteria. A potential compromise regarding Britain also emerged: the final decision on British participation in a single currency would be reserved for the Parliament at Westminster. This provision seemed to placate the British, who had been insisting all along that they would not commit themselves irrevocably to a single currency.

The last contentious issues concerned the European Monetary Institute to be set up in stage 2 (specifically, its responsibilities and the procedures for naming its officers) and how to decide on the final move to stage 3 (full monetary union). The final compromises were hammered out during a flurry of bargaining just before the Maastricht summit and at the summit itself. The result was a new treaty on EMU.

Eleven states committed themselves to rapid and irreversible movement to a single currency and a common central bank. EMU would be fully in place by 1999 at the latest, and possibly as early as 1997. During 1996, the European Council (the heads of state or government) may decide by unanimity to move to stage 3 (a single currency and an operational European central bank) provided a simple majority of EC states meet the economic criteria for full participation. If the governments did not agree on the final move to EMU by the end of 1997, stage 3 would begin on 1 January 1999 with whichever states meet the economic criteria (whether they comprised a majority or not). The monetary union would be managed by a European central bank, which would be independent of national governments and EC authorities and whose primary goal would be to ensure price stability. National central banks would become independent of their governments before the transition to stage 3, at which time they would become, in effect, branches of the ESCB.

The treaty also lays out the economic criteria that states must meet in order to participate fully in the EMU. States moving on to stage 3 will display:

1. a rate of inflation in the consumer price index no more than one and one-half percentage points higher than the average of the three states with the best performance in price stability;
2. interest rates on long-term government bonds no more than two percentage points higher than the average of the three countries with the lowest rates;
3. a central government budget deficit no greater than 3 percent of gross domestic product (GDP);
4. a public debt of no more than 60 percent of GDP;
5. a national currency that has remained within the narrow (2.25 percent) fluctuation margins of the ERM for the previous two years and has not been devalued against any other member state currency over the same period.

Ironically, though the Germans insisted on tough convergence indicators, Germany itself would not presently (autumn 1992) qualify under the agreed terms. However, governments committed themselves to meeting the criteria in time to join the first wave of entrants into full EMU. For some states (Greece, Portugal) that will be virtually impossible, and they will make the transition later. Other governments (especially Italy's) will find it severely challenging to meet the requirements. And, once in the EMU, states will have to keep public sector deficits and debt within the guidelines or face penalties provided in the treaty.

Finally, the reluctant British were accommodated with a special protocol allowing them to opt out of stage 3, presumably by a vote of Parliament. Denmark and Ireland also declared their intention to place the Maastricht treaties before the voters in national referenda.

Interestingly, the broad framework for EMU remains largely intact from the Delors Report: a federal ESCB, independent of political authorities, with a mandate to pursue price stability, and rules against the monetizing of public deficits. What remains to be explained is why EC governments chose the EMU path rather than unilateral or multilateral options as the basis for a European monetary regime.

• EXPLANATIONS OF POLICY CHOICES

In this section, I present and discuss five propositions that might explain the movement toward monetary union. This is not intended to be one more "contending theories" approach, in which the "contenders" are set up merely as foils for the preferred explanation, and the result of the "test" is known in advance. The approach in this study is to take preferences as endogenous and requiring explanation. Thus the analysis that follows should allow me to assign relative weights to the propositions to justify conclusions about which factors are more important in explaining the outcome. Each proposition offers a different explanation of the motives behind the drive for monetary union, and each is based on one of the following factors: (1) spillovers from the 1992 process; (2) domestic political economies; (3) interstate politics in the EMS; (4) EC foreign policy beliefs and German unification; and (5) rational institution building (the effort to "tie one's hands").

○ Spillovers from the 1992 Program

The "spillover" proposition is that the 1992 single-market process increased the level of support, among publics and political leaders, for EC-level initiatives. Widespread enthusiasm for the 1992 project tilted preferences toward programs that could be seen as cementing the gains from the single-market program. Whether or not EMU was a necessary complement (in terms of economic theory) to the 1992 project, the EC Commission tried to sell it as such, and many EC politicians and societal groups were receptive.

The theoretical case for spillovers was initially developed in neofunctionalist theories of integration. The spillover argument was that integration in one issue-area would reveal functional linkages to other issues-areas; as a result, the desire to obtain the full benefits of integration in the first area would lead to pressure for integration in a second, linked sector. The notion of spillovers underwent substantial revision, but it is worthwhile to remember what was scrapped and what was not. What was dropped was the notion that spillovers were unidirectional, pushing steadily toward further integration and, ultimately, political union. Thus theorists wrote about "spill-backs" and "spill-arounds." What was not refuted was the notion that spillovers could occur; indeed, if issues are linked, then the potential for spillovers always exists. The process is simply not automatic or one-directional.

The neofunctionalist spillover argument appears at first glance to explain much of the drive for EMU. Certainly Jacques Delors and the EC Commission portrayed EMU as functionally linked to the internal market program and necessary for its success. In 1988 and 1989 Delors, EC Commission president, took on a leading role in the campaign for EMU (similar to the role played by Roy Jenkins, then EC Commission president, in the origins of the EMS). Though the Commission had traditionally deferred to national governments on monetary policy, in June 1988 Delors spoke out in favor of rapid action on a study concerning a European central bank. After the April 1989 Delors Report, EMU became the EC Commission president's favored project. The official EC Commission line has been that monetary union is a necessary counterpart to the 1992 single market program. The August 1990 EC Commission document, *Economic and Monetary Union,* argued that EMU

> can be seen as the natural complement of the full realization of the Single European Act and of the realization of the 1992 objective: the internal market without frontiers. . . . [T]he Member States and the citizens of the European Community will only fully benefit from the positive effects of the creation of the large common market and cooperation if they can use a single currency—the ECU.

The report later declares: "A single currency is the natural complement of a single market. The full potential of the latter will not be achieved without the former. The EC Commission's economic assessment of EMU, "One market, one money," declares that "the economic advantages of 1992 are certainly not fully achievable without a single currency."

The basis for the Commission's case is that there is a functional linkage between the 1992 project and EMU. The argument is that complete capital liberalization (undertaken in July 1990) and exchange-rate stability (in the EMS) are incompatible with divergent national monetary policies. With stable exchange rates, cross-border capital flows would compel monetary policy adjustments (through interest rates, for example) in countries that are inflating. The movement of money would create pressure for interest rates and levels of inflation comparable to those in other EC states. As the EC Commission's economic analysis states, "If the move to EMU were not to take place [given 1992], it is quite likely that either the EMS would become a less stable arrangement or capital market liberalization would not be fully achieved or maintained." Tomasso Padoa-Schioppa advances a similar argument in his discussion of the "inconsistent quartet." He asserts that the EC cannot simultaneously enjoy a single market for goods and services, complete capital liberalization, fixed exchange rates, and national monetary policy autonomy. One of the four would have to give. Since the first three bring about gains in efficiency and transaction cost savings, Padoa-Schioppa urges the submersion of national monetary policy autonomy in a monetary union.

The spillover argument faces two major difficulties, however. First, there is not an unambiguous functional linkage between the internal market and monetary union. The economic logic is not compelling. A fully liberalized EC market could operate effectively with existing national currencies. Indeed, market forces (currency competition) would provide a powerful incentive for national governments to maintain low inflation. Among economists, there is no consensus on the desirability of monetary integration, much less on its functional necessity. Second, the neofunctionalist argument holds that spillovers involve a learning process; once an integrative step has been taken, actors discover that they must integrate further in order to realize the benefits. In the case of EMU, that kind of learning cannot yet have taken place. The target date for the single market was, after all, 31 December 1992, though actual market integration would take longer. The learning process postulated by neofunctionalist spillover theories has not had time to occur.

Nevertheless, it would be absurd to think that the 1992 project had no bearing on the EMU initiative. The drive for EMU got underway in 1988 and 1989, the years in which EC 1992 became a major public phenomenon. A more modest spillover proposition (not involving functional linkages) is that the 1992 program generated a broad pro-EC enthusiasm that benefitted the EMU initiative. That is, EC 1992 increased the credibility of the community as a source of solutions to common problems.

Poll data show that there was a rise in pro-EC sentiment in the late 1980s. A Eurobarometer poll in autumn 1989 found that communitywide, 74 percent of those questioned had "read in the papers, seen on television or heard" about 1992. The high was 93 percent in Belgium and the low, 58 percent in Spain. Among those who replied, 56 percent thought the single market in 1992 would be "a good thing," 36 percent thought it would be "neither good nor bad," and only 8 percent thought it would be "a bad thing." Regarding the EC itself, public approval was climbing dramatically after reaching a nadir in the early 1980s. Support for the EC moved markedly upward in each member country as the 1992 project was defined (1985–86) and stayed at high levels thereafter.

The data do not permit us to establish a decisive connection between rising support for the EC and its 1992 program and favorable opinion for the EMU initiative. Nevertheless, public opinion clearly supported further integration in some areas. Regarding currency policy, the percentage of respondents who thought it should be handled at the EC level (as opposed to the national level) rose from 43 percent in 1987 to 57 percent in 1989. *Eurobarometer* surveys showed broad support for monetary integration in the late 1980s. The survey of October 1990 asked the question: "In the framework of the European Monetary Union it is envisaged that there will be a Central Bank of the European Community, where national central banks would be represented. Would you be favorable or unfavorable to the creation of such a European Central Bank?" For the EC as a whole, 66 percent responded favorably.

The 1992 program produced a strongly positive attitude toward the EC, and the general enthusiasm for the EC was fertile soil for the EMU initiative. The strength of that proposition can be probed with a counterfactual hypothesis: Without EC 1992, the high level of pro-EC opinion—in the public, in business, and among political elites—would have been lacking, making serious discussion of monetary union impossible. It bears remembering that the goal of monetary union had been established at the Hague summit in 1969, yet the EC made no real progress in that direction in the 1970s. The member states reaffirmed monetary union as their objective at the creation of the EMS in 1979, but in succeeding years they failed to take any of the steps foreseen to achieve it. In 1988 and 1989, however, EMU became a movement. What had intervened was the 1992 project. Without it, EMU would still be merely a ritual invocation.

o *Domestic Politics*

A second proposition is that the move toward EMU was driven by changes in the domestic politics of EC states. The argument comprises two dimensions. The first highlights the distributional effects of economic policies; the second turns to the constraints set by the weight of opinion in the electorate.

Jeffry Frieden has employed a general analytic framework centering on the economic interests of social groups whose demands influence national policy. Frieden suggests that because they would benefit most from EMU, "Europe's leading financial and multinational firms have been the stronghold of support for breaking down remaining barriers to EC financial and monetary integration. Unfortunately, the data do not permit us to reach conclusions on Frieden's most specific proposition, that support for EMU should be high among those segments of business that would benefit most (financial institutions, multinational corporations, exporters) and low among those that might lose (firms producing goods and services for national markets). Still, we can point to suggestive pieces of evidence showing that business leaders in the EC favored EMU.

François Perigot, president of the French employer's association (the CNPF), declared that he considered monetary union the most necessary step in the creation of a true European community. Perigot stated that "single currency rhymes with single market," and that businesses would benefit if states would introduce more discipline in their joint monetary policies." Walter Seipp, chairman of Commerzbank, said that he believed the EMS would eventually lead to a European central bank with the ECU as a European currency and the sooner, the better." EC corporate officials in 1987 formed the Association for Monetary Union in Europe to lobby for EMU; its leaders have come from such companies as Philips, Société Générale de Belgique, Fiat, Total-CFP, Rhône-Poulenc, and Agfa-Gevaert. The smaller Committee for the Monetary Union of Europe, chaired jointly by Valéry Giscard d'Estaing and Helmut Schmidt, was founded in late 1986 and brought together government officials, industrialists, and bankers (including a Deutsche Bank chairman) to pressure EC governments toward monetary union. In 1990, the EC-wide employers' association UNICE endorsed the effort.

As the 1992 program progressed, many EC enterprises began to position themselves to compete in the larger EC market. The number of cross-border mergers and acquisitions involving EC firms was increasing yearly; the record set in 1989 (1,266 mergers and acquisitions worth 45 billion ECU) was broken in 1990 (1,467 mergers and acquisitions worth 48 billion ECU). A growing number of firms engaged in trans-EC business would swell the ranks of those who could save on currency-exchange costs and risk premiums if a monetary union were established. In fact, surveys reveal broad business support for monetary integration. A Gallup poll of 1,428 EC company presidents in July 1989 found that 83 percent were in favor of a common European currency and that only 10 percent were against it. The survey covered seven countries, with positive responses ranging from 65 percent in the United Kingdom and 69 percent in Germany, to 92 percent in Spain and 94 percent in Italy. France and Belgium fell between the two extremes. The poll also found that 75 percent of the respondents thought that national currencies would progressively disappear. A separate poll conducted by Ernst and Young for the Commission found similar results. EC businesspersons were asked their opinion on the prospects for the business climate with the 1992 program, and with 1992 plus a single currency. The total positive response rate rose from just over 80 percent for 1992 alone to almost 90 percent for 1992 plus a single currency; within that, the "very positive" response rate increased from about 16 percent to over 45 percent.

Though the movement toward monetary union has received political support from business groups, this is not a sufficient explanation of the political process that led up to Maastricht. To begin with, that the creation of the two lobbying groups (the Committee for the Monetary Union of Europe and the Association for Monetary Union in Europe) preceded formal discussion of EMU by EC governments is not as significant as it might appear. Their calls for monetary union were by no means startling or unique; the idea of monetary integration as the next step after 1992 was already circulating among EC and national officials. Finally, the notion of EMU has been around since 1969 and was a declared goal at the founding of the EMS in 1979. Groups with an economic interest in monetary union in the late 1980s would have had the same motives ten or even twenty years earlier. The interest group approach does not explain why the groups that would benefit from EMU were heard in 1989–91 but not earlier. However, it does appear that once national leaders decided to pursue monetary integration, their efforts benefitted from solid business support. So, though interest groups endorsed the EMU project, we must look elsewhere for the origins of governments' interest in monetary union.

A second domestic politics approach centers on public opinion and picks up the theme that the 1992 program had boosted public support for integration. Politicians, the logic runs, are guided by the preferences expressed by the electorate. And, as mentioned in the previous section, public support for the EC rose in the late 1980s. At the same time, public opinion in most member countries favored a single European currency. Most countries showed a solid majority to be supportive of a single currency, with opinion in Germany and Luxembourg usually hovering just shy of an absolute majority in favor of it. In early 1991 even the United Kingdom had a majority in favor of a single currency, and Denmark came close.

Still, favorable public opinion could not be the driving force behind the EMU project. National political leaders did not undertake discussions of monetary union to satisfy the demands of pro-EMU publics. Indeed, opinion surveys sought the views of the electorates concerning EMU only after the initiative was well under way. Thus, mass opinion was not a cause of the drive for EMU but was a permissive condition. Generally favorable public opinion granted national leaders wide leeway in which to work on EMU.

By the same token, public opinion did signal potential trouble spots for EMU. Domestic politics are important not just in how they constrain or empower national leaders entering into international negotiations but they must also be a factor in ratifying international agreements. As Helen Milner puts it, "States may devise internationally cooperative solutions . . . only to find that their domestic situations will not support them." Certainly the low levels of public support for EMU in Denmark and the United Kingdom marked potential obstacles, since the Maastricht treaty was supposed to be ratified by all twelve member countries. Strong support for EMU by the Danish government, as well as by the major opposition parties and the labor unions, did not jibe with a distinctly more reluctant electorate. Domestic politics, in the form of mass opinion, will continue to be the crucial factor during the ratification process. For instance, in Germany support for the single currency fell from 50 percent in October 1990 to 24 percent in February 1992. The precipitous decline seriously complicated government's campaign to ratify the treaty.

○   *Politics in the EMS*

The proposition discussed here is that the drive for EMU came largely from France and other states that wanted a greater voice in EC monetary policymaking than they enjoyed in the EMS. The theoretical basis for this approach derives from Albert Hirschman's insights into the tradeoffs between exit and voice. If the costs of exit are perceived to be high, then the use of voice to change the status quo is more likely. The government of François Mitterrand in 1983 had reached the conclusion that withdrawal from the EMS would be too costly for France. In the late 1980s, however, French leaders chafed under what they saw as German dominance of the EMS. They proposed monetary union because it would increase the French voice in the formation of EC monetary policies. Other governments with similar concerns supported the French initiative.

By the late 1980s, the EMS appeared to be fulfilling much of its early promise: inflation rates for most states had converged to low levels, and exchange-rate realignments had become less frequent and involved fewer countries. After traditionally high-inflation countries like France were able to cut inflation to 3 percent and lower, the widespread perception was that the EMS could provide external discipline to countries seeking price stability. Indeed, British entry into the ERM was largely motivated by the expectation of benefitting from its disciplinary effects. But with the objective of generally low inflation largely achieved, some countries began to express discontent with EMS modes of operation.

The French government, in particular, was becoming dissatisfied with what it perceived as a fundamental asymmetry in the system, namely, that the burden of adjustment so as to maintain parities was predominantly on the weak currency country. (Similarly, the French consistently argued in the 1960s that the Bretton Woods agreement contained a basic asymmetry of adjustment pressure.) Indeed, whereas other EMS countries sometimes faced major adjustments when the Bundesbank tightened policy (for example), the Germans needed only consider domestic objectives and consequences. The perception of asymmetry was the heart of the debates in 1987 over EMS revisions, leading up to the Basle-Nyborg reforms and the December 1987 realignment. Whether or not the system did in fact impose fundamentally unequal burdens is an open question; the *perception* that it did became the basis not just for the 1987 EMS reforms but also for calls to replace the EMS with a monetary union.

Continuing dissatisfaction with German dominance of European monetary policy was reportedly a major motive behind the French proposal in January 1988 to move beyond EMS. Finance Minister Edouard Balladur circulated a letter to his EC counterparts proposing that it was time to discuss a European central bank "that will manage a common currency, the ECU." Balladur argued that Europe should avoid having one country set economic and monetary policies for all and was reportedly critical of German policies as hampering growth. Governments in Belgium and Italy expressed similar concerns, and even the Dutch (most tightly linked to German monetary policy) were reportedly concerned about Germany's inflexibility. This was not the first time that monetary union had been proposed for the EC. The notion dates back to the Hague summit of 1969 and the Werner Report of 1970. EMU was reaffirmed as a goal when the EMS was established in 1979, and the Single European Act in 1985 made reference to it again. However, monetary union was not actively being considered in EC institutions until the French proposal was made and subsequent support from other states placed it on the agenda.

From the French point of view, the proposal for monetary union represented a bid to gain a seat at the monetary table, a table that under the EMS was located in Frankfurt. Of course, if the French wanted more control over monetary policy, unilateralism would have given it to them. That option, however, had been ruled out in 1983 when the Mitterrand government concluded that withdrawal from the EMS would be more costly than continued participation. Assuming that the European regime continued to provide for price and exchange-rate stability, full monetary union in which each country had some say would be preferable to one in which Germany was perceived to dominate.

The effort to dilute German control of European monetary policy did not necessarily indicate on the part of the other countries either a relaxed commitment to macroeconomic discipline or a desire for higher inflation. There can be legitimate differences of opinion on how restrictive monetary policy needs to be, given current economic conditions, in order to maintain price stability. The Bundesbank tends to lean to the tight side, even when economic conditions might justify a less restrictive policy. Indeed, many remember the artificial recession created by overly restrictive policies at the Bundesbank in the late 1960s. Furthermore, the type of EMU that Belgium, France, Italy, and the others supported was one in which governments would not be able to dictate monetary policy to a dependent European central bank. If pursuing monetary union were simply a ploy to gain political control over monetary policy so as to inflate, then the "pro-inflation" countries would not have supported an ESCB that would be committed to price stability and independent of all political authorities. Yet a stable consensus has existed on precisely that kind of ESCB.

The proposition, then, is this: the drive for monetary union resulted from a decision by the French first, and supported by other countries, that a greater voice in EMU would be preferable to continued German dominance in the EMS. Although this approach seems to account partially for the French proposal on monetary union in January 1988, it is not sufficient. First, it does not explain German support for EMU. Indeed, by the same logic, Germany could be expected to oppose changing a system in which it had the predominant role. Second, greater voice for the other EMS countries did not require the dramatic step of sacrificing monetary sovereignty to EMU. Greater symmetry in the ERM could be achieved via reform of the existing system. The Basle-Nyborg reforms, in fact, did ease the burden on the weak-currency countries by permitting increased access to financing and greater interventions in ECUs. The reforms also required strong-currency countries, not just weak-currency countries, to participate in intramarginal interventions. In short, the goal of a greater voice for France and other countries in EC monetary policy could have been achieved by other means and did not require movement toward EMU.

○ *Foreign Policy Beliefs and German Unification*

The premise for the approach presented here is that European integration at present, as in its origins, is motivated by a broad foreign policy goal, namely, to bind Germany to its western neighbors so as to prevent conflict or aggression. The proposition is that such foreign policy objectives largely explain German support for EMU and account for the rapid steps toward monetary union taken during the period of German unification.

On purely economic grounds, German motives for pursuing EMU would remain puzzling. Germany underwent no conversion to macroeconomic discipline and low inflation, because it could already boast of a solid record in achieving both goals for a period of four decades. As mentioned in the second section, the Bundesbank is independent of German political authorities and is legally committed to price stability as its policy priority. For the other states, the conversion to monetary discipline was a necessary prerequisite for discussion of monetary union, but that logic does not apply to Germany. On the contrary, German officials could be expected to oppose EMU on the grounds that it would decrease German control over a fundamental aspect of postwar economic policy and that there would be no assurance that a European central bank would perform as well as the Bundesbank in ensuring price stability.

Yet, the French proposal in January 1988 received prompt and enthusiastic support from the German Foreign Minister, Hans-Dietrich Genscher. The Bundesbank was much more cautious. Bundesbank president Karl Otto Pohl supported EMU as a long-term goal but stressed that a European central bank had to be independent of political influences and committed to price stability as its first priority. Pohl also argued that the various national economies had to converge more before monetary union would be practicable. Not surprisingly, German monetary authorities consistently have voiced doubts about EMU and insisted on strict prior conditions. Still, Genscher, in a speech to the European Parliament in January 1988, declared that a European central bank was "essential" and "logical" for the EC and implied that EMU would be on the Council of Ministers' agenda during Germany's presidency. Economics Minister Martin Bangemann sided with Genscher, while Finance Minister Gerhard Stoltenberg followed Pohl's more cautious line. The German cabinet in February endorsed monetary union as a long-term goal. Chancellor Kohl moved closer to the Genscher position and announced that monetary union would be on the agenda for the Hanover summit in June 1988. It was Genscher who called for the summit to create a committee of experts to draw up a plan for currency union—the proposal that led to the Delors committee.

How does one explain the interest of German political leaders—first Genscher but also Kohl—in EMU? One hypothesis ties their support for EMU to long-standing foreign policy ideas and goals. Genscher believes that integration was important for Germany and for Europe.

Together with Italian foreign minister Emilio Colombo, he sponsored an initiative in 1981 proposing new steps toward full European union. Though less overtly a "Europeanist," Chancellor Kohl consistently supported integrationist proposals in the 1980s. Genscher's enthusiasm for EMU must in large part be traced to his personal belief in the political importance of European integration, especially as a necessary counterpart to Germany's expanding ties to Eastern Europe.

The political (that is, foreign policy) salience of EMU moved to the foreground in 1989 as each month seemed to witness some Eastern European country slipping out from under Communist party rule and Soviet domination. The growing prospect of German unification proved to be a most effective stimulus for progress on monetary union. There were two considerations. One was the prospect that eventual EC membership for the Eastern European countries would lead to decision-making paralysis in EC institutions in which unanimity remained the rule. Many political figures perceived a need to solidify the core of the EC (that is, to "deepen") and saw EMU as a key part of that program. The other consideration related to the "German problem." Many leaders, including key Germans, desired to bind Germany irrevocably to the EC, and monetary union was a crucial means of doing so.

French President Mitterrand stepped up his campaign for more rapid progress on EMU after the breaching of the Berlin Wall. In October 1989, Mitterrand declared that the collapse of the communist order in Eastern Europe required that the EC "accelerate its own construction." The following month Mitterrand undertook a tour of the eleven other EC capitals to drum up support for EMU. Prime Minister Michel Rocard asserted that France was determined to attain European monetary union "regardless of who the partners might be." Foreign Minister Roland Dumas, after the East German elections in March 1990, suggested moving up the conference on EMU given the rapid pace of change in Germany. Given historical French worries about German power, it is not surprising that German unification should increase French interest in strengthening EC ties.

The French were not alone in this concern. Just prior to the Maastricht summit Andre Szasz, deputy president of the Dutch central bank, declared that it was essential to bind Germany to a European monetary union. Otherwise, he argued, there was a danger that "Germany, in the next two decades, will become a different country." Szasz, though not fully comfortable with all of the provisions being outlined for EMU, asserted that most of the EC member states understood that "if we do not grasp this opportunity [to ensure continued German integration in Western Europe] there may not be another one."

German officials also proclaimed a desire to push ahead on EMU;

committing to further integration was a vital way of proving that Germany would remain a loyal EC partner. Genscher argued for an early conference on EMU, declaring that setting dates would bind Germany to the West. Chancellor Kohl repeatedly stressed that German unification would proceed in the context of European integration. In November 1989, as Kohl prepared his ten-point plan for unification, he also strongly endorsed Mitterrand's proposal for rapid movement on EMU. According to some reports, German support for monetary (and political) union was a bargain, the other one-half of which was French assent to rapid German unification. Finally, in the days preceding the summit, Helmut Schlesinger, president of the Bundesbank, stated that EMU offered Germany no major economic benefits and acknowledged that German support for the project was largely political. In short, foreign policy ideas seem to provide the best explanation for German support for EMU, especially the enthusiasm evinced by Genscher and Kohl.

The concerns evoked by the prospect of German unification brought about an acceleration in the movement toward EMU. France, Germany, and other states favored rapid progress on EMU, and only Britain expressed reservations. In December 1989, in the wake of Kohl's ten-point plan for German unification, the Strasbourg summit voted to convene an Intergovernmental Conference on EMU in 1990. The Rome summit in October 1990, in which the heads of state (except Thatcher) agreed to an agenda for EMU, followed on the heels of German unification on 3 October. Events in Eastern Europe thus pushed to the fore one of the political objectives that the EC had originally been designed to address, namely, binding Germany to the West. In short, the acceleration of the EMU process in 1989 and 1990 can be explained by the beliefs of European political leaders concerning a desirable European order.

Still, the foreign policy goals do not explain the origins of the EMU movement, especially the interest shown by Belgium, France, Italy, and other countries in 1988 and early 1989. Also, it is not clear that the spur of German unification, in the absence of other motives, could propel EC states over the difficult hurdles involved in designing supranational institutions and transferring to them monetary sovereignty. The hypothesis on foreign policy objectives must therefore be combined with others for a satisfactory explanation.

○   *Concerns About Credibility and Binding Commitments*

The key premise in this next approach is that the shifts toward monetary discipline in the 1980s represented a decisive change in the economic beliefs of policymakers. Specifically, by pursuing low inflation above all other macroeconomic goals—including full employment—political leaders in essence abandoned the notion that there was an exploitable Phillips curve, or a stable tradeoff between inflation and unemployment. Prior to the shift of the 1980s, governments often implemented expansionary policies to stimulate growth and sustain employment, at the "cost" of high inflation. The new belief was that price stability was the foundation for growth and employment in the long term (that is, that the long-term Philips curve might have a positive slope).

One of the critical challenges for governments pursuing price stability is establishing credibility. It would be impossible to review the extensive literature on this issue, but the fundamental point is quite straightforward and has to do with expectations. If economic actors do not find the government's commitment to low inflation credible, then their decisions will produce inflationary pressures. For instance, if there is an expectation that the government will permit inflation, demand for the currency will fall, unions will demand higher wage settlements, and producers will set higher prices—all increasing inflationary pressures. Part of the debate about central bank independence is that central banks subject to instructions or demands from political authorities will not be credible in pursuing low inflation because politicians will inflate for electoral advantage.

One way credibly to insulate national monetary policy from polit-ical influences would be to eliminate it—to create a single currency and transfer monetary policymaking to international institutions that would be aloof from national politics. The proposition is that European governments favored EMU because it would provide the highest possible level of credibility; monetary union would once and for all "tie their hands." Richard Burdekin, Clas Wihlborg, and Thomas Willett have argued that even if the case for monetary union is open to question, the EMU process may lead countries to grant their central banks genuine independence—something that governments would otherwise be incapable of achieving. The result would be anti-inflationary national "monetary constitutions." If it were implemented, monetary union would be more credible than unilateral pegging to a strong currency because the latter could be undone at any time, even in response to temporary electoral concerns. In fact, monetary union would provide price stability for governments that would be unable, for domestic political reasons, to achieve it on their own. EMU would also tie the hands of future governments, as it would be extremely costly to withdraw once the transition to monetary union had been made. Furthermore, national leaders could escape electoral punishment when restrictive policies caused economic distress by pointing out that they had no control over those policies.

The evidence favoring this proposition is both direct and indirect. The Germans have insisted all along that the European central bank be as committed to price stability and as independent as the Bundesbank has been. German policymakers want to keep their own monetary hands tied. Italian support for monetary union is in large part an attempt to gain via European institutions the policy credibility that Italy has found difficult to forge at the national level. European monetary union would enforce discipline on all future Italian governments.

Indirect evidence for the "tying hands" hypothesis is the broad consensus on the *nature* of the monetary union. EC governments concurred that a future ESCB must be independent of political authorities, be they national or EC. They agreed that this independent ESCB should be constitutionally committed to price stability above other goals and (with the exception of Britain) that the final objective was the replacement of national currencies by the ECU. Both the Delors Report and tile Draft Statutes for the European Central Bank adhered to the principles of independence and price stability. In fact, part of the EMU bargain was that governments would grant independence to their central banks prior to moving to stage 3. Pursuant to this requirement, the Italian parliament in January 1992 passed a law granting the central bank exclusive competence over the setting of interest rates, in which the bank had previously been subject to the Treasury.

- ## CONCLUSION

The treaty on EMU was always fragile but not only because some governments, given substantial political leeway, ran faster than their publics were willing to go (though in the German case, public opinion did not turn against EMU until after the treaty was signed). Government enthusiasm despite public reluctance intensifies the puzzle of the Maastricht treaty. The monetary accord was tenuous in another way, as well: it was based on domestic coalitions across the EC in the late 1980s that supported monetary and price stability. The EMU project depends on those coalitions remaining intact. In the end, perhaps only a small core of EC states will have both the anti-inflationary political coalition and the public support to make the transition to monetary union.

I have argued that the conversion to monetary discipline in several European countries in the 1980s was a necessary prerequisite for discussion of EMU. As long as some governments embraced policies that entailed inflation and devaluation, monetary union remained not just on the back burner but locked in the cupboard. The breadth and strength of the shift to discipline on the part of national governments shows up in the convergence to low inflation rates that occurred in the EMS during the late 1980s. This shift was not due to any institutional EMS change that rendered it more effective. Rather, the success of the EMS derived from the newfound inclination in a number of member countries to commit to low inflation. Indeed, the Delors Report noted that the success of the EMS could in part "be attributed to the participants' willingness to opt for a strong currency stance."

Systemic analyses arguing that the internationalization of financial markets caused the drive for EMS claim too much. International financial interdependence is essential to explain why European governments turned to low-inflation policies in the mid-1980s; but EMU was by no means the only regime compatible with the objective of monetary and price stability. In fact, this article outlined three broad options: a unilateral order, a multilateral approach (the EMS), and an integrative regime (EMU). The international system can present challenges and opportunities; it cannot determine how governments will respond.

From the point of view of traditional realist political theories, which emphasize the compelling urge for national sovereignty and independence, monetary union should have been the option least likely to be chosen by national leaders. Since systemic approaches are inadequate, we must look to national decision makers and the sources of their motives and preferences. This article examined five propositions that might explain why EC governments chose a path toward monetary union. My goal has been to show why national preferences overlapped enough to make an EMU accord possible. I have not tried to explain the actual bargaining, nor have I examined the international leadership, by the EC Commission and some national officials, which was necessary to define a point of agreement among the overlapping national preferences.

The first two propositions, concerning 1992 spillovers and domestic politics, are necessary but insufficient to explain why national leaders desired monetary union. The 1992 project produced a renaissance in pro-EC sentiment. That enthusiasm, coupled with broadly supportive public and business opinion, gave national governments broad scope in which to discuss EMU. The EC Commission's depiction of EMU as a necessary complement to the single market could reach a receptive EC audience. Furthermore, the liberalization of capital flows (part of the 1992 program) combined with the fixed but adjustable exchange-rate system of the EMS to place new constraints on independent national monetary policies. Of course, in principle, states could opt for monetary autonomy and retreat from the EMS, restore capital controls, or both. In practice, the EMS was widely perceived as a major success: inflation rates in the late 1980s had generally converged at low levels and the number of exchange-rate realignments had declined and involved fewer countries. Rightly or wrongly, the EMS was associated with that success. Similarly, capital liberalization was an important part of the 1992 project, which enjoyed broad support. Since abandoning the EMS and reimposing capital controls were, at that time, out of the question, states found that monetary integration appeared to be the most viable option. I conclude that 1992 momentum and favorable domestic opinion constituted permissive conditions; they were necessary (the EMU initiative could not have proceeded without the optimism surrounding the EC 1992 venture or without supportive domestic opinion in the vast majority of countries) but not sufficient.

The third proposition explains an important part of the motivations of the French and other governments: they desired a greater voice in EC monetary policy. The cost of exiting the EMS was too great (as the French explicitly decided in 1983). The French (and the Belgians, Dutch, and Italians) have more say (as they saw it) in a European central bank than they had in an EMS dominated by the Bundesbank. However, there would have been ways to achieve greater "symmetry" within the EMS; the Basle-Nyborg reforms in 1987, in fact, took some steps in that direction. The desire for greater voice in monetary affairs was a proximate cause of the call for monetary union in early 1988.

Without the fourth proposition, German motives must remain mysterious. Monetary union offered Germany few if any economic benefits. The staunch commitment of Foreign Minster Hans-Dietrich Genscher to European integration explains much of the German support for EMU, especially at first and especially given Bundesbank skepticism. Stronger EC bonds were the counterbalance to growing German ties to Eastern Europe and the reforming Soviet Union. When German unification became a genuine prospect, EMU became a tailor-made means for Bonn to prove that a larger Germany would remain a good European citizen. German unification also focused the thinking of other EC states on ways to keep Germany in the family. Germany sought to reemphasize its commitment to the EC; France (and other states) wanted to tie the enlarged Germany more firmly to the EC. Traditional EC political goals therefore account in large part for the German government's commitment to monetary union and for the general acceleration in the EMU process that occurred in 1989 and 1990.

The final proposition was the EMU appeared to be the best choice, in the context of the late 1980s, of governments seeking to institutionalize their commitment to low inflation. Crucially, from 1988 to 1991 national governments enjoyed ample political leeway in which to negotiate EMU, as the discussions of the first two propositions showed: the 1992 project had boosted pro-EC sentiment, and domestic public and business opinion were broadly favorable. Government leaders therefore enjoyed considerable political autonomy during the EMU negotiations; we would expect the design for monetary union to reflect their policy beliefs and objectives. The primary economic goal since the mid-1980s had been to maintain price stability. Monetary union appeared to offer distinct advantages in assuring price stability. National politicians could not cause inflation for political purposes if a European central bank controlled the monetary levers. EMU would tie the hands even of future governments. For governments that found it difficult domestically to achieve monetary discipline, EMU offered the chance to have it implemented from without. Governments could even escape the blame when tight monetary policies pinched.

This is precisely the kind of monetary union about which EC governments enjoyed consensus. It would be built on an independent European central bank committed to price stability. Such a European central bank could hardly be understood except as the product of EC governments seeking to tie their hands in monetary policy. This proposition accounts for the fundamental policy objectives driving EC governments as they marked a path toward monetary integration. However, it can only explain the signing of the EMU treaty in combination with the other propositions.

The propositions examined in this article account for different parts of the outcome; only together are they sufficient to explain why there existed space for international agreement among the various national preferences. Discussion of three of the propositions—spillover from 1992, EMS politics, and the search for credible commitments—demonstrated that EC institutions and policies can influence the formation of national preferences. Strictly intergovernmental approaches to analyzing the EC, focusing on national interests, neglect the impact of EC membership on how states define their interests. Finally, treating preference formation as endogenous leaves us with little prospect of a neat, unitary theory of national preferences. This analysis has demonstrated the futility of trying to collapse the distinct perspectives into one. Perhaps our explanatory goals are best served by specifying the analytical strengths—and limitations—of approaches that work better in combination than alone.

Index

About the Book and Editors

Designed for classroom use, this anthology introduces and places in context a selection of the most important contributions to our understanding of the European Union.

From the world of politics, the voices of Winston Churchill, Robert Schuman, Jean Monnet, Charles de Gaulle, Margaret Thatcher, and Jacques Delors present their visions—often conflicting—of a united Europe. From the academic world, the classic works of David Mitrany, Leon Lindberg, Bela Balassa, and others ask key questions and lay the theoretical foundations for more recent contributions by such respected scholars as Robert Keohane, Stanley Hoffmann, Philippe Schmitter, Wolfgang Streeck, Andrew Moravcsik, and Wayne Sandholtz, who explore a variety of questions regarding decisionmaking in the Union and the origins of the Single European Act and the Maastricht Treaty.

The collection offers the student of the EU a chance to be party to and engage in a long-running, sometimes congenial, sometimes heated, but always engaging conversation among some of the best minds dedicated to creating, maintaining, or simply understanding the European Union.

Brent F. Nelsen is assistant professor of political science at Furman University. He is author of *The State Offshore: Petroleum, Politics, and State Intervention on the British and Norwegian Continental Shelves* and editor of *Norway and the European Community: The Political Economy of Integration.* **Alexander C-G. Stubb** is a graduate student at the College of Europe, Bruges, Belgium.